Lakeland Fell Running
for Mortals

John Myatt

 Pesda Press LTD   www.pesdapress.com

First published in Great Britain 2022 by Pesda Press
Tan y Coed Canol
Ceunant
Caernarfon
Gwynedd
LL55 4RN

© Copyright 2022 John Myatt

Maps by Bute Cartographics
Contains Ordnance Survey data © Crown copyright and database right 2022

ISBN: 9781906095888

The Author has asserted his rights under the Copyright, Designs
and Patents Act, 1988, to be identified as Author of this Work.
All rights reserved. No part of this publication may be reproduced, stored in a retrieval
system, or transmitted, in any form or by any means, electronic, mechanical, photocopying,
recording or otherwise, without the prior written permission of the publisher.

Printed and bound in Poland, www.lfbookservices.co.uk

Running over Latrigg summit (Latrigg route)

Contents

Introduction	6
Using this Guide	8
Getting Ready	10
Care for the Environment	16
About the Author	18
Mindfulness	18
Fell-run Summaries	19

THE EASTERN FELLS — 23

1 Clough Head	25
2 Gowbarrow Fell	29
3 Swineside Knott	33
4 Sheffield Pike	37
5 Birkhouse Moor	41
6 Birks and Arnison Crag	45
7 High Hartsop Dodd and Little Hart Crag	49
8 Seat Sandal	53
9 Great Rigg Triangle	57
10 Nab Scar	61

THE FAR EASTERN FELLS — 65

11 Askham Fell	67
12 Arthur's Pike	71
13 Hallin Fell and Steel Knotts	75
14 Beda Fell	79
15 Place Fell	83
16 Angletarn Pikes	87
17 Caudale Moor and Hartsop Dodd	91
18 Branstree and Selside Pike	95
19 Wansfell Pike and Baystones	99
20 Sour Howes and Sallows	103

THE CENTRAL FELLS — 107

21 High Rigg	109
22 Walla Crag	113
23 Bleaberry Fell	117
24 Raven Crag	121
25 Brund Fell	125
26 Armboth Fell and High Tove	129
27 Watendlath Tarn	133
28 Steel Fell	137
29 Silver How	141
30 Loughrigg Fell	145

THE SOUTHERN FELLS — 149

31 Rosthwaite Fell (Bessyboot)	151
32 Seathwaite Fell	155
33 Lingmoor Fell and Blea Tarn	159
34 Great Carrs, Swirl How and Grey Friar	163
35 Black Fell and Tarn Hows	167
36 Wetherlam	171
37 Holme Fell and Tarn Hows	175
38 Harter Fell (Eskdale)	179
39 Green Crag	183
40 Devoke Water Circuit	187

THE NORTHERN FELLS — 191

41 Binsey Double	193
42 High Pike (Caldbeck)	197
43 Uldale Fells	201
44 Bowscale Fell	205
45 Bannerdale Crags	209
46 Longside Edge	213
47 Souther Fell	217
48 Blencathra	221
49 Glenderaterra Valley	225
50 Latrigg	229

THE NORTH WESTERN FELLS — 233

51 Sale Fell and Ling Fell	235
52 Graystones, Broom Fell and Lord's Seat	239
53 Whinlatter Top and Brown How	243
54 Whiteside	247
55 Barrow and Outerside	251
56 Catbells Terrace	255
57 Causey Pike and Scar Crags	259
58 Maiden Moor and High Spy	263
59 Knott Rigg and Ard Crags	267
60 Rannerdale Knotts	271

THE WESTERN FELLS — 275

61 Fellbarrow and Low Fell	277
62 Burnbank Fell and Blake Fell	281
63 Gavel Fell and Blake Fell	285
64 Hen Comb	289
65 Murton Fell and Cogra Moss	293
66 Mellbreak	297
67 Crag Fell and Grike	301
68 Hay Stacks	305
69 Lank Rigg and Whoap	309
70 Middle Fell and Seatallan	313

APPENDICES — 319

Rating System Criteria	319
Fell Races	321
Acknowledgements	323
Index	325

Introduction

Why run the fells?

Fells are mountains or hills, sometimes referring to a whole mountain, sometimes to a summit and occasionally to the flanks of a large mountain such as Blencathra. The word comes from fjell, the Norwegian for hill so, to keep it simple, fell running is running in the hills.

Running the fells unleashes the inner runner. It becomes hard to look at a fell without wondering what it would be like to run over it. Running the fells is never boring. There is too much to focus on: the scenery; the ascents and the descents; the bogs and the rocks; the ghylls and the becks; the bracken and the heather. Your watch is the last thing you look at. Soon you become part of the landscape, alive with the seasons, following the spears of grass, the gorse, the mayflower, the bluebells, the wild garlic, the ling and the rowan berries.

Running the fells is elemental. You flow with the seasons. You learn to embrace the winter. Running through driving rain, battling a storm force wind, being the first to hear the crunch of virgin snow or feeling the sting of hail on your cheeks is strangely primordial. Then the leaves sprout, the blossom droops and the fern fronds unfurl, announcing a fleeting, temperate northern summer. The heather and bracken slowly brown and the leaves reluctantly turn yellow, red and bronze, heralding once more the long nights and a frost that clings to the grey brown bracken.

The great thing about the Lakeland Fells, that makes them ideal for short uncomplicated fell runs, is their accessibility. Most are easy to get to and to get up and down without the need for specialist equipment or skills. Many are clearly visible from the roadside. There are few long walk-ins and the 70 runs chosen in this guide avoid exposed terrain and scrambles.

Another attraction is that paths are optional. A number of runs in this book use routes that are not on the maps. Often, in reality, good paths exist on the ground even if they are absent from maps, formed over the centuries by walkers and runners. Sometimes paths are not necessary; sometimes running straight down a fellside is the best option.

Who is this guide for?

This book is aimed at parkrunners and club runners who run mainly on the roads but who would also like to run in the hills; roadrunners who want to head onto the fells but who are wary about taking the first step, maybe even a little intimidated by fell-running mountain goats who might seem almost like another species.

This book is here to debunk a myth. Everyone can be a fell runner. This book is for mortals who want to feel the freedom and wildness of the Lakeland Fells.

I have chosen shorter runs, ranging from 7 to 11 kilometres, which in the main can be completed in between an hour and an hour and half of steady running. These 70 runs are for runners who want to take the plunge but are not sure where to start. If I can run these routes, almost any runner can.

Introduction

There are many books and websites that describe walking routes and many people still rely on Wainwright's distinctive sketches. There are few guides exclusively about fell runs though, and fewer directed at the fell novice. You can choose a route from a walking guide and decide to run it, but this might leave too many questions unanswered. How long will it take me to run it? What is the terrain like for running rather than walking? How runnable are the inclines and the declines? How easy is it to lose your way when you are covering the ground at speed rather than strolling along with map and guidebook in hand and talking to your companions about route choices?

Many hikers also enjoy running, but finding a shorter run to inspire, maybe at the start or the end of the day, might not be easy. Of course, all of these routes can be walked; they are perfect circuits when a morning, afternoon or evening is all the time you have or all that the weather allows.

Disclaimer

Every effort has been made to ensure that the information given in this guide is accurate. However, mistakes happen and routes are subject to change. The author welcomes updates and corrections.

As with any activity, fell runners must accept responsibility for their own actions, know their own limits and stay within these. The author, publisher and distributer of this book do not accept any liability for any injury or damage or injury to person or property arising from the use of this guide.

Jumping for joy on Walla Crag summit (Walla Crag route)

Using this Guide

Many visitors to the English Lake District National Park will be familiar with Alfred Wainwright's *Pictorial Guide to the Lakeland Fells* with his legendary idiosyncratic descriptions of the fells (214 in total) that have become known as Wainwrights.

To capitalise on this familiarity, I have grouped the runs in this guide according to the Wainwright sections. There are ten runs in each of the seven areas. Within each region I have included at least one run that is easy to navigate and relatively easy to run. I have designated these as entry level fell runs.

This guide is too big to carry in your backpack. Keep it at home or in the car. Photocopy the relevant pages and mark the routes on a paper map or create an online version using a mapmaker. Familiarise yourself with the route and the landmarks before you set out and make a note of features to aim for if you get off route, such as walls, fences, rivers and roads.

Route descriptions

There is a quick reference guide at the start of each route description, which lists the length of each route in kilometres and cumulative ascent (height gain) in metres. The distances and height gain have been calculated using GPS and online Ordnance Survey mapping, and while there will be discrepancies between data collected by different runners the differences will be small. The rating system, explained below, is a relative system comparing each of the runs described in this guide. The distance on the road is given to assist in planning, especially with the choice of footwear.

Setting the bearing for Blakeley Raise (Lank Rigg and Whoap route)

The descriptions are 'real-time' written on the day the route was run, so the conditions detailed are for that day. The photographs were taken at different times so the views don't always match the conditions described. The numbering in the descriptions matches the numbers shown on the route maps.

The rating system

I have graded each run on a scale of 1 to 5 according to its relative level of exertion, how easy it is to navigate and the conditions underfoot, using the criteria given in the appendices to this guide.

Following the routes

Naturally, runners go faster than walkers and often they don't want to be spending too much time stopping to check which way to go. For this reason, using a GPS is important as the route descriptions refer to distances travelled between landmarks and changes of direction. Often compass directions are given and these become more important when beginning descents, especially if the visibility is poor.

Using this Guide

Signposts and waymarkers are used where available, in conjunction with other useful aids to navigation such as walls and fences, water features, sheepfolds and other structures. Elementary compass skills are needed on a number of runs and you should take a paper map with you and know how to use it.

Start of Great Carrs route

How long will the runs take?

If you are an inexperienced fell runner, it can be hard to judge how long a run in the mountains might take. Bear in mind that the times I give are those of a just above average 60(+)-year-old-male fell runner. All the times I have recorded are for runs I completed within a six-month period. As a guideline to how long they may take you it might be useful to know that, at the time of writing, I average 21 minutes for flat 5 kilometre parkruns and 45 minutes for 10 kilometre road races.

A younger, fitter runner than me will obviously complete these runs faster than the times I have given. There is no rush. Walking the up-hills is normal and on some of the steeper gradients inevitable.

The weather will have a major part to play in how long you will be out. Wind and rain will slow you down, as will snow and ice.

Eden Runners on Heughscar Hill (Askham Fell route)

Getting Ready

Fell running requires more preparation than road and trail running. You are going to be more exposed to the elements, you will be further away from roads, dwellings and settlements, and you may occasionally stray from your intended route.

The visibility can suddenly change. The terrain is likely to be more demanding. You are more likely to twist an ankle running down a fell than when jogging around your neighbourhood.

The key is to plan ahead. Take more than you think you will need, make sure you know your route and tell someone else where you are going before you set out.

Equipment

Use your common sense and prepare for the worst.

What can go wrong? This is not something you normally think about when going for a road run or a run in the park.

The Fell Runners Association (FRA) has a mandatory minimum kit requirement for its long and medium races. This consists of waterproof jacket and trousers (with taped seams and integrated attached hood on the jacket), hat, gloves, compass, whistle, emergency food and a map of the route.

The FRA would classify the vast majority of runs in this book as short and so the mandatory minimum kit would not apply. Though it is good practice to carry this bare minimum, you should judge the conditions and consider what you might need based on the run and the weather forecast.

Ready to go

On a hot summer's day with no chance of rain, you might look no further than your normal road-running kitbag for most of the runs I have described in this book. You might decide to dispense with the waterproofs and take extra water. If the sky is clear, you have checked the forecast, you are not heading out just before the sun goes down and you have taken the precaution of telling someone where you are going, or switched on the Strava's Beacon app so someone knows where you are, you are going to be pretty safe.

However, in the Lake District, perfect sunny days are few and far between and you will need to take more precautions. As a matter of habit, when I'm running in the fells, I always have a compass, a whistle, a thermal survival bag and some energy bars already packed no matter where I'm going and no matter what the weather is like. This way I won't forget to take them.

In the winter you might be wearing running tights and a base layer, a waterproof jacket, gloves and hat when you set off, so you are going to need to carry extra warm, dry gear as a back-up. Waterproof mitts are useful, as is a buff, and an extra base layer.

Getting Ready

Footwear

In dry conditions, all-terrain running shoes are good enough. I have worn them for years on a mixture of ground from the rolling grassy summits of the Northern Fells to the craggiest rocky peaks of the Borrowdale hills. You may even welcome the thicker cushioning when scrambling over scree and bounding down stony slopes. However, when the weather changes it's a different story. On wet moorland and muddy trods, it has to be a fell shoe. On a lot of the runs in this book, I wore Inov-8 X-talon 200 trail running shoes. Though described as a trail shoe they have a studded sole, which definitely makes them into a fell shoe.

Fell shoes

On rocky ground or stony paths and trails, a more robust shoe is needed. Trail shoes offer grip and cushioning and are more forgiving on any road sections. On steep grassy fells, especially when the ground is soft and wet, they don't offer the same degree of purchase as fell shoes but they perform well when it is dry and provide greater versatility.

Fell shoe lugs

No matter what the manufacturers may claim, I find that nothing really gives you a lot of traction on wet or icy rocks.

And wet feet are inevitable.

Trail shoes

Microspikes

On snowy days when I expect to run on icy trails, I always throw a pair of running microspikes into my bag. They are light to carry and easy to slip onto the bottom of your fell shoes. They won't help me out in the fiercest of winter conditions but they make me feel a lot safer on moderately steep slopes, especially on compacted granular snow. A good pair of fell shoes and some microspikes should get you around most of the runs I have included in this guide.

Kahtoola Microspikes have served me well over the past few years; they are easy to slip on and off, a little over 300g and very compact.

Waterproofs

You will need a waterproof jacket and waterproof running trousers. The make doesn't matter, but the quality is important. The FRA insists on taped seams and integrated attached hood. Some jackets are very light but what you gain in weight loss you lose in durability. I use a Gore-Tex waterproof to give me protection from the wind even when it isn't raining.

Getting Ready

I generally use waterproof running trousers less frequently, relying on my tights to keep my legs warm and dry when the rain is light or when it's snowing.

Headgear

Hats are the warmest option, reflective beanies being my choice. When it is cold and windy, I also wear a Buff (tubular neck scarf) to keep the chill off my neck. On top of a mountain on a cold winter's day, my face is the only part of me that is exposed to the elements.

Gloves

My hands get cold so I have two pairs of gloves for the winter; a pair of lightweight gloves for warmer days and a pair of mitts for when it gets chillier. Mitts might be bulky and prevent you doing fiddly jobs like tying your laces but when the temperatures fall, they can stop your fingers going numb. Mitts, such as the Inov-8 All Terrain Pro Mitts, have a wrist loop, which means you can slip them off without fear of losing them. They easily pack down and are waterproof.

Baselayers

In the summer a short-sleeved T-shirt will suffice but as the weather cools, I move to a long-sleeved thermal top. Merino wool is the warmest and I will always pack a long-sleeved wool baselayer even if I don't wear it to start with.

Equipment checklist

FELL RUNNERS ASSOCIATION MANDATORY MINIMUM FOR MEDIUM AND LONG FELL RACES	WATERPROOF JACKET WITH TAPED SEAMS AND INTEGRATED ATTACHED HOOD
	WATERPROOF TROUSERS WITH TAPED SEAMS
	HAT
	GLOVES
	MAP OF THE ROUTE
	COMPASS
	WHISTLE
	EMERGENCY FOOD
ADDITIONAL EQUIPMENT FOR COLDER WEATHER	EXTRA BASE LAYER(S)
	RUNNING TIGHTS
	WATERPROOF MITTS
	THERMAL SURVIVAL BAG (THIS IS **NOT** A REFLECTIVE SURVIVAL BLANKET)
	BUFF OR NECK SCARF
	MICROSPIKES
EXTRAS	PHONE
	HEAD TORCH (IF HEADING OUT LATE IN THE AFTERNOON)
	BANKCARD AND MONEY
	EMERGENCY CONTACT DETAILS
	DRYSTORE BAGS FOR PHONE, MAP AND MONEY

Getting Ready

Food and drink
All of the runs in this guide are short enough for you not to worry about fuel; I always carry some energy bars just in case I have to walk for some reason. On a hot day, I take water.

Carrying equipment – backpack, vest or waist belt?
You will want to travel as light as you can. How you carry the essentials is a matter of preference and down to the season. Using a waist belt is fine when you can travel light and are not overly worried about taking water. Your gear is easy to access and you don't feel encumbered by straps around the shoulders and chest.

Running vest

Running vests have more space and should have enough volume to carry the minimum recommended equipment. They often have space for hydration bladders and front storage pouches for soft flasks, which means you can drink without having to remove the pack.

Running backpacks are often bigger, offering more capacity when it is cold and you need to bring extra gear. However, your equipment is not very accessible, requiring you to stop to take off the pack when you need something.

Running backpack

Maps
A map based on Ordnance Survey mapping with the scale varied to fit the whole route onto a one-page spread accompanies each route. You should not depend on these maps; they are intended to help you to plot the route onto Ordnance Survey or other published maps.

You should always carry a sheet map of the area in which you are running. All the routes in this guide are covered by the 1:25,000 scale Ordnance Survey Explorer maps of The English Lakes. There are four maps numbered OL4 (north-western area), OL5 (north-eastern area), OL6 (south-western area) and OL7 (south-eastern area). The maps relevant to the runs are listed in the quick reference at the start of each route description.

The lack of phone signal in the fells means you should not rely on the mapping provided on a smartphone. If you download maps, ensure that your device has sufficient charge. Remember, you will need enough battery life for emergencies. Your phone has to work hard when using a map app, so it uses a lot of charge. The longer you leave the map open on the screen, the more it drains the battery.

Getting Ready

Weather

You should check the weather forecast before planning a route. Your choice of route should be made according to the visibility in the fells, the rainfall expected, the temperature and the wind.

Check the wind-chill temperature and make sure you know the temperature and wind speed at the height you will be running. Choose low-level alternatives when the forecast is poor. Useful weather sites include *www.mwis.org.uk/english-welsh-forecast/LD* and *www.metoffice.gov.uk/public/weather/mountain-forecasts/lake-district*

Safety

Because the runs in this book are short, they are relatively safe. You are never going to stray too far from a road, dwellings or villages.

The weather is the major factor in terms of navigation and safety. On a sunny day in summer with clear fell tops, route finding is massively easier than on a misty, rainy day and if you are forced to stop or walk rather than run, you are unlikely to be worrying about hypothermia.

Cloud changes everything. It is very easy to become disoriented even on a route you know well, especially when descending.

> **Better safe than lost**
>
> If the cloud level is likely to be lower than the height you have planned to run at, choose a lower level run or wait for better conditions. Even experienced navigators can get lost in low cloud.

Hay Stacks summit (Hay Stacks route)

Getting Ready

Always plan for injuries in advance. What will happen if you turn over on an ankle and can't continue running? It is easy to underestimate how quickly you can become cold if you stop moving.

Running with a group or a friend is always going to be safer than running on your own and it will feel more secure, especially if you are new to fell running.

The safety list
- Always tell someone where you are going and when you expect to be back.
- Carry a phone, but don't rely on it for route finding.
- Plan the route beforehand.
- Take a sheet map.
- Check the weather, avoid running in the clouds – choose a low-level run when the visibility is poor.
- Know the escape routes.
- Know how to read a map.
- Be prepared for the worst. If you twist an ankle and have to walk or, even worse, you are unable to walk, it is amazing how quickly you can get cold. Don't wait until you feel cold before putting on your warm clothing.
- Take a bankcard and carry some cash.
- Carry details of your address and the details of someone who can be contacted in an emergency.
- Always carry a compass and whistle and know how to use them. Know how to run on a compass bearing.
- If you are running late, call someone as soon as you get reception.
- Wear something bright.
- Beware of trods (paths forged by sheep), which often promise much and then disappear.
- Beware of rights of way (the green dots or dashes on OS maps) that often don't actually exist on the land.
- Check for ticks on your legs if you have been running through ferns.

Emergencies
In the event of emergency, where you can make a call, phone 999 and ask for mountain rescue. You can register your phone at *www.emergencysms.org.uk*. This way you can contact the emergency services by text when you are in an area where signal strength is weak.

Care for the Environment

The Lake District is packed into a small area, stretching just 50 kilometres east to west and 60 kilometres north to south. This compact mountainous region attracts 20 million tourists each year, many wishing to walk, cycle, climb and run in the fells.

Such a volume of visitors inevitably puts pressure on this fragile environment. Footpath erosion, litter, water pollution and traffic congestion are growing issues threatening the very landscape that attracts so many tourists.

Like others enjoying the mountains and lakes, fell runners have a responsibility to help sustain the environment and therefore should aim to leave no trace.

Access

The Countryside and Rights of Way Act (2000) allows a freedom to roam over wild, open countryside in England and Wales. The legal right of open access over mountains, moors, heaths, downs and common land extends to those wishing to walk, watch wildlife, climb and, most importantly for the context of this guide, run without having to stick to paths. Over 50 percent of the park has statutory open access rights.

Dogs

If you are using the open access rights and running with your dog on open access land, you must keep your dog on a lead no more than 2 metres long to protect ground nesting birds between 1 March and 31 July, and at all times around livestock.

On public rights of way, your dog does not have to be on a lead but it must be under close control. Your dog must be with you on the path, not straying off to one side, or in front of you. If there are livestock present, your dog must remain on a short lead.

Countryside Code

As a fell runner, adhere to the Countryside Code, for example by shutting gates and not climbing walls or fences. Respect private property and other users of the fells.

When running the fells share the space; be considerate to others living in, working in and enjoying the countryside. Maintain the natural beauty by caring for nature and leaving no trace. Take your litter home and remove other people's litter when you can.

Swaledales on Bowscale Fell

Care for the Environment

Running off Gowbarrow summit (Gowbarrow route)

Erosion control

Over 10 million people use the Lake Districts paths annually, so not surprisingly many of the popular routes have become badly eroded, with some routes becoming huge open gullies. The damage and scarring caused by erosion is not just ugly, it can also cause habitat loss and a reduction in biodiversity.

The majority of the runs in this guide avoid the most badly eroded paths, the paths with the heaviest footfall over the major hiking routes.

When running on footpaths, avoid erosion by keeping to the path surface and do not take shortcuts.

Look out for donation boxes for Fix the Fells or consider a donation to the teams working on the fells.

Erosion control

Path repairs

About the Author

Having spent most of his career overseas, living and working in Sudan, Cairo, Hong Kong, Amsterdam and Bahrain, John Myatt now lives in the Lake District in the north of England. Since his retirement from teaching and school administration John has devoted his time to researching running routes in the Cumbrian Mountains. He is passionate about the benefits of running on physical and mental health, especially running in wide-open spaces over beautiful and varied terrain. He runs every day, a streak reaching back to 1994, often over the fells close to his door, and hopes to open up the magic of running over mountains to a wider section of the running community.

John often runs with a camera, taking photos to sustain his enthusiasm for the natural world. He is a member of Penrith based Eden Runners and is also a member of the Outdoor Writers and Photographers Guild.

Mindfulness

As a runner, you know the benefits of running for your mood and mental health. Running in the fells, in contact with the natural world and the elements, adds another dimension to this positivity. Be aware of where you are in the present moment. Be alive to your surroundings and use all your senses.

Cherish these fell runs. Observe the shifting clouds, the flights of the soaring ravens, the brilliance of the tumbling waters and the intensity of the colours as they change in a perpetual rhythm through the seasons.

Enjoy the fragrance of the forests and the meadows, and inhale the rich sweet scents of silage and newly mown pasture.

Catbells Terrace (Catbells Terrace route)

Listen to the crunching of the bracken fronds, the piping of the lapwings, the bubbling water as it crashes over rocks and pebbles, and enjoy the silence of the fell summits.

Embrace the wind and the rain against your face, the warmth of the sun on your neck and arms, and revel in the freshly fallen snow as it crumples beneath your fell shoes.

For one hour, become part of the landscape.

Fell-run Summaries

The Eastern Fells

	Run	Start	Distance (km)	Time	Elevation gain (metres)	Exertion level	Navigation level	Terrain level	Nearest town / village
1	Clough Head	NY 315 232	7.9	1hr 13min	602	4	3	2	Threlkeld
2	*Gowbarrow Fell	NY 392 216	7.8	1hr 12min	359	3	1	3	Pooley Bridge
3	Swineside Knott	NY 392 216	8.7	1hr 16min	396	3	3	1	Glenridding
4	Sheffield Pike	NY 386 188	6.9	1hr 13min	526	4	3	4	Glenridding
5	Birkhouse Moor	NY 392 161	9.4	1hr 19min	581	3	2	2	Glenridding
6	Birks and Arnison Crag	NY 392 161	7.3	1hr 11min	503	4	4	2	Glenridding
7	High Hartsop Dodd and Little Hart Crag	NY 402 133	9.1	1hr 22min	481	4	3	3	Patterdale
8	Seat Sandal	NY 335 095	8.2	1hr 22min	657	4	3	2	Grasmere
9	Great Rigg Triangle	NY 340 084	7.7	1hr 16min	685	4	3	2	Grasmere
10	Nab Scar	NY 364 061	6.9	1hr 00min	431	3	3	3	Rydal

The Far Eastern Fells

Run	Start	Distance (km)	Time	Elevation gain (metres)	Exertion level	Navigation level	Terrain level	Nearest town / village
11 *Askham Fell	NY 512 236	9.2	57min	217	1	1	1	Askham
12 Arthur's Pike	NY 478 236	10.3	1hr 11min	352	2	2	1	Pooley Bridge
13 Hallin Fell and Steel Knotts	NY 435 192	8.2	1hr 23min	537	4	3	1	Pooley Bridge
14 Beda Fell	NY 434 184	7.8	1hr 07min	388	2	2	1	Pooley Bridge
15 Place Fell	NY 392 161	7.3	1hr 13min	554	3	3	3	Patterdale
16 Angletarn Pikes	NY 410 130	10.1	1hr 27min	505	4	3	3	Hartsop
17 Caudale Moor and Hartsop Dodd	NY 402 133	9.8	1hr 25min	638	4	2	1	Hartsop
18 Branstree and Selside Pike	NY 469 107	9.3	1hr 19min	528	3	3	1	Bampton
19 Wansfell Pike and Baystones	NY 376 042	11.3	1hr 32min	606	4	1	1	Ambleside
20 Sour Howes and Sallows	NY 412 026	8.3	1hr 09min	440	3	3	2	Troutbeck (Windermere)

*Entry level runs

Fell-run Summaries

The Central Fells

Run	Start	Distance (km)	Time	Elevation gain (metres)	Exertion level	Navigation level	Terrain level	Nearest town / village
21 *High Rigg	NY 306 225	7.4	56min	310	2	2	2	Threlkeld
22 Walla Crag	NY 266 233	8.4	1hr 05min	400	3	2	1	Keswick
23 Bleaberry Fell	NY 287 227	8.7	1hr 15min	442	2	3	1	Keswick
24 Raven Crag	NY 306 189	6.3	50min	365	3	2	1	Keswick
25 Brund Fell	NY 256 176	8.5	1hr 22min	422	3	3	2	Grange
26 Armboth Fell and High Tove	NY 305 102	7.3	1hr 16min	685	3	3	1	Grasmere
27 Watendlath Tarn	NY 256 148	8.1	1hr 15min	419	3	2	2	Keswick
28 Steel Fell	NY 320 129	6.5	1hr 08min	366	3	3	1	Grasmere
29 Silver How	NY 336 075	6.9	1hr 15min	406	3	3	1	Grasmere
30 Loughrigg Fell	NY 375 044	9.2	1hr 12min	361	2	3	1	Ambleside

The Southern Fells

Run	Start	Distance (km)	Time	Elevation gain (metres)	Exertion level	Navigation level	Terrain level	Nearest town / village
31 Rosthwaite Fell (Bessyboot)	NY 245 138	10.5	1hr 32min	452	4	3	3	Rosthwaite
32 Seathwaite Fell	NY 235 122	8.4	1hr 26min	525	4	3	3	Rosthwaite
33 Lingmoor Fell and Blea Tarn	NY 295 043	7.9	1hr 12min	425	3	3	3	Chapel Stile
34 Great Carrs, Swirl How and Grey Friar	NY 277 027	8.5	1hr 29min	649	4	3	3	Skelwith Bridge
35 Black Fell and Tarn Hows	SD 321 998	8.7	1hr 11min	294	2	3	1	Coniston
36 Wetherlam	NY 306 010	8.4	1hr 32min	620	5	3	5	Coniston
37 *Holme Fell and Tarn Hows	NY 328 018	7.5	1hr 09min	354	2	2	2	Coniston
38 Harter Fell (Eskdale)	NY 213 011	7.2	1hr 19min	546	3	3	2	Eskdale Green
39 Green Crag	NY 190 009	7.9	1hr 23min	459	3	3	2	Eskdale Green
40 Devoke Water	SD 170 977	7.6	1hr 19min	396	2	4	1	Eskdale Green

*Entry level runs

Fell-run Summaries

The Northern Fells

Run	Start	Distance (km)	Time	Elevation gain (metres)	Exertion level	Navigation level	Terrain level	Nearest town / village
41 Binsey Double	NY 236 351	7.7	1hr 05min	464	3	3	1	Bassenthwaite
42 High Pike (Caldbeck)	NY 345 358	8.1	1hr 08min	380	2	4	1	Hesket Newmarket
43 Uldale Fells	NY 266 358	9.2	1hr 12min	592	3	4	1	Uldale
44 Bowscale Fell	NY 359 316	7.3	57min	484	3	3	2	Mungrisdale
45 Bannerdale Crags	NY 368 302	11.5	1hr 45min	630	3	3	1	Mungrisdale
46 Longside Edge	NY 234 281	8.25	1hr 23min	710	4	2	2	Bassenthwaite
47 Souther Fell	NY 343 269	9.1	1hr 31min	559	3	3	1	Threlkeld
48 Blencathra	NY 318 256	11.0	1hr 38min	783	5	2	1	Threlkeld
49 *Glenderaterra Valley	NY 302 256	9.8	1hr 10min	448	2	1	2	Threlkeld
50 *Latrigg	NY 267 241	8.8	57min	381	2	2	1	Keswick

The North Western Fells

Run	Start	Distance (km)	Time	Elevation gain (metres)	Exertion level	Navigation level	Terrain level	Nearest town / village
51 Sale Fell and Ling Fell	NY 185 293	7.9	59min	437	2	3	1	Embleton
52 Graystones, Broom Fell and Lord's Seat	NY 181 255	8.0	1hr 10min	494	3	3	1	Braithwaite
53 Whinlatter Top and Brown How	NY 208 244	8.7	1hr 12min	363	3	3	1	Braithwaite
54 Whiteside	NY 168 241	8.3	1hr 22min	622	5	2	5	Lorton
55 Barrow and Outerside	NY 231 236	7.3	1hr 14min	599	3	2	1	Braithwaite
56 *Catbells Terrace	NY 252 228	10.5	1hr 08min	253	2	1	2	Keswick
57 Causey Pike and Scar Crags	NY 232 217	8.0	1hr 17min	606	4	2	5	Braithwaite
58 Maiden Moor and High Spy	NY 231 193	11.0	1hr 31min	538	4	1	3	Braithwaite
59 Knott Rigg and Ard Crags	NY 192 176	7.4	1hr 09min	432	2	3	1	Buttermere
60 Rannerdale Knotts	NY 174 169	8.0	1hr 06min	457	2	2	1	Buttermere

*Entry level runs

Fell-run Summaries

The Western Fells

Run	Start	Distance (km)	Time	Elevation gain (metres)	Exertion level	Navigation level	Terrain level	Nearest town / village
61 Fellbarrow and Low Fell	NY 118 224	8.4	1hr 19min	516	3	3	1	Loweswater
62 Burnbank Fell and Blake Fell	NY 109 228	8.0	1hr 04min	439	3	3	1	Loweswater
63 Gavel Fell and Blake Fell	NY 134 210	9.2	1hr 12min	531	3	3	1	Loweswater
64 Hen Comb	NY 142 211	9.4	1hr 18min	407	3	3	1	Loweswater
65 *Murton Fell and Cogra Moss	NY 085 198	8.2	1hr 00min	282	1	2	1	Lamplugh
66 Mellbreak	NY 142 211	9.8	1hr 28min	531	4	2	5	Loweswater
67 Crag Fell and Grike	NY 070 159	10.2	1hr 13min	467	3	2	1	Ennerdale Bridge
68 Hay Stacks	NY 194 149	7.7	1hr 27min	544	4	2	5	Buttermere
69 Lank Rigg and Whoap	NY 066 130	9.1	1hr 12min	477	3	3	1	Ennerdale Bridge
70 Middle Fell and Seatallan	NY 144 055	7.2	1hr 22min	726	4	4	1	Nether Wasdale

* Entry level runs

The Eastern Fells

Dominated by the massifs of Helvellyn and Fairfield, bounded by Thirlmere and Dunmail Raise in the west and Ullswater and Kirkstone Pass in the east, these Eastern Fell routes are easily accessible and eminently runnable. Classic Lakeland views of perfect calm waters and crowded peaks abound, rocks are not a hindrance and grassy summits prevail.

Stile on Birkhouse Moor (Birkhouse Moor route)

Eden Runners, Clough Head

Clough Head 1

Clough Head from St John's in the Vale

1 Clough Head

Park / Start	Wanthwaite, junction of the B5322 and the road to St John's Church (NY 315 232)		
Map	OS Explorer OL5		
Exertion	●●●●		
Navigation	●●●		
Terrain	●●		
Distance	7.9 kilometres	Time	1 hour 13 minutes
Ascent	602 metres	On road	200 metres

A satisfyingly uncomplicated traverse across a craggy mountain face

There is room for three or four cars on the west side of the road just by the turn-off for St John's Church and Youth Centre. From here, the western face of Clough Head looks daunting. Red Screes, Buck Castle, Wanthwaite Crags and Bram Crag seem to form a forbidding fortress to all except intrepid climbers. Despite this, the route I am taking to the summit is on clear, mainly grassy paths.

START The signpost at the start of the trail is visible from where I am parked, a hundred metres south.
❶ I turn left up the track marked *'Public Way Old Coach Road Dockray (5 ½ mile)'* and follow the lane past Hill Top Farm. For ease of navigation, avoiding the disused Hill Top Quarries, I continue on the Old Coach Road until I reach a five-barred gate.

25

1 Clough Head

❷ Through the gate I immediately turn right climbing up the pasture alongside the fence; there is no path. I cross a track and keep climbing with the disused quarry behind the wall on my right. Four hundred and forty metres from the Old Coach Road there is a gate in the wall with a sign warning of the quarry ahead. **❸** This is my signal to turn left up the fell along a grooved path that looks like an old wagon run. The path is clear, a steep winding grass furrow, which attacks the slope in broad sweeps to reduce the gradient. Once I have gained the same height as Threlkeld Knotts, a subsidiary summit 400 metres due north, the path switches back south-west across Red Screes. A smooth, well-worn path, and a steep but straightforward run that did not seem possible from the road below.

❹ Above the scree, I hairpin back again, left, onto a grassy track, the gradient eases and the summit trig point comes into view. Significant as being the most northerly fell of the Helvellyn Range, Clough Head drops away to the Glenderamackin valley offering a grandstand view of the Blencathra Massif. On a calm spring evening, I can pause to locate a score of overlapping peaks from Skiddaw to Coniston Old Man. A bleak spot in a westerly wind, a raw day in winter would force a quick retreat.

Clough Head 1

Eden Runners on Clough Head on a summer's evening

My route of descent is down to the Old Coach Road, aiming for Hause Well. ❺ The path I want, not marked on the OS map, follows a north-northeasterly line. I run on a bearing of 30 degrees on a path that is virtually a continuation of my route of ascent. I avoid the more northerly, indistinct path that would lead me too close to Red Screes.

Red Screes, Clough Head

Once beyond the summit, the grassy north-easterly ridge falls away directly and quite steeply. However, on a soft route bereft of rocks I can bound down the kilometre to the Coach Road without concern.

I veer to the east of White Pike; there are a number of paths down but my actual route choice is not crucial. ❻ I will soon reach the Coach Road, where I will turn left and head back to Wanthwaite. I actually arrive at the byway too far to the east at a point where there is no gate in the fence. I run west along the fence line until I reach the gate beyond Hause Well.

The Old Coach Road ... a route of mystery, with no evidence of it ever being used by coaches. A drover's road,

Signpost for the Old Coach Road, Wanthwaite

1 Clough Head

Clough Head summit looking west

a route for miners, a track for peat diggers? Whatever its former use, today it is a rocky trail heading west towards the old Threlkeld Quarry, hard on my fell-shoe lugs. I should have worn my trail shoes.

The running is easy though, past incongruously placed old railway carriages scattered across the common. Above the Iron Age settlement, I cross the track leading to the quarry face, still strewn with discarded granite.

As I round the flank of Threlkeld Knotts, I reach the gate I passed through an hour ago on my way up to the summit, leaving me with a five-minute trot down the track, back to the road and my car.

St John's in the Vale from Red Screes, Clough Head

Eden Runners training run, Clough Head

Gowbarrow Fell 2

Gowbarrow from Arthur's Pike

2 Gowbarrow Fell

Park / Start	The Royal Hotel, Dockray (NY 392 216)		
Map	OS Explorer OL5		
Exertion	●●●		
Navigation	●		
Terrain	●●●		
Distance	7.8 kilometres	**Time**	1 hour 12 minutes
Ascent	359 metres	**On road**	0 metres

An entry-level loop through Wordsworth's daffodil country

Shooting boxes and stalkers' huts betray Gowbarrow Park's past as home to a large herd of deer. Today the main attraction is the thunderous waterfall at Aira Beck.

START A fingerpost across the road from The Royal Hotel pointing to Airy Crag and Ulcat Row takes me down to Riddings Beck. The track becomes a path, which today is a stream. Storm Christoph has saturated the fells and the water has nowhere to go.

Over the footbridge, then splash through the beck. I reach the gate that opens into Gowbarrow Park, Lord Greystoke's old hunting ground. ❶ Once through the gate at the three-fingered sign I head west, upwards, in the direction of Airy Crag and Gowbarrow summit.

2 Gowbarrow Fell

I am now on the Ullswater Way, waymarked by yellow daffodils in a nod to Wordsworth, following the alternative route around the north side of Gowbarrow Fell, and my climbing begins.

A lone Herdwick ewe, grey and bristly, gazes at me quizzically, following my ascent through the surface runoff, the greasy mud and peaty quag. I am moving slowly here, straining because of the slope and the slippery surface. Mist, sombre and atmospheric, swirls around me, but ahead I can make out the bumpy knolls of Airy Crag – the fell summit.

I have to take a slight detour to reach the trig point. I continue past the pillar and re-join the path I left 100 metres further on. Down the twisting, well-maintained path through the heaps of heather, brown and woody, stressed by midwinter's struggle. Again, a single Herdwick raises its head, its piercing eyes tracking me as I step carefully down to the gate leading to Swinburn's Park.

I am at the point where the Ullswater Way divides. ❷ At the fingerpost I turn south in the direction of Aira Force (1.5 miles). I ascend into the still, lugubrious cloud across waterfalls and down slick rocks. I tread cautiously today. As I reach the southern face of the fell, yet another Herdwick gives me puzzled look.

Gowbarrow Fell 2

Heading towards Gowbarrow summit

The start of the Gowbarrow run

Running over Gowbarrow

I am beginning to think it's the same one, stalking me. On the contour path west on a summer's day, the view up and down Ullswater is one of the finest in the English Lakes. Today the scene is grey. Then I gasp out loud. There is no one to hear me. The mist drifts away, the lake is revealed, a silver sheet, a pool of mercury. By some optical illusion, it appears to be above the clouds, floating.

I turn and see Lyulph's Tower – an old hunting lodge – at the point where Dorothy Wordsworth inspired her brother to write of "... *a host of golden daffodils*". I splash through puddles, joyously, like a young boy. I keep on the path, through the gate and down to Aira Beck. ❸ I can see the stone bridge ahead, but I turn sharply right, keeping the rushing water to my left. ❹ Thunderous water, white and moss green as it bounds down the rocks towards the lake.

❺ At the plunge pool beneath the force, I take the well-cut steps upwards and away from the rapids, but soon I am back by the swollen water. I can hear bird song and crashing torrents, nothing more. Peaty water droplets

2 Gowbarrow Fell

Lyulph's Tower from the path towards Aira Force

linger in the air. Soon, away from the beck, through flooded fields to Dockray, I pass the fingerpost I met an hour earlier directing me to Airy Crag. I continue through the gate, paddling up to the footbridge and along the track to The Royal Hotel.

An accessible fell, one that can be run in all seasons. A straightforward, well-marked route, almost impossible to go wrong on even in the densest of mist.

Aira Force tumbling towards Ullswater

Route to Gowbarrow from Dockray

Swineside Knott 3

Swineside Knott from Lucy's Wood

3 Swineside Knott

Park / Start	The Royal Hotel, Dockray (NY 392 216)		
Map	OS Explorer OL5		
Exertion	•••		
Navigation	•••		
Terrain	•		
Distance	8.7 kilometres	Time	1 hour 30 minutes (in deep snow)
Ascent	396 metres	On road	800 metres

A little visited fell with the best vistas of Ullswater

Swineside Knott is not one of Wainwright's fells, which probably explains why this is a moor of such tranquillity compared with Gowbarrow Fell, its more famous neighbour.

START Just south of The Royal Hotel in Dockray on the A5091 road to Ullswater there is a phone box and an artist's studio where I turn right onto a broad track leading towards open moorland. ❶ Once through the gate and past the National Trust sign for Watermillock Common, I follow the track for 90 metres before turning left onto a grassy path that begins to climb up the fell ❷.

After another 300 metres the path branches, continuing straight on towards the mound of Round How or right to climb Common Fell. I proceed right, cross Pounder Sike, and within 60 metres branch right again onto a broad path that begins to climb steeply.

33

3 Swineside Knott

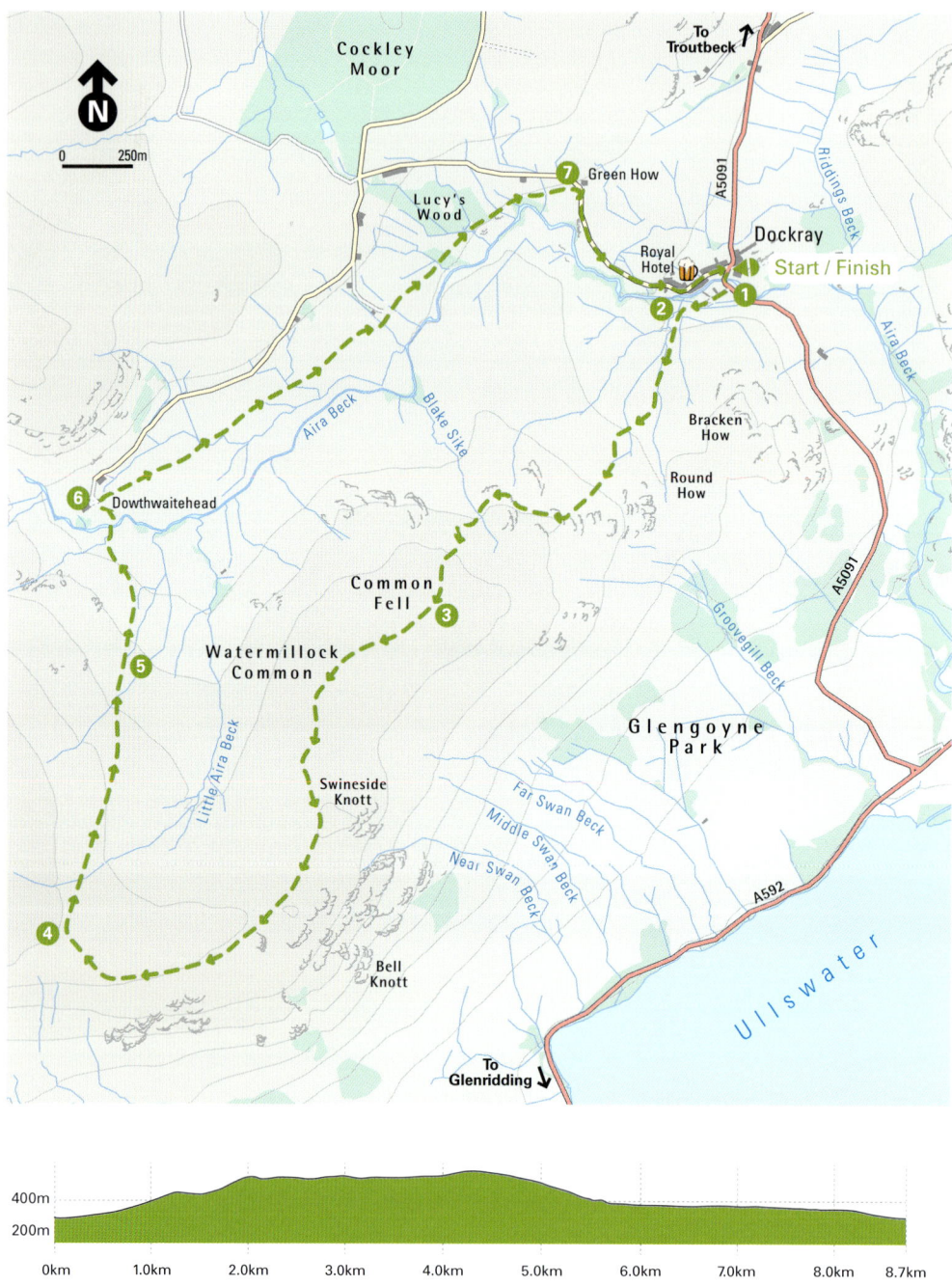

It is not long before I am wading through snow at least 20 centimetres deep. In parts, I sink into drifts of soft snow that reach beyond my knees. My attempt to run is quickly scuppered. I am not sure where the path lies. I see paw prints, like those of a dog, but there are no footprints so I can only guess that I am following the nocturnal track of a fox.

Swineside Knott

I'm in the shade of the afternoon sun. I traverse icy springs, crack frozen scales upon hardened bogs, seeking the higher ground, which is swathed in bright sunshine. The snow hides the tufted grass; I stumble and fall, knowing that I am not on my intended path. I know I have to resist all routes that try to lure me left away from the higher ground. I keep climbing. My progress has slowed to walking pace.

Then with height gained the sun flashes into my eyes, bouncing off the white, making it hard to see. After a kilometre of steep ascent, I reach a large anvil-shaped boulder, then a small cairn. This is Common Fell. ❸ Back on my intended route, I take the south-westerly path, hidden by drifts of untouched snow, in the direction of Swineside Knott.

The route undulates over Watermillock Common, veering south to reveal the sweeping panorama of Ullswater. Climbing under a deep blue sky, warmed by the afternoon sun, I eventually reach a trail of footprints and I sense that beneath the crunching white powder is a path. I follow the route to the highest point of the moor. Walkers and their dogs have been here earlier but I see no one. The rolling hills are silent, intensely white and still. Ahead, the unruffled surface of Ullswater, reflecting the blue of the sky, seems even bluer in contrast to the frosted peaks.

I can run freely now that I am on top of the ridge. The snow is still deep here but trampled by earlier visitors. Once beyond the high point of the fell the path veers to the west. I reach a drystone wall, turn right and run north-west for 150 metres. Ahead in the distance, gleaming silver, is Blencathra's saddle. ❹ I reach a stile in the wall and I know this is the point where I turn right to begin my descent towards Dowthwaitehead. With the marshy ground an ice rink in places, I keep to the edge of the path, crossing Little Aira Beck heading for the enclosed pastures.

❺ Over a stile I veer slightly west of north down to Aira Beck, down to the valley. Gentle slopes across a moor,

The Artist's Studio at the start of the Swineside Knott run

Leave the track to start the climb Swineside Knott

The anvil rock on Common Fell, Watermillock Common

Ullswater from Common Fell

Entering Lucy's Wood

3 Swineside Knott

Running through Lucy's Wood with Swineside Knott in the background

frosted and hard, interspersed with patches of soft mud trapped beneath polygons of thick ice. When I reach the wall the fingerpost by the gate points to Dowthwaitehead (¾ mile) across farm fields into the damp valley bottom. A footbridge over Aira Beck leads me to the farm at Dowthwaitehead. ❻ I turn right onto the path meandering through fields and numerous gates in the direction of Green How, following yellow arrows and slate signs. Through Lucy's Wood and high above Aira Beck as it races towards Dockray.

❼ I reach the road at Green How and turn right. Usually I can hurtle down here but today glassy ice makes me wary. Less than one kilometre on tarmac takes me back to The Royal Hotel in Dockray.

Entering Watermillock Common

Sheffield Pike from Ullswater

4 Sheffield Pike

Park / Start	Glencoyne Bay, Glenridding (NY 386 188)		
Map	OS Explorer OL5		
Exertion	●●●●		
Navigation	●●●		
Terrain	●●●●		
Distance	6.9 kilometres	Time	1 hour 13 minutes
Ascent	526 metres	On road	600 metres

Surrounded by shafts and levels, and two classic glacial valleys with views along a serene ribbon lake

This is a figure of eight run, which can be completed in either direction. Today I have chosen to run the Sheffield Pike section of the double loop clockwise, thinking that the wind will be behind me on the way up and over the top.

START From the car park, I take the path south towards Glenridding. This is part of the Ullswater Way. I only stay on here for 170 metres and, unfortunately, the last 20 metres are flooded so I have to wade through knee-deep water. At least I no longer have to bother trying to keep my feet dry.

1 After Glencoyne Bridge, I turn right down the tarmack driveway to Glencoyne Farm. At the farm, the

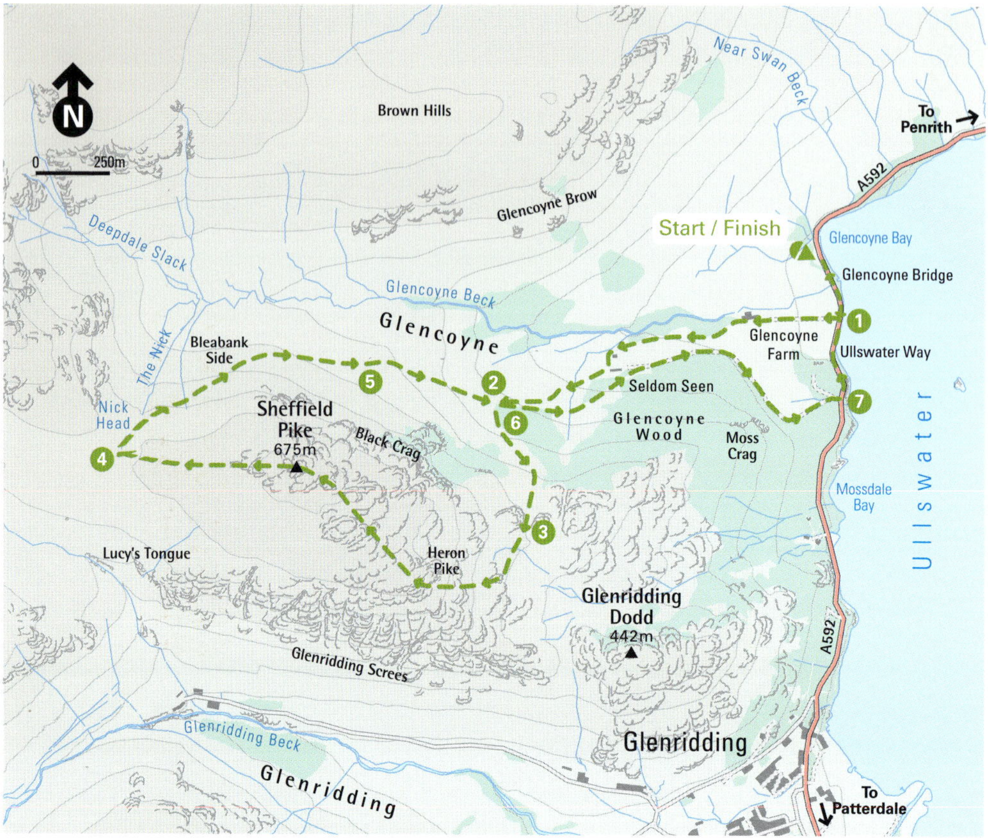

4 Sheffield Pike

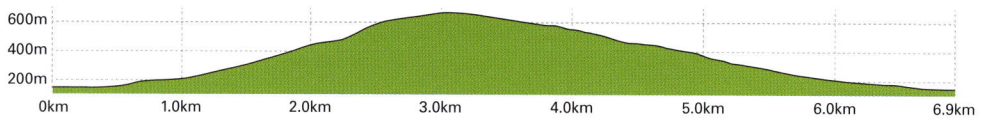

path passes through the garden and the state of the gate fastenings makes me think walkers are not encouraged to come this way.

Through the garden, I veer up the bank on the left and follow the path alongside Glencoyne Beck until I reach Seldom Seen – ten mineworker's cottages built in the heyday of the Greenside mine. The path passes alongside the plantation at the back of the cottages rising up to a wall. ❷ I pass through the gate in the wall and labour straight ahead, taking the path (not on the map) heading south. The footpath hugs the wall, climbing gradually at first. Ahead, though, is an arduous slog. A 30 percent incline for 1.5 kilometres, I will have my head down and I won't be running.

My views here are restricted, by the plantation on my left and the sun directly ahead, which means I lose track of the path each time I raise my head. I keep close to the wall until I pass between a gateway formed by two rocky hillocks, the one on my left on the other side of the wall ❸. Just beyond the two protuberances, 600 meters on from the gate, the path branches off to the right and continues to climb towards the southeast ridge to Heron Pike.

Sheffield Pike

The route back to Glencoyne Bay

Now my view is fixed on the rocky trail in front of me. I follow the path as it climbs towards a break between two rocky outcrops, sweeping below and to the left of the highest point of Heron Pike.

At last, the gradient eases and the vista opens up with Glenridding Beck to my left and the broad ridge of Sheffield Pike ahead. Beyond the heather across soft, boggy ground, I run on more gentle slopes towards the peak. Brown-black peat and mossy swamps hamper my journey to the summit cairn. Now the outline of the surrounding fells is in my field of view; Stybarrow Dodd, Raise, White Side, Helvellyn. An undulating landscape, providing a feeling of space and freedom. I am alone in the wilderness.

The driveway to Glencoyne Farm

It's all downhill from here. The path continues on, directly west. I splash across the sodden moor, picking up the pace, unaware of time. Seven hundred metres on from the summit I reach Nick Head, at an obvious col between the heights of Sheffield Pike and Stybarrow Dodd ❹. Various paths cross, I veer right, north-east then east, keeping high above Glencoyne with the meandering beck snaking towards Ullswater several hundred metres below.

Seldom Seen, miners cottages at Glencoyne

The descent is steep yet steady. I can see the wall ahead. The path passes across rocky ground, through a high pasture of boulders. ❺ When I reach the wall, I

4 Sheffield Pike

Eden Runners ascending Sheffield Pike

pass through the gate and drop quite sharply towards Glencoyne Wood.

Five hundred metres on from the wall, I am back at the gate I passed through 45 minutes earlier. However, I don't retrace my steps back down to the valley towards Seldom Seen. Instead, I keep going east through another gate into Glencoyne Wood ❻. After a few hundred metres of negotiating branches and protruding roots, I am above the miner's cottages and I turn right onto a track that takes me all the way to the road at Mossdale Bay. Only now on a smooth gravel trail can I pick up my pace. For me, this loop doesn't give much opportunity for anything approaching moderate running speed. It is a straight up and down journey with no flat ridges to canter across. An hour has flown by, though. An hour in a tranquil valley and over a little visited summit.

Running down from Sheffield Pike to Nick Head

The route down from Sheffield Pike to Glencoyne

❼ When I reach the road, I cross with care, picking up the path directly in front of me, part of the Ullswater Way. I meander north by the lakeside for a couple of hundred metres, then the path crosses back over the road. I follow the wall, past the driveway to Glencoyne Farm, through the flooded field back to the car park.

5 Birkhouse Moor

Glenridding from Birkhouse Moor

5 Birkhouse Moor

Park / Start	St Patrick's Church, Patterdale (NY 392 161)
Map	OS Explorer OL5
Exertion	● ● ●
Navigation	● ●
Terrain	● ●
Distance	9.4 kilometres
Time	1 hour 19 minutes
Ascent	581 metres
On road	2.4 kilometres

A rolling moor between two perfect glens

Two hours free parking in the lay-by in front of the church should be plenty of time, unless something goes wrong.

START I head towards Glenridding and after 250m turn left ❶ along the Grisedale Road. At the road bend, a signpost to Helvellyn and Grisedale Tarn is confirmation, if I need it, that I am heading in the right direction.

Beside the falling waters of Grisedale Beck, I run for a kilometre into the gloomy valley with the claustrophobic masses of the surrounding mountains hemming me in. At the start of the farm track a slate sign points to Grisedale Tarn and Grasmere. ❷ Here I turn right down a private road, towards the kennels, on a public footpath towards Helvellyn. Over the bridge and straight on through a gate where there is a

5 Birkhouse Moor

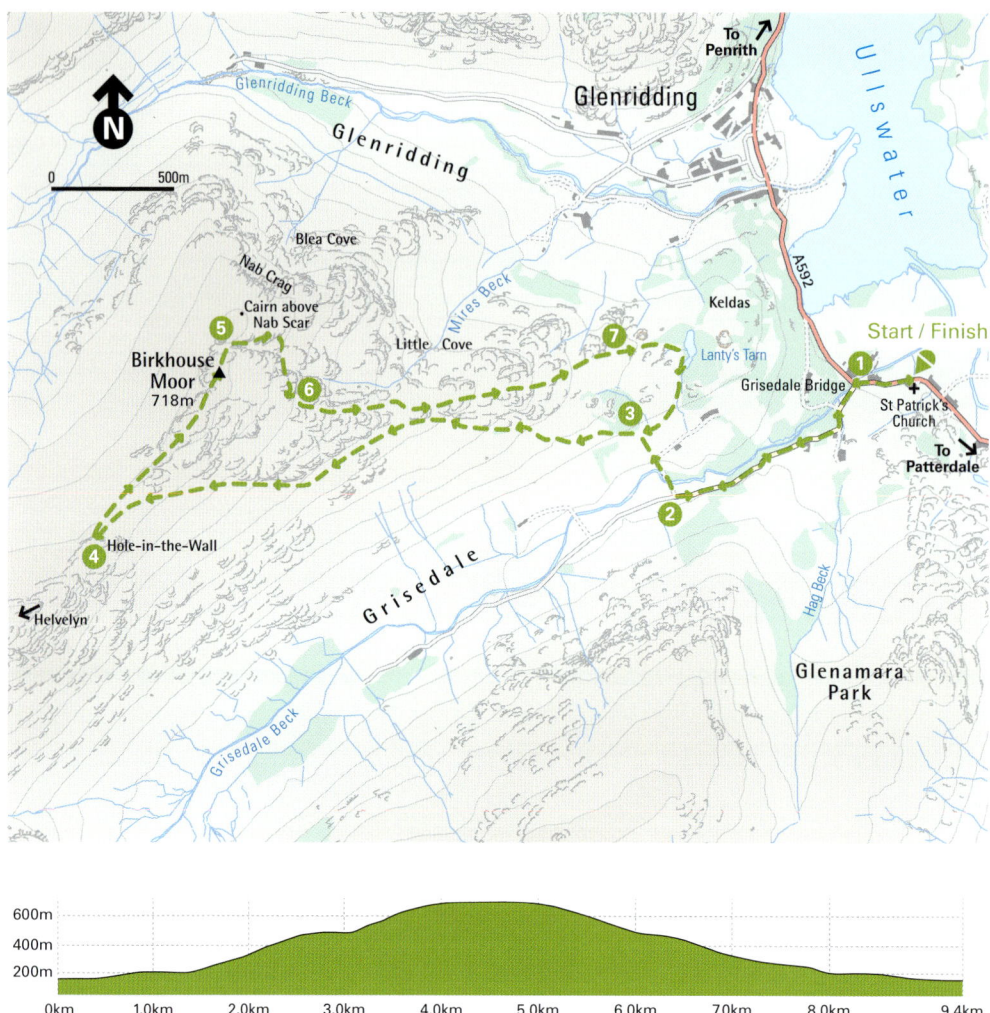

wordless finger sign. ❸ Across a field to another gate and then the valley opens up. I climb away from the wall in a westerly direction. It gets brighter; the sun, as pale as a moon, tries to push through the clouds. I feel released from the valley.

So far, it has been easy, but you have to be prepared for a long slog up to the Hole-in-the-Wall. Most of the way the gradient is consistent. For nearly two kilometres I struggle along at the same pace managing something resembling a run.

The path is fairly smooth so it's easy to make progress, until you pass a large cairn. Beyond this point, the route becomes progressively rocky and more arduous. The gradient increases a notch and some of the boulders are a struggle to climb without a lot of effort and some thigh pushing. The ascent is a good cardiovascular workout but it does nothing for your leg speed.

I glimpse a wall rising over the slope to my left; the Hole-in-the-Wall is not far off now. A set of stone steps and a final gruelling effort, then a wall junction and two stiles come into view. Mountaineers turn left towards Striding Edge and the summit of Helvellyn. ❹ I head for the stile straight ahead, relieved to

Birkhouse Moor 5

Looking back towards the Hole-in-the-Wall

Birkhouse Moor from the lane to the kennels

Nearly at the Hole-in-the-Wall

be close to the summit of the moor. Once over, I immediately turn right following the path alongside the wall. At last I am on rolling moorland, with most of the climbing behind me. My quads are lumps of lead and I am still gasping for air so even the small inclines seem tough. I trudge on, not sure of where the highest point is, but there is a flattish pile of stones just before the turn in the wall and I assume this is it.

As the wall turns right (to the east) I carry straight on for 180 metres towards Nab Crag. These days this is the recommended route as the path by the wall is getting badly eroded. ❺ One hundred and forty metres before the cairn I turn right to follow the route east and shortly I'm running alongside the wall again towards Lanty's Tarn ❻. At first, the path is craggy and steep – not a path I can bound down. Soon the terrain gives way to grassy moorland, wet but more grippy. I try to pick up the pace.

Segments of Ullswater drift into view, like pieces of a jigsaw puzzle, and Place Fell is directly in my eyeline across the water. I'm close to Glenridding here. I peer

5 Birkhouse Moor

Greenside Road from Birkhouse Moor

down at the Greenside Mine road and the miner's cottages. Under dank oppressive clouds, I can almost hear the haulers and the washers and the separators and dressers at the end of their shifts, returning to their lodging shops or the stone cottages that reach deep into the narrow valley overlooked by looming fells.

Lanty's Tarn, an old Patterdale Hall fishing haunt, appears nestled in a woodland west of Keldas. I keep on

Heading down to Lanty's Tarn from Birkhouse Moor

the path, hugging the north side of the wall until, 1.7 kilometres on from where the wall turns to the east, I meet the footpath leading up from Grisedale. ❼ At this point, I cross the wall by a stone stile and once over continue to follow the wall in an easterly direction. In just 300 metres, I reach the tarn, turn right, and jog along the water's edge. The track beyond the small dam leads back to the gate where I began my grind up to the Hole-in-the-Wall. I can now retrace my steps back to the church.

Birks and Arnison Crag   6

Arnison Crag from Glenridding Pier

6 Birks and Arnison Crag

Park / Start	St Patrick's Church, Patterdale (NY 392 161)		
Map	OS Explorer OL5		
Exertion	••••		
Navigation	••••		
Terrain	••		
Distance	7.3 kilometres	Time	1 hour 11 minutes
Ascent	503 metres	On road	1.1 kilometres

An old deer park and magnificent views of the head of Ullswater

The mountains and lakes in the English Lake District are small, even on a European scale. This is what gives them their beauty.

Within one field of view, an abundance of distinctive peaks is visible, both in the foreground and in multiple layers reaching back in all directions. Entire bodies of water can be surveyed in a single sweep, encircled by green sloping shorelines and timeless hamlets and villages.

Many of the peaks are small enough to get up and down quite easily and most of them are close to a road. Today I will run over the summits of two Wainwright fells in just over an hour. There is something satisfying about running up and down a mountain on your daily run. Around here, this does not have to be an epic journey.

6 Birks and Arnison Crag

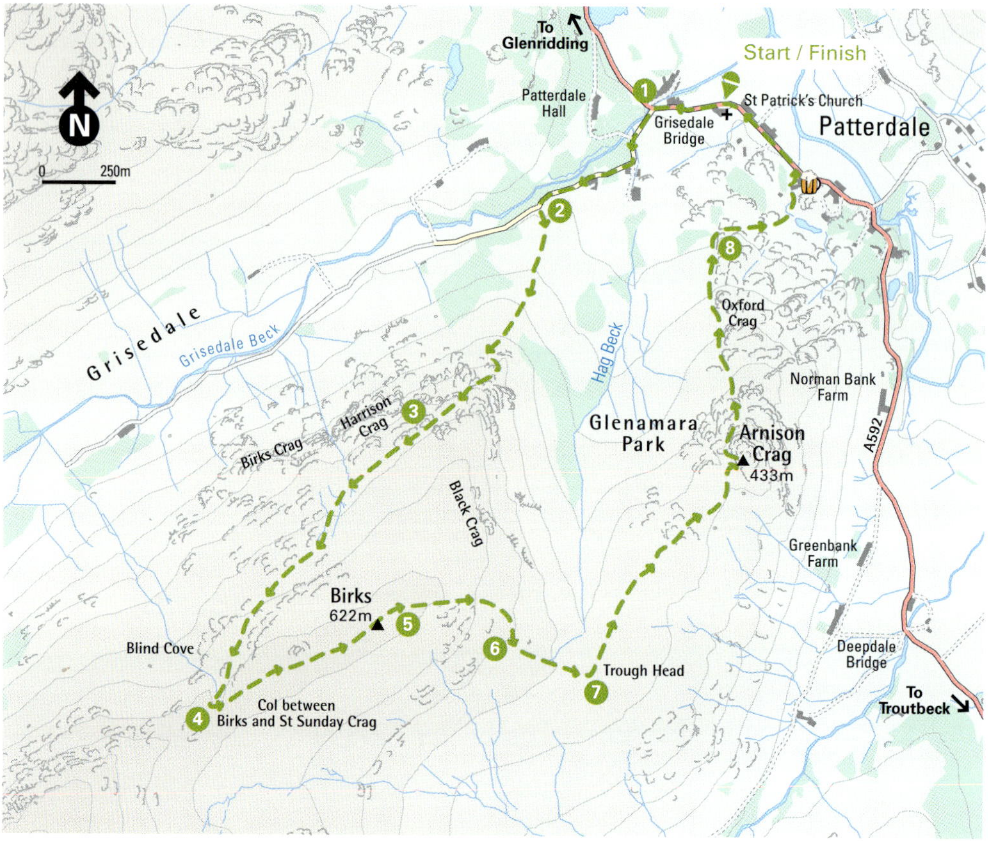

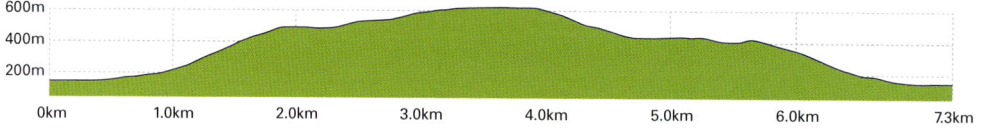

🚶 **START** From the parking space in front of St Patrick's Church, I head north towards Glenridding for 250 metres before turning left down the lane to Grisedale. ❶ Past Patterdale Hall, alongside Grisedale Beck, I continue on the road for another 500 metres until I reach a field gate on my left with a public footpath sign. ❷ Ahead is a gate through a fence and a National Trust sign telling me I am entering Glenamara Park.

I continue straight ahead, climbing steeply. The sound of the dogs howling at the kennels across the valley follows me up. It is a strenuous ascent to begin with, through another gate with views of Birkhouse Moor to my right and the peak of St Sunday Crag in front of me. I am in a tranquil corridor of low-lying fells. The summit of Helvellyn lies beyond Striding Edge and Grisedale Beck flows along the valley below. The dogs are still barking.

❸ A faint path leads off to my left but I ignore this, keeping south-west towards the col between Birks and St Sunday Crag. The col is an obvious junction. ❹ I turn a sharp left so that I am now heading north-east towards Birks summit.

Birks and Arnison Crag 6

Heading towards Birks summit

From the col, it is just 700 metres to the highest point. I reach an insignificant cairn, which I assume is the top. Place Fell dominates the skyline in front of me. It has been easy navigation until this point. Now I need to focus more – I'm entering an amber leg of an orienteer's traffic lighting system. Beyond the summit I continue on the path north-east for 200 metres. I reach a small pile of stones and see an indistinct path to my right. ❺ I follow the path until I reach a wall, broken to begin with. I keep to the right side of the wall descending a steep grassy slope, lamenting my lack of speed, irked by my over-caution.

Ullswater from the path down from Arnison Crag

The wall becomes more intact. Three hundred and seventy metres from the turn-off at the pile of stones, the wall turns left and the path branches. ❻ I take the right-hand branch, soft grassy ground down to the head of Hag Beck.

Arnison Crag from Patterdale

Trough Head is ahead of me; I climb up to reach the ridge path over Arnison Crag. ❼ Turning left, undulations and bogs abound, I am heading north-northeast on easy to run terrain. I take the short diversion up to the top of the crag. Ullswater spreads before me. From a distance, the moored steamers at Glenridding jetty seem like toys floating on a model boating lake.

6 Birks and Arnison Crag

The route down from Arnison Crag

I retrace my steps and follow the path north, keeping an impressive drystone wall to my left. ❽ I ignore the gate leading back into Glenamara Park, follow the trail down the slope and pass through the gate in front of me. Once through the gate, I bear left and almost end up in the kitchen of the Patterdale Hotel!

I am now back at the road where I turn left to cover the 250 metres back to the church and my car.

Patterdale Hotel

7 High Hartsop Dodd and Little Hart Crag

High Hartsop Dodd and Caiston Glen from the Kirkstone Pass

Park / Start	Cow Bridge, Patterdale (NY 402 133)		
Map	OS Explorer OL5		
Exertion	●●●●		
Navigation	●●●		
Terrain	●●●		
Distance	9.1 kilometres	Time	1 hour 22 minutes
Ascent	481 metres	On road	0 metres

A sharp climb gives stunning views over Brothers Water

Brothers Water, lake or tarn, is glittering today.
The things we claim as beauty are hard to analyse. Sunlight flicking the wavelets of a body of water, surrounded by green fields and folded mountains. White clouds floating across an azure sky. A fresh northerly wind chills my back and neck. April sun warms my face. It is a day when it is hard to get the clothing right.

START From where I am parked, the start of this run is difficult to miss. Over the old bridge at the southwest corner of the car park, I pass through the gate onto the path leading south alongside the west bank of Brothers Water. Surprisingly on such a beautiful afternoon, the path is deserted. Through the trees,

7 High Hartsop Dodd and Little Hart Crag

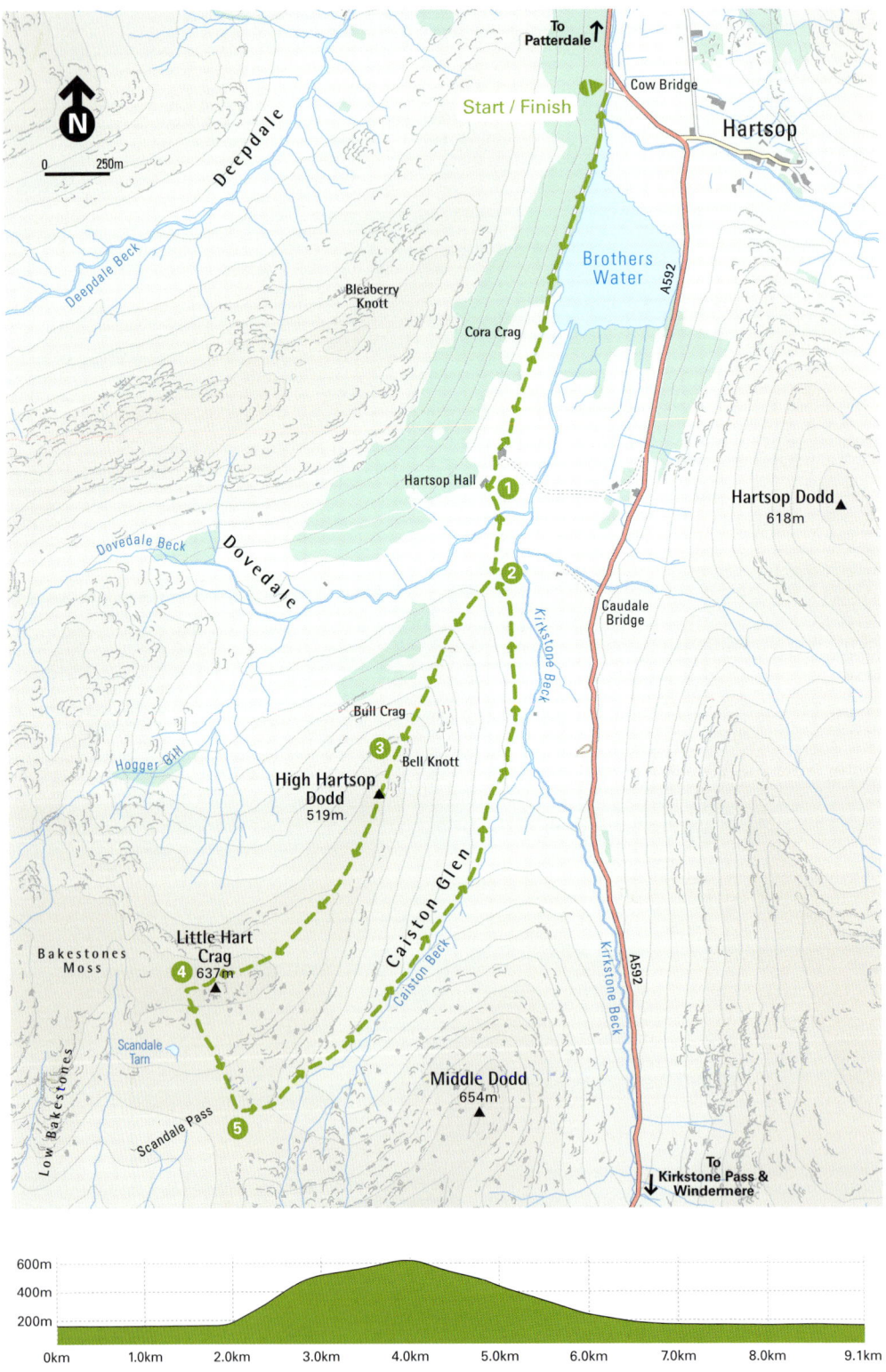

High Hartsop Dodd and Little Hart Crag

I have the picture of the lake and the folds of the mountain summits to myself.

It is 1.5 kilometres along the lakeshore to Hartsop Hall. Once through the farm there is a choice of paths. Straight on is the route to Dovedale; I take the left-hand branch signposted to Kirkstone Pass and Scandale Pass. ❶ Through the gate with the farm outbuildings on my right, I run across the field to the bridge over Dovedale Beck, then through the next field littered with impressive boulders.

Through the gate, I am in an enclosure in front of a barn. ❷ I turn off the route to Caiston Glen taking instead the path directly ahead, which leads straight up the north ridge of High Hartsop Dodd. I now have a tough kilometre in front of me, steep – a 40 percent gradient until I reach the top of the craggy Bell Knott. My heart rate rises and my pace drops. The terrain is grassy though and the view behind me becomes increasingly impressive as Brothers Water, enveloped in a cauldron of mountains, becomes a small angular mirror of water.

Beyond the crag, the slope eases. ❸ I reach a wall, which straddles the ridge, and pass through the gap to complete the final 170 metres to the small cairn that marks the summit of High Hartsop Dodd. A Wainwright, but not a summit at all. Beyond the cairn, the path continues to rise but it is a relatively easy incline. I can see the twin turrets of Little Hart Crag, less than a kilometre away and just 100 metres of ascent.

The summit of Little Hart Crag yields views of Windermere to the south and the Hartsop valley to the north, and I am surrounded by summits of higher fells: Red Screes, Scandale Fell, Dove Crag, St Sunday Crag. From the top of the western peak, the highest point, the path drops down sharply, west, to a small, unnamed tarn ❹. Water features are useful navigation markers in the mist. Beyond the small tarn lies a broken wall and the metal fence posts of the parish boundary line; more useful navigation tools.

Start of the High Hartsop Dodd run

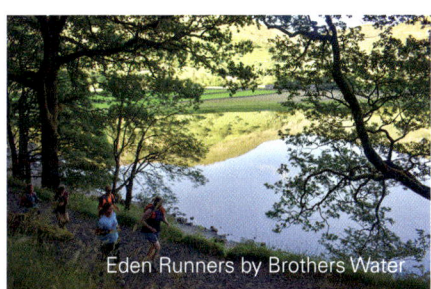
Eden Runners by Brothers Water

Hartsop Hall

High Hartsop Dodd, boulder and barn

Route to Little Hart Crag from High Hartsop Dodd

7 High Hartsop Dodd and Little Hart Crag

Path back to Cow Bridge

Brothers Water, the path to Hartsop Hall

A path follows the wall and fence posts south to Scandale Pass. I turn left and descend. I can see Scandale Tarn to my right on the other side of the wall. It is 500 metres down to Scandale Pass. ❺ When I see the stile over the wall, which would take me in the direction of Ambleside, I turn left and head east-northeast down Caiston Glen.

I can't go wrong if I keep Caiston Beck to my right. The path is rocky with occasional grassy strips; I have to watch my foot placement and I seem be to working the 'tear-drop' quads just above my knee quite extensively. The path improves as I descend and edge north, running below the High Hartsop Dodd ridge. I reach the intake wall. The terrain is smoother and the gradient gentler but I don't start running freely until I am retracing my steps across the pastures, back towards Hartsop Hall. I am now heading back to the car park on the flat track alongside Brothers Water. The sun is still shining, a perfect spring afternoon. Again, I am alone.

Seat Sandal

Approaching Hause Gap

8 Seat Sandal

Park / Start	Lay-by on the A591, 400 metres north of Mill Bridge (NY 335 095)
Map	OS Explorer OL5
Exertion	●●●●
Navigation	●●●
Terrain	●●
Distance	8.2 kilometres
Time	1 hour 22 minutes
Ascent	657 metres
On road	1 kilometre

The legendary resting place of the crown of the last king of Cumbria

A wide, grass verge makes this a safe start alongside the busy A591. **START** I run south for 400 metres to Mill Bridge before turning left into the lane where a fingerpost points to a public bridleway to Patterdale. ❶ I run past the cottage signed *'1 Tongue Ghyll'* and I can now move away from the main road, onto a more peaceful major route from a different era.

Beyond the cottages, through the first gate, I pass the Tongue Gill hydro scheme building. The stony packhorse route climbs, the rippling of the gill to my left soothes and a warbling of dippers fills the afternoon air. ❷ I reach the second gate after 1.15 kilometres and immediately see the two footbridges I must cross to reach the higher ground to the right of the gill. Within 150 metres of the gate a sign informs me

8 Seat Sandal

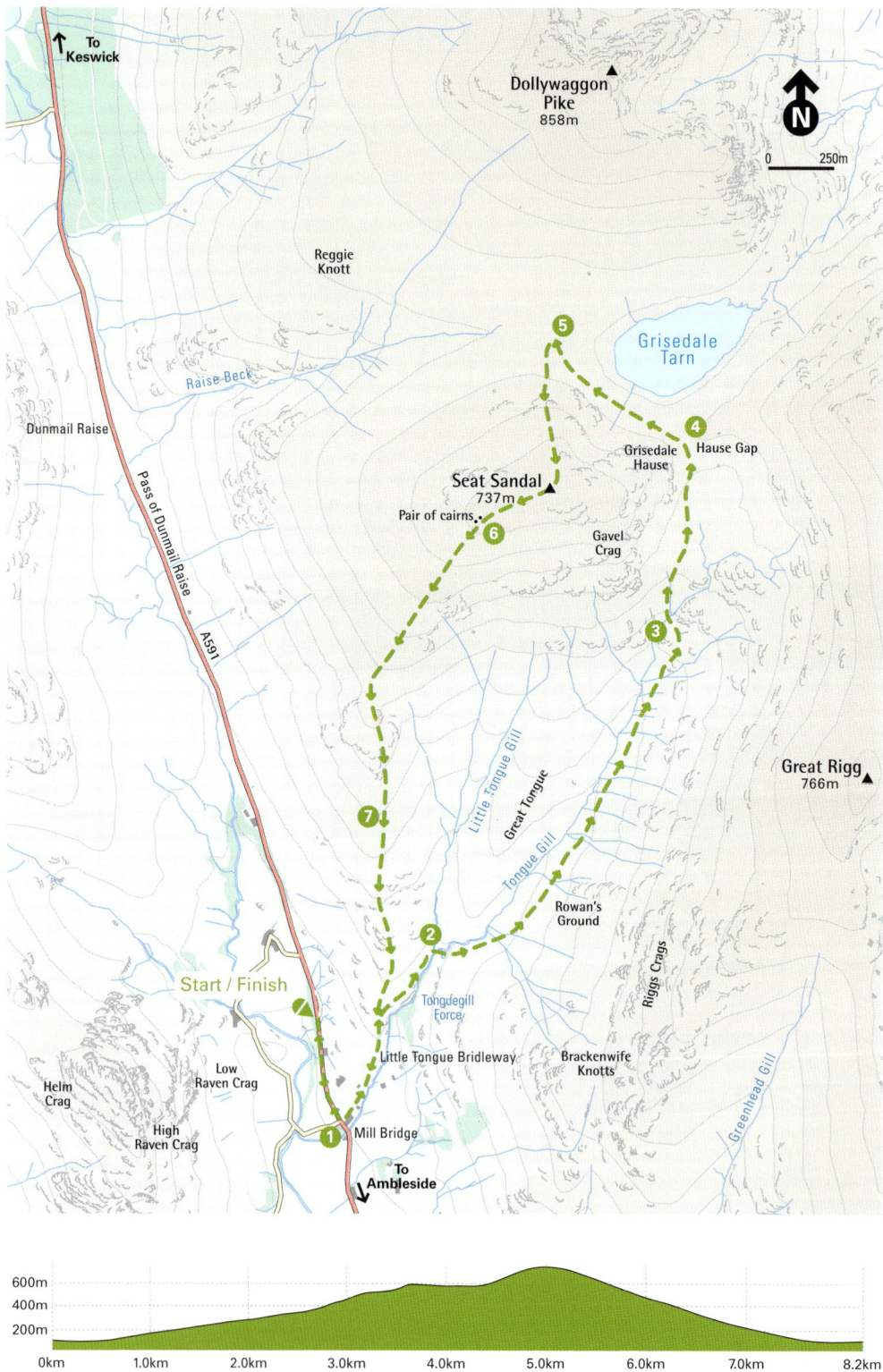

Seat Sandal

of erosion control and directs me on to the Coast-to-Coast footpath.

To begin with, the path climbs gently past a rectangular enclosure. I pause to remove my jacket. Under a celestial sky, fluffy white cumulus clouds float above the peaks of the glacial valley. Behind me, framed by the jaws of the gill, a portrait of the valley is displayed: Easedale, Grasmere, the craggy hills of Silver How and Helm Crag, a mosaic of woodlands and a patchwork of cramped fields hemmed by neat drystone walls.

Footbridge over Tongue Gill

Beneath the giant black molar of Gavel Crag, I pass a large cairn on my right; from here the route gets steeper and I get slower. A carefully laid stone-pitched path, easy to ascend, brings me to Tongue Gill beneath the waterfalls. ❸ Nonchalantly, the water tumbles into the pool; it has been dry so the beck is easy to cross.

From here, three kilometres into my loop, the path gets craggy on its way to Grisdale Hause, much easier to climb than descend, especially when wet. I have only 600 metres though, until I reach the wall at Hause Gap, a few minutes of hard slog over angled rock. ❹

The route to Hause Gap along the Coast to Coast path

Through the gap in the wall Grisedale Tarn, the home of Dunmail's crown, appears as if by magic. From this point, rather than turning sharp left and opting for the more direct route to the summit across jagged scree, I run in a north-westerly direction 30 metres above the shore of the tarn. Seven hundred metres on a runnable, wet path beneath the southern flanks of Dollywaggon Pike brings me to a junction of routes and walls. ❺

Passing the walled enclosure on the way to Hause Gap

The path across from west to east is the route from Dunmail Raise to Patterdale. Ahead is the climb to Dollywaggon Pike. I turn sharp left (south) to begin my clamber to the top of Seat Sandal, only another 150 metres of ascent on a grassy slope. I'm heading along a broken wall, an obvious route, with the squid-ink blue tarn down to my left.

Gavel Crag, approaching Hause Gap

As the gradient eases towards the summit, I pass through a gap in the wall to reach the cairn, which stands 30 metres west of the wall. There is a profusion of peaks in

Grisedale Tarn from Hause Gap

8 Seat Sandal

The gates through to the pastures leading to Little Tongue Bridleway

view from the top and a glimpse of Ullswater to the east, a reminder of the narrowness of the Helvellyn Range. I'm descending via the southern ridge. From the highest point, I run west-southwest and within 250 metres, I reach a pair of cairns a few metres apart. ❻ From here on a clear day like today, the line is easy; I head towards Grasmere Island. In the mist, a compass bearing of 210 degrees will take me to the intake wall above Mill Bridge. I pick up the faint path (not on the map) which follows the ridgeline. A kilometre bound down a grassy slope, freewheeling, my eyes drawn towards Grasmere and a spectrum of greens – lime and fern and forest – in the valley below.

The path becomes more distinct and meets a wall at a gate. ❼ Once through the gate I keep left to meet a second gate straight ahead at the corner of the enclosure. Through the gate, I follow the path across three more soft pastures and through three more gates. There is a small barn ahead and to the left another gate opens onto the Little Tongue bridleway.

Turning right down the bridleway, I can now retrace my steps down to the A591 and back to the lay-by.

On the Coast to Coast route

The path to the top of Seat Sandal from Grisedale Tarn

9   Great Rigg Triangle

Great Rigg from across Grasmere

9 Great Rigg Triangle

Park / Start	The start of the lane to Greenhead Gill behind The Swan Hotel, Grasmere (NY 340 084)		
Map	OS Explorer OL7		
Exertion	●●●●		
Navigation	●●●		
Terrain	●●		
Distance	7.7 kilometres	Time	1 hour 16 minutes
Ascent	685 metres	On road	500 metres

A superb undulating ridge with views across a multitude of lakes

There is some roadside parking at the end of the lane leading up to Greenhead Gill. If there is no space here, it means parking in Grasmere Village and running 700 metres on the road from the nearest car park to the start.

At the bottom of the lane, a public footpath sign pointing to Greenhead Gill and Alcock Tarn confirms I am heading in the right direction. **START** Compared with a circuit of one of the outlying fells, a run from Grasmere has a touch of suburbia about it. I run past driveways leading to expensive looking houses and within 250 metres I reach a gate. Here, another signpost points left to Stone Arthur and straight on to Alcock Tarn. I turn left. **1**

9 Great Rigg Triangle

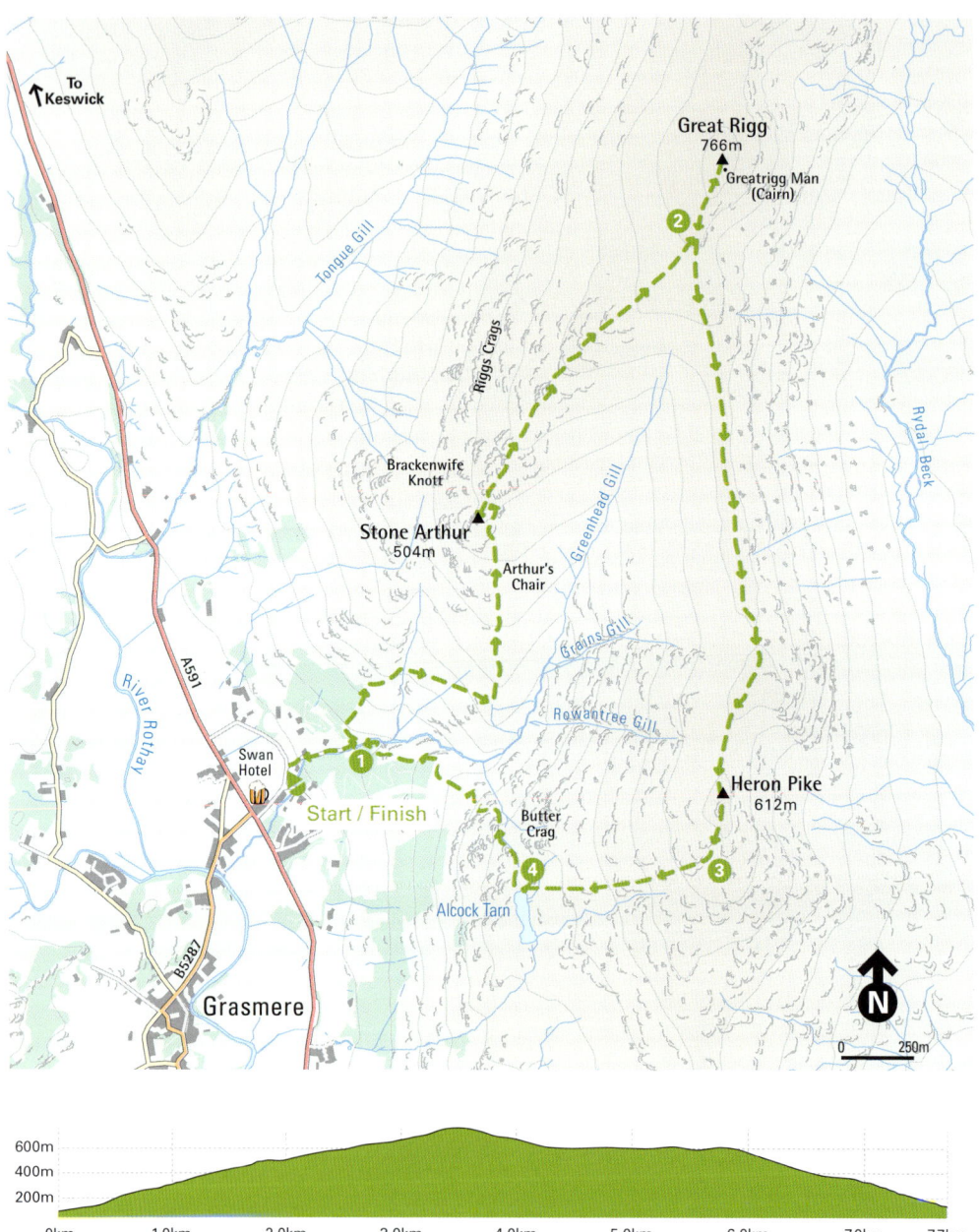

The old stone steps and the repaired eroded sections of path hint at the enduring popularity of the views from the rocky tor of Arthur's Chair. I sweep right to cross a beck and rise steadily with a low-level wall to my right.

Just beyond the kilometre mark, the hard work begins. An obvious path turns left and begins to climb up the ridge, a twenty percent gradient all the way to Great Rigg summit. I get into a rhythm, the constant grind absorbs me, I am detached from my surroundings. I pass the top of Stone Arthur, merely a blip in the ridge profile, without noticing.

Great Rigg Triangle 9

Arthur's Seat, Stone Arthur summit

The path, easy to follow even in cloud, has veered right and I am travailing northeast, lost in the effort, only faintly aware of a string of lakes – Grasmere, Rydal Water, Windermere – stretching away from me in the valley below.

The top of the Stone Arthur ridge is marked by a cairn. It is the point where the path meets the path from Heron Pike. ❷ From here, it is only 300 metres distance and 60 metres of ascent to Greatrigg Man, the highest point on Great Rigg.

The path to Stone Arthur and Great Rigg

I have reached the summit; I have hauled myself to the top of a roller coaster arch and I am about to descend. Two kilometres to Heron Pike, a steep downhill, followed by a gently undulating ridge. I retrace my steps down to the path junction at the top of the Stone Arthur ridge but now I bear left and head due south on a clear path.

Grasmere from Stone Arthur

❷ Down the back of a sleeping green lizard, heading towards the tail at Rydal. A surfeit of lakes fills the view ahead: Windermere, Grasmere, Elter Water, Coniston Water, as well as a multitude of tarns.

There are sufficient rocks and grassy steps to mean that I cannot run at full pelt but after three kilometres of climbing, I feel unshackled. There is a small rise to the summit of Heron Pike and from here, it is an easy descent to Nab Scar and Rydal beyond but my car is in Grasmere so I need to complete the triangle.

Great Rigg Triangle

Greenhead Gill

Beyond the summit of Heron Pike, I continue on the path towards Nab Scar for 200 metres then begin my descent towards Alcock Tarn. ❸ At this point, I go off-path down the side of the fell heading just south of west. It is a fairly steep descent but grassy, not hazardous, and Alcock Tarn is quite a large target to aim for. On the west bank of the reedy water is a clear path, south to Dove Cottage or north to Greenhead Gill. ❹

Alcock Tarn on the descent from Heron Pike

I turn right (north) to the gill. The path zigzags down towards the ravine and once over the footbridge I am back at the gate at the top of the lane. Two hundred and fifty metres on hard tarmac and I am back at the road where I am parked.

Nab Scar from across Grasmere

10 Nab Scar

Park	Pelter Bridge car park, Rydal (NY 364 061)
Start	Opposite the Rydal Lodge Hotel, junction of A592 and road up to Rydal Mount (NY 364 061)
Map	OS Explorer OL7
Exertion	•••
Navigation	•••
Terrain	•••

Distance	6.9 kilometres	Time	1 hour
Ascent	431 metres	On road	800 metres

A short canter through Wordsworth's country

A wild crag on a winter's day, benign and glorious on an afternoon in summer. A short burst up Nab Scar, a summit gained quickly, and then an easy trail past the length of Rydal's spindle-shaped water.

A dazzling dry day, I have put on my trail shoes; there is only one section in the middle of the loop where fell shoes might be an advantage, and then only in the wet. **START** I head north on the road with Rydal Church on my left and Rydal Hall on my right. ❶ At 240 metres there is a fingerpost pointing left to Grasmere via the Coffin Route, this will be the route of my return. The hiker-sign on the small wooden arm points up the concrete slope (north) and, within 40 metres, a public footpath sign confirms I am

10 Nab Scar

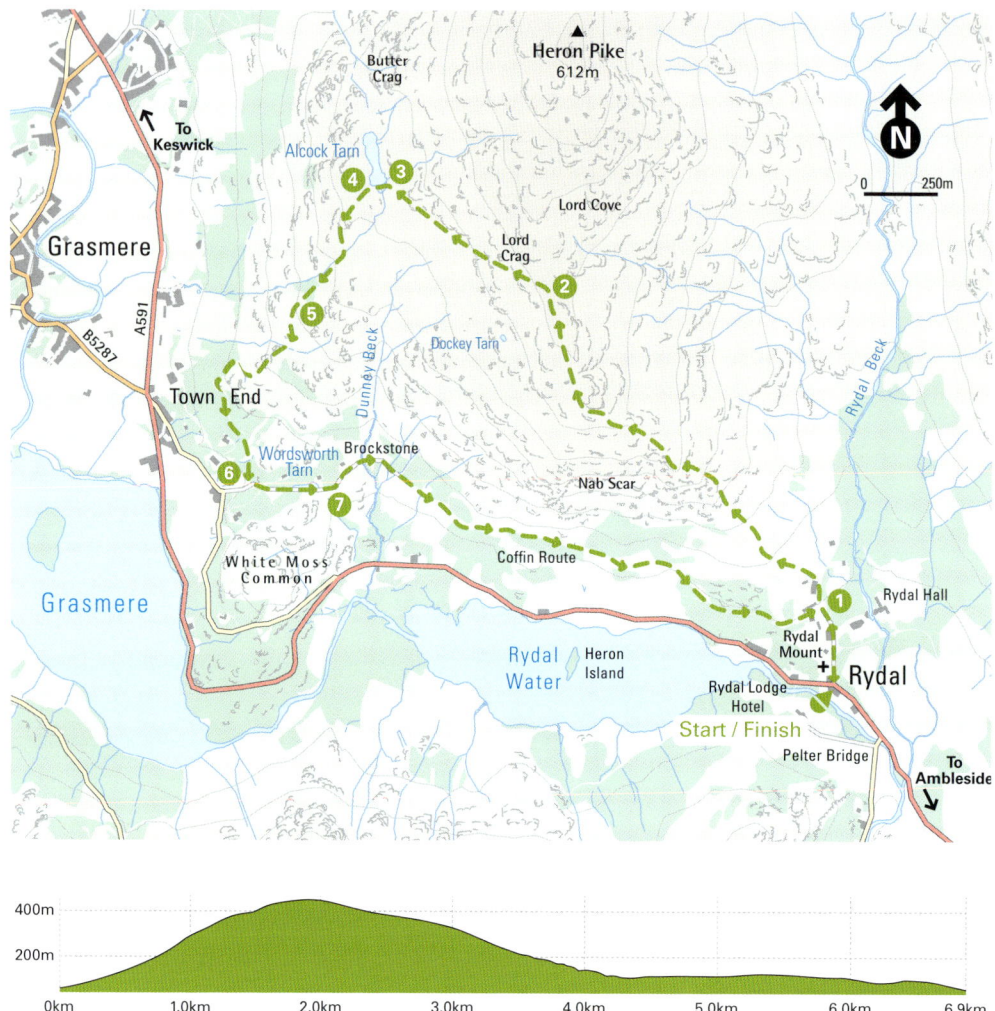

going in the right direction. Often the start of a trail can be the hardest part of a run to find, especially when starting from a village.

A further 50 metres ahead, on the left-hand side, I pass through a kissing gate adjacent to a five-barred field gate; I am now on a clear path leading up to Nab Scar and beyond. On a well-used route by Wordsworth's backdoor, I scale well-maintained rock steps. Over a ladder stile, I am now on the fell side, climbing steeply under the watchful eye of a herd of curious Herdwick.

There are no route choices, I can plough on upwards unshackled, and the gradient eases as I come alongside a wall on my left. Once over a neat stone stile I am surprised how quickly the summit cairn comes into view. On my left there is pile of stones set on a small mound, merely a shoulder on the ridge to Heron Pike, which Wainwright managed to elevate to a separate fell.

Stopping briefly on the summit, I glance back at the views to the west and south, across Grasmere and Windermere, a perfectly balanced portrait. A panorama that explains why, for centuries, this has been such a popular chunk of rock on which to stand.

Nab Scar 10

Nab Scar from across Rydal Water

St Mary's Church, Rydal

Now, though, I have to be more careful with my navigation. I continue on the route to Heron Pike, looking out for a large cairn perched on a mound on my left. Just beyond this, 250 metres on from the summit cairn, another pile of stones comes into view to my left. ❷ Set on the other side of a broken wall, this cairn marks the start of a faint path, not on the map, leading off in a north-westerly direction down the fell.

Although indistinct to start with the path soon becomes more defined. With the southern portion of Alcock Tarn visible on my left, I descend on a runnable route across open pasture, a path with sufficient rocks to force me to clip my stride and focus on my footing.

❸ I climb the wooden portcullis contraption that leads me into the walled enclosure surrounding the tarn, cross the dyke-like dam at the southern outfall and head for the hole in the wall on the other side.

❹ Out of the enclosure, I turn left onto the footpath down to White Moss Common. The path winds down to the base of the western flank of Nab Scar. Five hundred metres on from the tarn there is a path off to my right, which I ignore. ❺ I keep left to pass through the National Trust Alcock Tarn gate. The path swings around sharp chicanes and once I pass a small pond I can see a lane ahead.

Path junction-turning left to Alcock Tarn

10 Nab Scar

Rydal Water from the Rydal Coffin Route

🞄 At the lane, I again turn left to run past Wordworth's Tarn, unnamed on the map, and on to Brockstone. 🞄 I pass through the gate to the right of the house and I am now on the corpse route between Ambleside and Grasmere. I run east on the path along which coffins were hauled on their way to St Oswald's consecrated ground in Grasmere.

I avoid any paths to my right, which would take me down to the road. From Wordsworth's Tarn, it is two kilometres on an undulating trail through greening, burgeoning woods and open pastures running parallel to Rydal Water. At Rydal Mount, I reach the Coffin Route fingerpost I passed nearly an hour ago on my way up to the summit. Turning right it is a quick 250 metres downhill, past the church to the Rydal Lodge Hotel.

Descending to Alcock Tarn from Nab Scar

Leaving Alcock tarn and heading down to White Moss Common

The Far Eastern Fells

These runs are never too far away from the water's edge, with many straddling the eastern shores of Ullswater and Brothers Water, on routes characterised by moorland ridges and slopes with fast descents. Stretching from Askham Fell above Pooley Bridge in the north to Sallows overlooking Windermere in the south, these gallops are predominantly over rolling moorland.

Windermere from Wansfell Pike (Wansfell Pike and Baystones route)

Descent to Askham, heading to the corner of the plantation

The Cockpit stone circle and Askham Fell

11 Askham Fell

Park	Askham Village car park, adjacent to the swimming pool (NY 512 236)
Start	Opposite The Queen's Head Inn (NY 512 236)
Map	OS Explorer OL5
Exertion	•
Navigation	•
Terrain	•
Distance	9.2 kilometres
Time	57 minutes
Ascent	217 metres
On road	700 metres

**Cairns, burial mounds, stone circles and
a descent to die for on this entry level run**

Some fells are runnable all the way – rolling moors with gentle gradients and grassy slopes. Cover them like a cross-country runner, unshackled, ungirded, liberated.

I park in the village car park next to the swimming pool and from The Queen's Head Inn **START** I run west through the village towards Askham Fell. I pass the farm and the unofficial car park at the top of the village and, beyond the gate, I take the bridleway track on the right following the signpost for the Lowther Cycle Loop. ❶

11 Askham Fell

It is a perfectly still day. The air is dry and the sky on a winter's afternoon is so much bluer than on a summer's day. Fresh scents of livestock and sweet silage drift across from the adjacent farms. A stony path soon gives way to a smooth grass incline stretching all the way to a five-barred field gate, which leads onto the open fell. Through the gate, I immediately veer left, this time ignoring the sign for the Askham Fell Cycle Loop, which points straight ahead towards the enclosed plantations. ❷ Instead, I follow the broad green path to my left, south-west across the fell, gentle, easy running to Moor Divock. This is a moor littered with Bronze Age cairns, stone circles and burial mounds as well as a multitude of limestone sinkholes.

A couple of paths cross at right angles, but I keep heading south-west until, after three kilometres, I reach the main thoroughfare, the bridleway from Pooley Bridge to Helton. ❸ Here I turn right, heading north-west in the direction of Pooley Bridge.

On a lowland fell path, I continue with Ullswater visible in the valley below and the comparatively imposing peaks of the Helvellyn Range: the Dodds, White Side, Lower Man, Catstycam and Helvellyn itself,

Askham Fell

Eden Runner on Heughscar Hill.

towering white and magnificent like an Alpine landscape. The fell ponies ignore me; they are basking in the sun, perhaps, like me, dreaming of spring.

Just beyond White Raise Cairn, at Ketley Gate, I reach the parish boundary where a four way fingerpost points ahead to Pooley Bridge (2 miles) and back to Lowther Castle (2½ miles). ④ I turn left following the sign for Howtown (3¼ miles), picking up a grassy path stretching away west-southwest over Moor Divock and the Bronze Age Cockpit stone circle.

⑤ At the stone circle, high above Ullswater, on a broad, bright moor of golden grasses, I turn right onto High Street heading north on a clear track towards Heughscar Hill. After 500 metres, I am back at the Pooley Bridge to Helton bridleway. ⑥ At the path junction I continue north, following the signpost to Celleron (1¾ mile); I begin to gently climb.

At Ketley Gate turn towards Howtown

Two hundred metres beyond the crossroads I approach another wide path junction where, set up on the grassy bank on my right, a large cairn resides. I carry straight on, north, towards Celleron. Within 700 metres the path branches, I bear right heading for the limestone outcrop of Heugh Scar.

⑦ The path winds beneath the white clint, climbing up the bank to hairpin back towards Heughscar Hill. The

Hay bales on Heughscar Hill.

11 Askham Fell

The summit of Heughscar Hill

path climbs southwards, a green ribbon through dormant ferns and woody heather to the top of the small mound that is the hill summit.

❽ By the cairn on the hilltop, I stop to admire the panorama. To the south-west, the congested peaks of central Lakeland; to the east, beyond the Eden Valley, the distant Pennine Hills; and north-east Beacon Hill and the sprawling market town of Penrith.

From the summit cairn, I run straight ahead, towards the south-western corner of Winder Plantation.

❾ Like a child careering down a moorland slope I race a Roman mile* trying to get some speed and bounce out of my inflexible frame. The ground is soft – I don't worry about falling. One kilometre down to the gate, a gentle descent running directly east. Two mountain bikers sweep past me almost out of control. On the other side of the river valley, Lowther Castle is perched in the woods, a great gothic monument watching over Askham village.

Running towards Askham

Beyond the gate, the smooth clipped sward continues before merging into a stony, icy track. I am soon at the farm to the west of the village and from here, I continue down the road to the village store.

Ponies on Heughscar Hill

A Roman mile was a thousand paces, roughly 1.5km.

Arthur's Pike

Arthur's Pike sunset from Pooley Bridge

12 Arthur's Pike

Park / Start	Roehead, Pooley Bridge (NY 478 236)		
Map	OS Explorer OL5		
Exertion	●●		
Navigation	●●		
Terrain	●		
Distance	10.3 kilometres	Time	1 hour 29 minutes (in deep snow)
Ascent	352 metres	On road	0 metres

Running with the Romans across High Street

Under a grey sky, the water of Ullswater to my right is the colour of wood ash. The green fells ahead of me emit little more than a slate-grey hue. The sun is buried deep behind thick clouds.

START The fingerpost by the gate at Roehead points to Askham Fell (1 mile) and Lowther Castle (3¾ miles). It is a broad, stony trail traversing the moor to Askham and Helton in the east, a path crossing a landscape bearing its history upon its surface. Once through the gate I begin to run, slowly, inflexibly without a chance of a decent warm-up.

There is little snow remaining at this level, a few splodges here and there resisting the warming temperatures. It is just above freezing at this height but even on the low fells I am climbing, it will be a couple of degrees below zero in the easterly breeze. I am not sure how much snow I will find on the featureless

12 Arthur's Pike

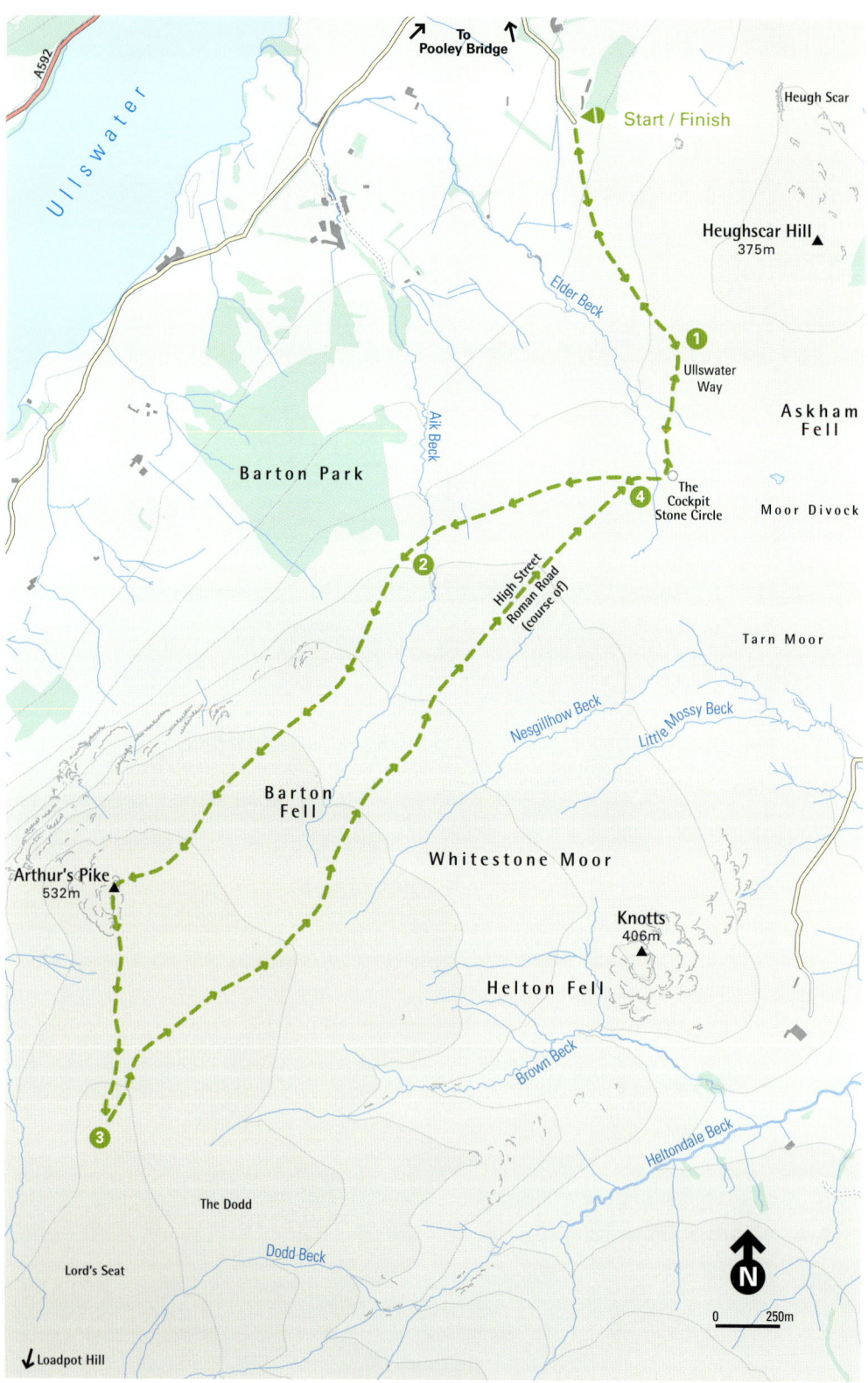

Arthur's Pike 12

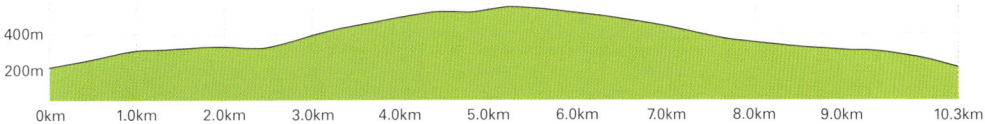

plateau. A mist has descended obscuring the view of the western flank of Arthur's Pike and although I know this moorland well, it is with slight apprehension that I begin my journey. This rolling moorland, this runnable country, a tranquil, unfettered space, can be bleak in winter.

After a kilometre, I reach a path junction marked by a surfeit of signs. The first part of this run is on the daffodil-waymarked Ullswater Way, which has been impressively signposted. The first signpost is just off the path to my right and since it is off-track, it is not much help. It points towards Brocavum (VII m.p.) to the north-east and Galava (XIX m.p.) to the south-east. This is Latin for the Roman forts of Brougham and Ambleside respectively, the two forts linked by High Street, the road built by the Romans across these hills. The abbreviation, m.p., stands for mille passus or a thousand paces – a Roman mile.

Ullswater Way, start of Arthur's Pike run

❶ The four-way fingerpost ahead is more useful. I turn right here in the direction of Howtown (3¼ miles), again on the Ullswater Way and again on a wide, unmissable bridleway. The fell is saturated. Water, with nowhere else to go, pours off the closely-cropped moor, falling in cascades, flooding the path, tumbling to find the easiest run-off towards the farmland below.

Looking across to Arthur's Pike from Roehead

I run through the water; my feet are already soaked. Small waves whisper to smooth pebbles, nudging them further down the fellside. I run through streams and gurgling springs and I have to avoid slicks of enduring ice. Beyond The Cockpit stone circle, at 1.5 kilometres, I ford through Elder Beck and just beyond here I continue on the Ullswater Way, ignoring any of the grassy paths off to my left. Aik Beck, today full and funnelling over the edge of the track by the corner of the wall that encloses Barton Park, tells me that soon I must leave this contour route and start to climb to the fell summit.

Take the Ullswater Way towards Howtown

Passing The Cockpit stone circle on the path to Arthur's Pike

73

12 Arthur's Pike

② Thirty metres on from the beck I turn left (south-west) onto an obvious path at a point where a finger-post points to Howtown (2½ miles) and Pooley Bridge (2 miles). It is not long before I am trudging through snow. This is normally a very runnable slope but today, the slush and ice trapped in the ruts and channels slow me considerably.

Arthur's Pike summit looking towards Pooley Bridge

Three hundred metres on from the fingerpost I reach a path junction where I keep left. Eventually I am running through deep drifts. I can no longer see the path clearly. I am running in mist. I can no longer see Ullswater or the fells on its western bank. Snow, sometimes knee deep, keeps my shoes saturated and my feet cold. Water seeps up my running tights chilling my ankles and thighs.

Approaching Roehead

After 4.2 kilometres I reach a snow-capped cairn, the path splits and I take the right branch continuing up the broad track to the top. It is not far to the summit cairn though, and once I am there I take the path on my left, in a southerly direction, toiling through the snow as if I am wading through water.

After 300 metres I reach a peaty, boggy hollow; I continue south climbing up the slope towards Lord's Seat. Nine hundred metres on from Arthur's Pike summit

Descending from Arthur's Pike towards Roehead

cairn I meet the bridleway from Loadpot Hill, a section of High Street. ③ A sharp left turn takes me in a north-easterly direction back towards Barton Fell. Still trudging through snow, still in cloud, I bounce over dormant clumps of heather by the edge of the path. A struggling heather with brown-mulberry coloured stems and moribund leaves.

I try to pick up some speed down the slope but I am still hampered by the snow. As the snow recedes, I run over bright rugs of strange psychedelic lime-coloured moss, a striking contrast to the overwhelming white surrounds.

Soon I drop below the snowline and emerge from the mist. After a 2.6-kilometre unbridled gallop down a gentle slope I have a choice of routes. ④ I take the right branch, continuing on High Street back to the Ullswater Way. I am back at The Cockpit having looped over Arthur's Pike and back down Barton Fell. I turn right, heading north to retrace my steps back to Roehead. I am with people again. I meet hikers, dog walkers and a couple of intrepid cyclists.

There is something profoundly pure about being out on these moors on your own. Never far from civilisation yet briefly aware of a natural world, one that will endure long after humanity's candle is extinguished. The snow will still fall and the mist will still drape these rolling hills.

13 Hallin Fell and Steel Knotts

Hallin Fell from across Ullswater

Park / Start	St Peter's Church, Martindale (NY 435 192)		
Map	OS Explorer OL5		
Exertion	●●●●		
Navigation	●●●		
Terrain	●		
Distance	8.2 kilometres	**Time**	1 hour 23 minutes
Ascent	537 metres	**On road**	200 metres

On the edge of Ullswater, a brace of fells with superlative views

Why anyone would want to build a church at the base of a hause (a pass between two high points) on a dead end road miles from the nearest village is baffling. Why anyone would want to build a new church half a mile from the old one in a valley where hardly anyone lives is an impenetrable mystery.

START I park at St Peter's, the new church on The Hause. My plan is to save the smooth grassy slope down off Hallin Fell for my descent. I jog down the road towards Howtown for a couple of hundred metres before picking up the obvious path on my left signposted to Howtown Lakeshore (½ m). **1** Gradually descending, with Ullswater pulling away to my right all the way to Pooley Bridge. **2** It's not long before I join the Ullswater Way footpath, which I follow towards the water's edge, around the north side of Hallin

13 Hallin Fell and Steel Knotts

Fell. I continue through the gate by Kailpot Crag, into Hallinhag Wood where the tree roots and jutted rocks seem to be positioned just to trip me up.

❸ Before I reach the gate on the other side of the wood, I cut up the slope through the trees following the wall to the kissing gate in the corner. ❹ Once through the gate I immediately head to my left (south-east), away from the wall and begin to climb steeply through dead, crunching bracken. There is a faint path of sorts, which I seem to keep losing and rejoining. It is surprisingly steep for a low-level, easy fell, which means I'm sweating in my many layers, despite it being several degrees below zero.

Above the trees, I turn to see virtually the entire length of Ullswater, deep blue against the clear winter sky. Then, ahead, I encroach upon a herd of red deer basking in the afternoon sun, grazing, undisturbed, sleek chestnut coats glinting; not many people approach this fell from this side. I advance, then one spots me, or hears my grunting, and within seconds, the herd is gone.

Hallin Fell and Steel Knotts

The four-metre obelisk on the summit is unmissable. The panorama is stunning. It's surprising sometimes how good a view can be from the top of a small fell. The grass path off to the south-southeast is a well-worn green carpet, 800 metres to the church and onwards to Steel Knotts.

Past the church, I avoid the route immediately to my left (Public Bridleway Howtown ¾ mile). This will be my route of return. Instead, I follow the wall for a while, keeping to the right of Lanty Tarn, before leaving the path at the wall ❺ to climb the ridge on the left (south-east) through Birkie Knott. Once on the summit ridge I turn right, directly south, with Fusedale on my left and Martindale on my right. ❻ On past the cairn. Snow flanked slopes of Loadpot Hill, High Raise, Red Screes and the Fairfield Horseshoe open up before me like a children's pop-up book.

The summit tor, Pikeawassa, worth visiting for the name itself, is hard to miss. I don't climb it. I return the way I came, back across the summit ridge, beyond the cairn but keeping north along the main path rather than retracing my route through Birkie Knott.

I head to Steel End, north-northeast, down towards Howtown. It is a rugged path and I am slow, circumspect, but it is only a short section and I can see the wall ahead where I will aim off to the left. ❼ At the wall, I join the bridleway that runs up to the church from Howtown. This is a sting in the tail, a short climb back up to the brow, less than a kilometre, but a hard effort. Over the grassy knoll on my right and there is the church, perfectly framed in a thicket of old trees, built from local stone, sheltered by Hallin Fell.

Hallinhag Wood by the shore of Ullswater

Reaching the summit of Hallin Fell

Steel Knotts from the path down Hallin Fell

Pikeawassa, the summit of Steel Knotts

13 Hallin Fell and Steel Knotts

Going for a dip off Kailpot Crag, Hallinhag Wood

14 Beda Fell

Looking across Martindale to Beda Fell

Park / Start	St Martin's Church, Martindale (NY 434 184)		
Map	OS Explorer OL5		
Exertion	●●		
Navigation	●●		
Terrain	●		
Distance	7.8 kilometres	Time	1 hour 7 minutes
Ascent	388 metres	On road	2.5 kilometres

Remote, off the beaten track, a lumpy fell standing between quintessential Lakeland valleys

Picture a scene from a gothic novel. I park opposite the old church and look up at the fell, or rather at the mist covering the place where I think the fell is. Atmospheric is how the scene would be described. The wind whips through the gnarled branches of the old yew tree overhanging the church, wispy clouds swirl around the flanks of Hallin Fell and a grey pall sits upon Winter Crag, where I will soon ascend.

START Crossing Christy Bridge over Howegrain Beck it begins to rain, a soft drizzle that will eventually soak me. ❶ At Winter Crag Farm, the footpath climbs behind a small enclosure, following the west side of the wall for 150 metres before heading up to the base of Winter Crag. ❷ At the metal bench, I turn left onto the ridge.

14 Beda Fell

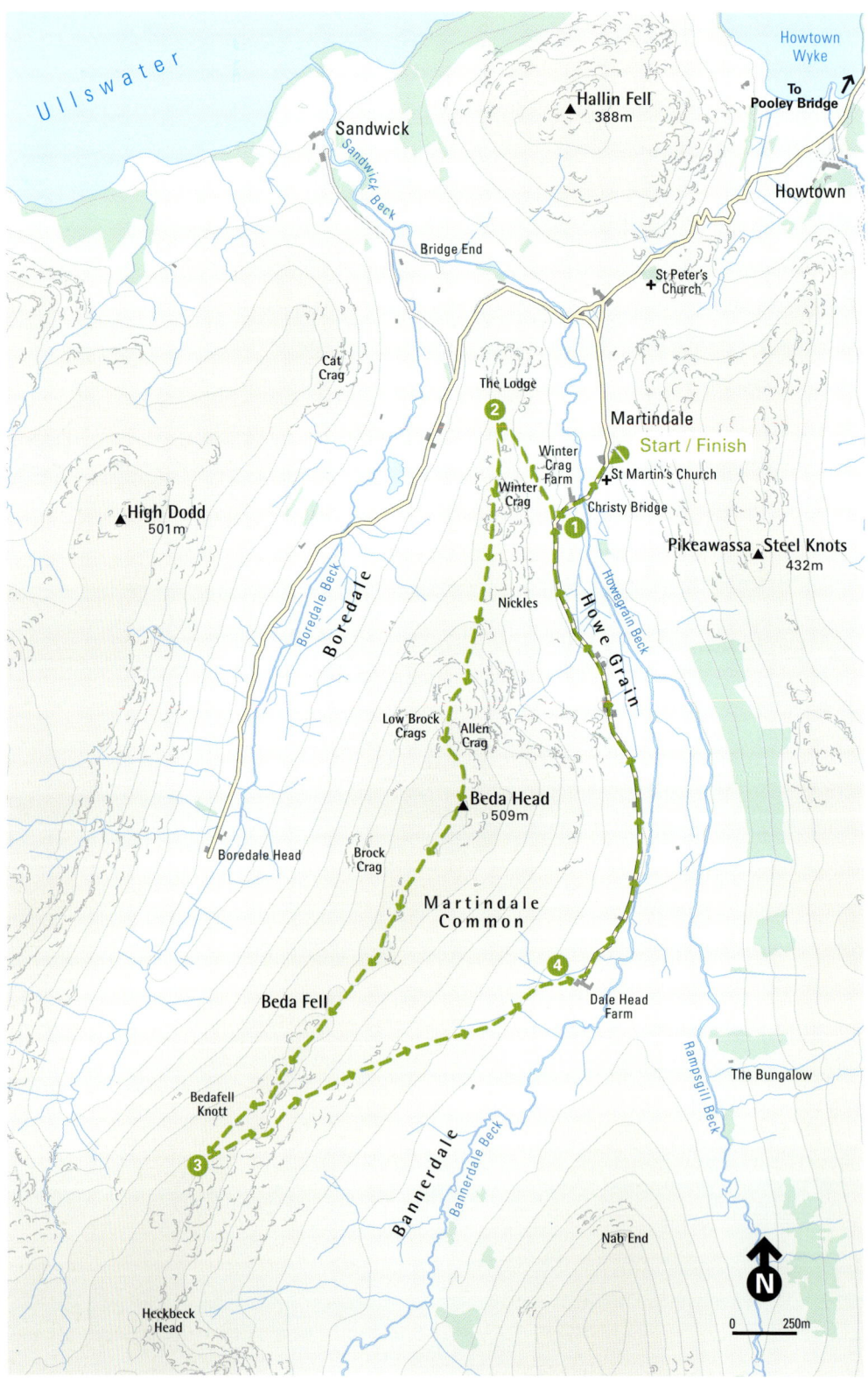

Beda Fell 14

I now travel just west of south for 1.5 kilometres to the highest point of the fell. Before the top of the ridge is reached, I face a steep climb through the rocky outcrops – a 40 percent gradient in parts, but not for long. For me at least, it isn't runnable.

On the back of a buried dragon, over knolls and through bogs, saturated with recent snowmelt. The mist obscures the summit but the glacial valleys of Howe Grain and Boredale stretch away in parallel, to the left and right respectively, each carrying a meandering beck, each supremely remote.

I push hard reaching the highest point in thirty minutes. In the cloud, the small cairn on the summit, Beda Head, is easy to miss, but the navigation isn't tricky. There is only one path. Through marshy areas, the route can disappear, but I keep running south-west and the path is always there, over grassy ground.

St Martin's Church, Martindale

There is something strangely exhilarating about being on your own in the silence of swirling clouds. The silence today is broken by the gentle patter of rain against my jacket. Occasionally I'm spooked by a sound from behind. I imagine there's someone following me, but it's just the swishing of my hood. I am alone on this ridge.

The old yew tree at St Martin's Church

Beyond the summit, my pace increases in spurts, but soon I am climbing once again, up Bedafell Knott. Once over the hump I quickly reach an obvious path junction, marked by a cairn. ❸ Running from east to west this is the bridleway from Martindale to Patterdale. Onwards is Angletarn Pikes, just a small ascent, a there-and-back jog, which would extend this run by two kilometres. Today I'm heading directly down to Martindale. My climbing is over.

Christy Bridge over Howegrain Beck

At the junction, I turn sharply north-east. It's good going, nearly two kilometres to Dale Head Farm. A more surefooted runner would make good time down here. Gradually the path improves; I can speed up along a

Looking over St Martin's Church to Winter Crag

14 Beda Fell

Looking towards Beda Head from Martindale

grassy slope towards the road. Bannerdale Beck meanders through the valley on my right. ❹ Dale Head comes into view and then The Bungalow incongruously emerges from behind Nab End like a lodge in a Malaysian hill station.

The two kilometres back to St Martin's Church is on road, first following Bannerdale Beck, then Howegrain Beck. Gradually the off-grid world becomes more connected. Electricity cables appear, the farms have satellite dishes and a message slips through on my phone. It is a quick finish after a slow start.

The Bungalow from Dale Head, Martindale

Bannerdale Beck alongside the road to Christy Bridge

Place Fell 15

Place Fell from Glenridding Pier

15 Place Fell

Park / Start	St Patrick's Church, Patterdale (NY 392 161)		
Map	OS Explorer OL5		
Exertion	●●●		
Navigation	●●●		
Terrain	●●●		
Distance	7.3 kilometres	Time	1 hour 13 minutes
Ascent	554 metres	On road	1.2 kilometres

A perfect lariat over an imposing lakeside mountain

From the eastern shores of Ullswater, Place Fell dominates the skyline. Its steep, juniper and heather draped western slope supports an alluring runnable ridge, which today I will traverse from north to south.

START From the church I run 150 metres south-east towards Patterdale village to the sign pointing across the road for Howtown via Side Farm (5¾ miles). ❶ I turn left and take the track across Goldrill Beck to the farm. I'm on the Ullswater Way route with its daffodil signs.

Once through the farmyard I turn left. Again, a daffodil fingerpost points left to Howtown (5½ miles). ❷ Immediately through the gate, though, I leave the daffodils behind, taking a sharp right-hand turn up the bank onto the fell. At the top of the bank, I meet a bridleway where I turn left to run just west of north.

15 Place Fell

I'm climbing up the fell side, across an old quarry on a path that soon heads due north. Parallel, below me, is the track to Sandwick – the Ullswater Way. I don't gain much height but the view north along the lake is spectacular. The flat water, a sheet of polished metal, reflects the sharp edges of the corrugated peaks. I pass a bench, and 800 metres on from this, beyond a cave, I reach the path on my right that will take me up to Hare Shaw. ❸ A large prism-shaped rock lies just before the path junction. Once on the trail it's a clear way through stones and larches and sprawling gorse bushes.

The first day of spring, 11 degrees Celsius in the valley under a cloudless sky. Five hundred metres up from the path junction I stop to take off my jacket. I turn to take in the view. It's difficult to imagine a more beautiful scene in England. The run is worth it just for this. An intensely blue sky, and lined up in a row across the lake are the mountains of Birks, Birkhouse Moor and Sheffield Pike, their peaks reflected in the mirror-glass water. The steamers, red funnelled, moored at Glenridding pier, framed by hanging branches of juniper trees. If I were a landscape painter, this is a place where I would rest my easel.

Place Fell 15

Eden Runners heading to Side Farm and Place Fell

I am high above the water now, pushing hard through a craggy section. There is only one other piece of navigation needed and this is straightforward. Once the gradient eases, with the protruding crag of Hare Shaw on my left, I look out for a branch in the path on my right, climbing up the grassy fell in a south-easterly direction. ❹ I keep to the right of the rocky turrets of The Knight and ahead I can see the higher ground of Place Fell summit.

The mossy, boggy ground gives way to rocky terrain and eventually I reach the top. The trig point on my left seems lower than the precariously balanced cairn I pass to my right. There are much bigger fells around me but none can offer better views than this waterside hump. Ahead of me, Brothers Water shines like a shard of broken glass. Deepdale and Goldrill Becks twist like silver ribbons across the valley floor.

Crossing Goldrill Beck on the way to Place Fell

Boredale Hause, descending to Patterdale

Onwards now in a southerly direction across the ridge, traversing a few undulations, before making the descent down Steel Edge. It's a steep drop with a few scrambles, not easy, until I reach Boredale Hause. Boredale Hause and a multitude of paths. The Coast-to-Coast footpath crosses this point. Ahead is the route to Angletarn Pikes. I turn right just in front of the ruined Chapel in the Hause, ❺ a place of mystery,

15 Place Fell

The route of descent down Steel Edge, Place Fell

a strange location for a chapel, and continue my descent. Under an hour to the Hause, 15 minutes back to Patterdale Church.

The path is less steep now. There are a few rocky sections interrupted by welcome gravelly stretches and soon I am closing in on the houses at Rooking. I have a choice of routes back. I can remain on the path behind the cottages towards Side Farm and retrace my steps the way I came. ❻ Or, I can drop down to the gate by the houses in Rooking and follow the road over Goldrill Bridge to the centre of the village. Today I take the latter option. Once I reach the A592 a right-hand turn and 600 metres takes me back to the church.

The path back to Patterdale from Place Fell

16 Angletarn Pikes

Looking across to Angletarn Pikes from Patterdale

Park / Start	Hartsop Village car park (NY 410 130)		
Map	OS Explorer OL5		
Exertion	●●●●		
Navigation	●●●		
Terrain	●●●		
Distance	10.1 kilometres	Time	1 hour 27 minutes
Ascent	505 metres	On road	1 kilometre

Craggy outcrops towering over a Narnian realm

The gate at the east of the small car park informs me that I am an entering a red deer conservation area. There has been a herd of deer on these fells for over 300 years, and Hartsop literally means 'valley of the deer'.

START The fingerpost on the other side of the gate points east along a public bridleway to Hayeswater. Once past the sheep pens I follow the gravel path east, (immediately right there is a track down to the old Myers Head lead mine, which I ignore). After 500 metres I reach a cattle grid, pass through the gate and from here I bear right down a stony track to the footbridge over Hayeswater Gill. ❶

Angletarn Pikes

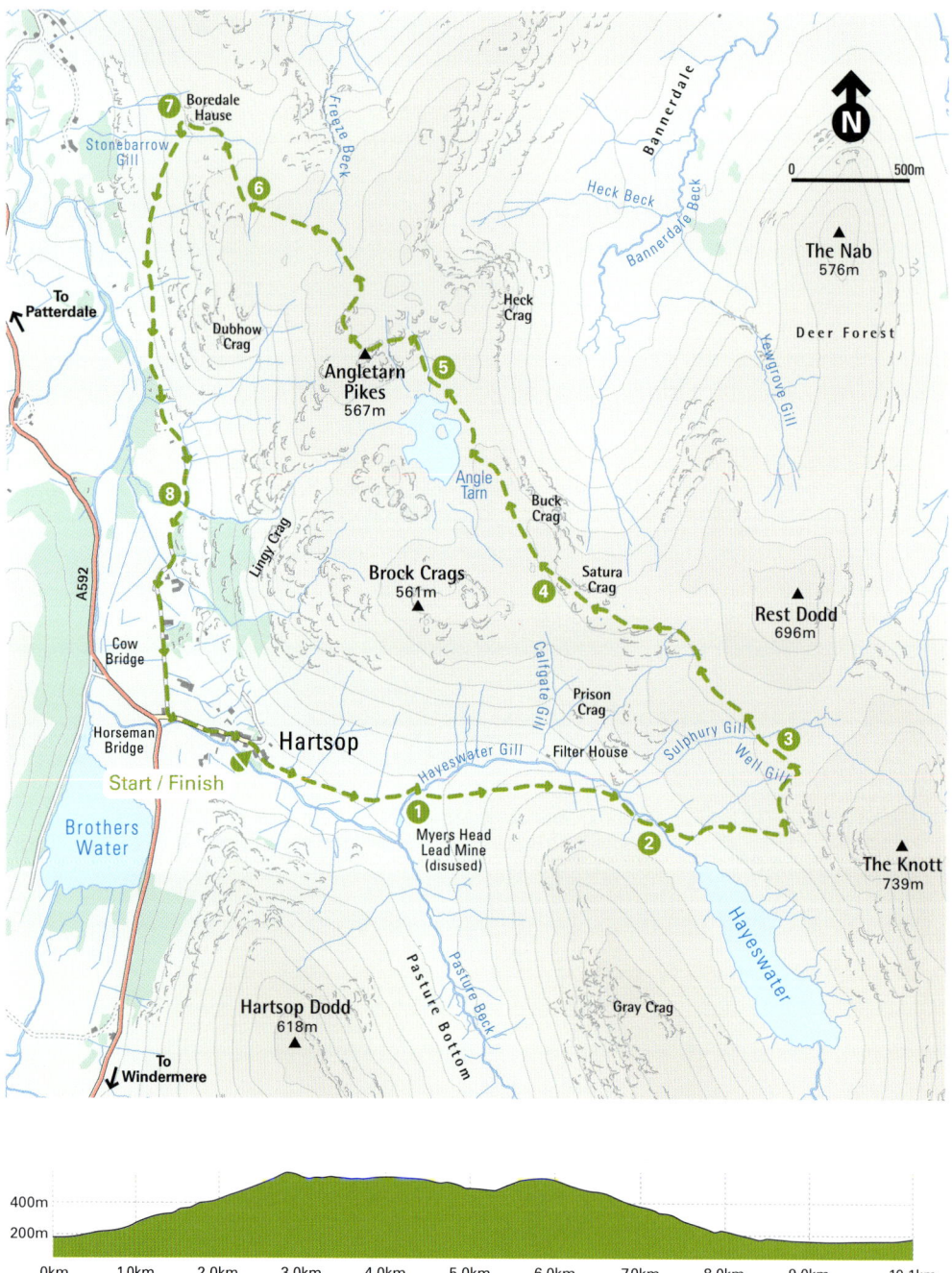

Beyond the footbridge, the path heads due east. The surprising aspect of the start of this route is the steepness of the track beyond the footbridge over the gill. It would not be particularly steep for a fellside path but I don't expect an access route to a reservoir, even an ex-reservoir, to be this precipitous. I slow down considerably.

Angletarn Pikes   16

Following the track into the valley, I'm looking for another footbridge. I ignore the first one that crosses the gill by the Filter House and continue up the slope past the falls. A path rises up the bank from the Filter House and 300 metres on from this point is the footbridge I am looking for. ❷ It is marked with bridleway waymarker discs.

Once over the bridge there's a path leading steeply up the fellside, which is the direction I need to travel. A 25 percent gradient, the most arduous section of the loop, awaits. The path heads away from the wall towards Hayeswater for 200 metres before heading north. The bridleway on the OS 1:25,000 map continues east in the direction of The Knott.

I can see the wall on my left and am moving slowly towards it. ❸ Just beyond the wall junction, I head towards a gap and run across Sulphury Gill to join the path down from The Knott. Now I am contouring beneath Rest Dodd, following the wall on my left; I pick up the pace.

I ignore the path on my right that heads north-east up to Rest Dodd; instead I follow the fence, west then northwest, through a plethora of small tarns keeping Satura Crag to my right. Beyond Satura Crag, I reach another wall and pass through a gap between two sturdy wooden gateposts. ❹ There is no gate.

At this point, if you have time and if you are collecting Wainwrights, it is possible to take a there-and-back visit west to the top of Brock Crags; the round trip is a flat kilometre across boggy ground. Today I carry straight on, and around the next bend Angle Tarn comes into view. Directly across from the tarn I can see Angletarn Pikes, standing 100 metres above the placid water.

Rather than dropping down to the tarn immediately, I take a grassy path parallel to its shore; it is easier running and the views of the tarn are more complete. A deep blue palette with two splodges of thick green acrylic. I hear a piercing caw, maybe a bird, but it sounds human. There are three green tents perched on the tiny peninsula and I half-believe there are swimmers in the tarn.

Looking across Brothers Water to Angletarn Pikes

Steep bridleway to Hayeswater

View of Hartsop Dodd from the bridleway to Hayeswater

Filter House on the bridleway to Hayeswater

Path alongside Angle Tarn

Angletarn Pikes

Angle Tarn from the west

I head down to the shore-path at the north end of the tarn. In the mist, to be safe, I would keep to the main path all the way. Today I decide to go over the pikes; I don't need to, it doesn't improve the run and on a cloudy day, I certainly wouldn't bother. As the path bears left, just across from the tip of the peninsula, there is a grassy path, distinct to begin with, running up the fellside to the left of a beck. ❺ I head up the

Boredale Hause, descending to Hartsop

path, following the beck, and soon find a way up to the highest point of the south top. Down the dip, I follow a distinct path up to the north top and then descend to the north-east before veering north-west as soon as possible. This brings me onto a clear path heading down the fell. I bear left and soon join the main Angle Tarn to Boredale Hause route again. ❻

❼ At the Hause I cross Stonebarrow Gill, turning left (west) and then left again to pick up the gravelly path south down into the valley. The stones glide beneath my fell shoes and I struggle to run at first, but soon the gradient becomes more gentle and the path more compact.

When I reach the main Patterdale to Hartsop track, I have two kilometres of gentle running with a few undulations. I keep striding south wearily with tired legs. Over Angletarn Beck, I take the lower of the two footbridges ❽ so that once I am beyond Hartsop Fold I reach a tarmac lane. At the end of the lane, I turn left and follow the road to the car park.

Hartsop Dodd and Caudale Moor from across Brothers Water

17 Caudale Moor and Hartsop Dodd

Park / Start	Cow Bridge, Patterdale (NY 402 133)		
Map	OS Explorer OL5		
Exertion	●●●●		
Navigation	●●		
Terrain	●		
Distance	9.8 kilometres	**Time**	1 hour 25 minutes
Ascent	638 metres	**On road**	800 metres

Following the footsteps of quarrymen and lead miners to a grassy plateau with a perfect descent

By the National Trust gate in the south-west corner of the car park, a fingerpost points along the Brothers Water shoreline path towards Hartsop Hall. **START** A gentle start to one of my longer and tougher fell runs in this collection. Across the unruffled water, through the budding trees, I can see a clearly defined path winding down the northern ridge of Hartsop Dodd; this will be the route of my descent.

One and half kilometres to Hartsop Hall, I pass the back of the farmhouse and into the farmyard with its shaggy Highland calves. ❶ Skirting left to the front of the house, I turn right to take the concrete track leading over Kirkstone Beck towards Sykeside Farm. Once across the valley and through the campsite,

17 Caudale Moor and Hartsop Dodd

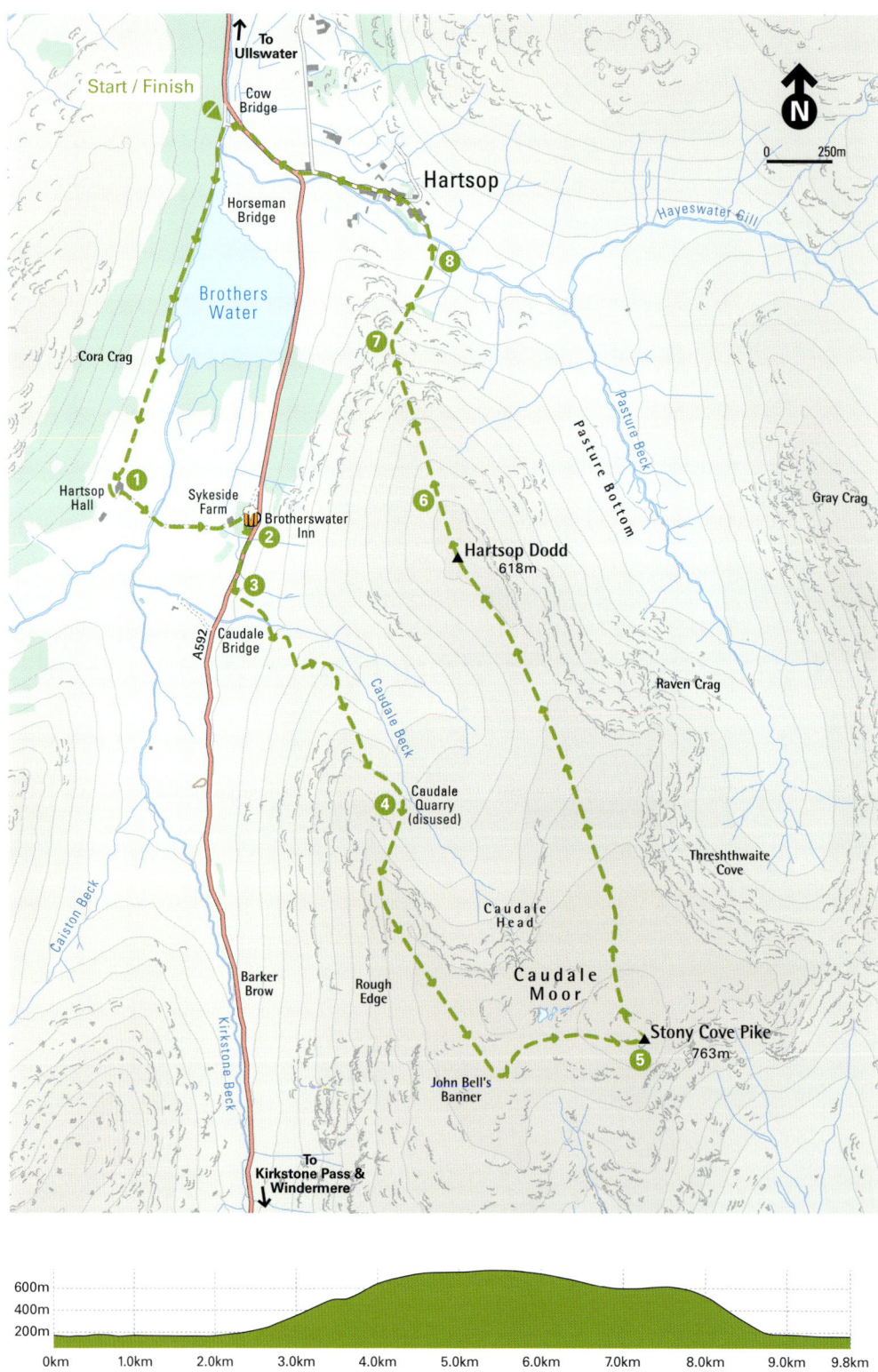

Caudale Moor and Hartsop Dodd

I turn right behind the Brotherswater Inn to reach the A592. More than two kilometres of running with hardly any climbing.

Over the road from the inn, I pass through a gate onto a footpath signposted to Caudale Bridge avoiding the road. ❷ Through the fields, two hundred metres south, I reach the main path, where a fingerpost by the road points up to Caudale Moor (1½ miles). ❸ Now the climbing begins, almost 600 metres of ascent in three kilometres of distance travelled. It's a twisting, convex slope, which means the gradient gradually eases as I rise above the valley into a world of space amongst the peaks and ridges.

As I start to climb, I ignore a path leading straight up the fell. Instead, I cross Caudale Beck and follow the wall south for 40 metres before picking up a clear path running south-east, parallel to the Caudale Beck ravine. I leave the valley behind; Brothers Water, a patch of indigo denim, recedes into the distance. I am now in a deep groove, a vertiginous luge run, once used to transport slate from Caudale Quarry to the pass below.

❹ Through the heaps of slate, past rusting wagons, blocked tunnels and tumbling sheds I emerge above the quarry and pick up a clear path leading high onto Caudale Moor. Down to my right, on the Kirkstone Pass, is the inn of same name – the third highest in England – and high above loom the peaks of Middle Dodd, Red Screes, Scandale Fell and High Pike.

The path veers left and I reach the wall that follows the parish boundary line across the top of the fell. I turn left and follow the route along the wall to the junction close to Stony Cove Pike, the highest point on the moor. ❺ The summit cairn, beyond the wall junction, is a large heap of stones.

I cross back over the wall and head due north down the ridge to Hartsop Dodd, two kilometres along a yielding grassy moor. I now have Caudale Beck on my left and above it, on the fell side, sits the old quarry – a cluster of dark grey warts.

Running alongside Brothers Water

The route of descent from Hartsop Dodd

Running down the ridge from Caudale Moor to Hartsop Dodd

Caudale Quarry from Hartsop Dodd

Hartsop Dodd summit cairn

17 Caudale Moor and Hartsop Dodd

Descending Hartsop Dodd towards Hartsop

There is hardly any climbing to the top of Hartsop Dodd, less than 30 metres ascent from the lowest point on the ridge. ❻ Just 140 metres beyond the final cairn the wall turns right, but the path and my route carries straight on (north-northwest). As I zigzag sharply down the ridge, Ullswater comes into view, filling the glacial valley floor. ❼ At the intake wall I turn right, run down to the wall junction, climb the stile and advance to the gate.

I continue on the path, cross the bridge over Hayeswater Gill and reach Hartsop village car park. ❽ Straight ahead through the car park, I turn onto the lane leading out of the village. It is five hundred metres to the A592, where I turn right to follow the footpath alongside the road back to Cow Bridge.

Brothers Water from the path down Hartsop Dodd

Eden Runners crossing Cow Bridge

Branstree and Selside Pike | 18

Looking towards Mardale Green and Mardale Head

18 Branstree and Selside Pike

Park / Start	Mardale Head car park (NY 469 107)
Map	OS Explorer OL5
Exertion	● ● ●
Navigation	● ● ●
Terrain	●
Distance	9.3 kilometres
Time	1 hour 19 minutes
Ascent	528 metres
On road	0 metres

Rolling moorland sweeping above the spectre of Mardale Green

A route for the living and a route for the dead.

START The gate to the south of the car park is impossible to miss. A few metres through the gate the fingerpost indicates that I should keep left, taking the Gatescarth Pass. This is the old Mardale to Longsleddale mountain pass, the route used for hauling wares out of the valley in the days before it was dammed and flooded.

I persevere with the rocky byway; I know that within a kilometre, it will become more runnable and that once I am out on the moorland this effort will have been worthwhile. For now, it's steep and hard on my feet. I am glad I'm not a packhorse and relieved I'm not pushing a mountain bike up the track, like the two people I pass.

18 Branstree and Selside Pike

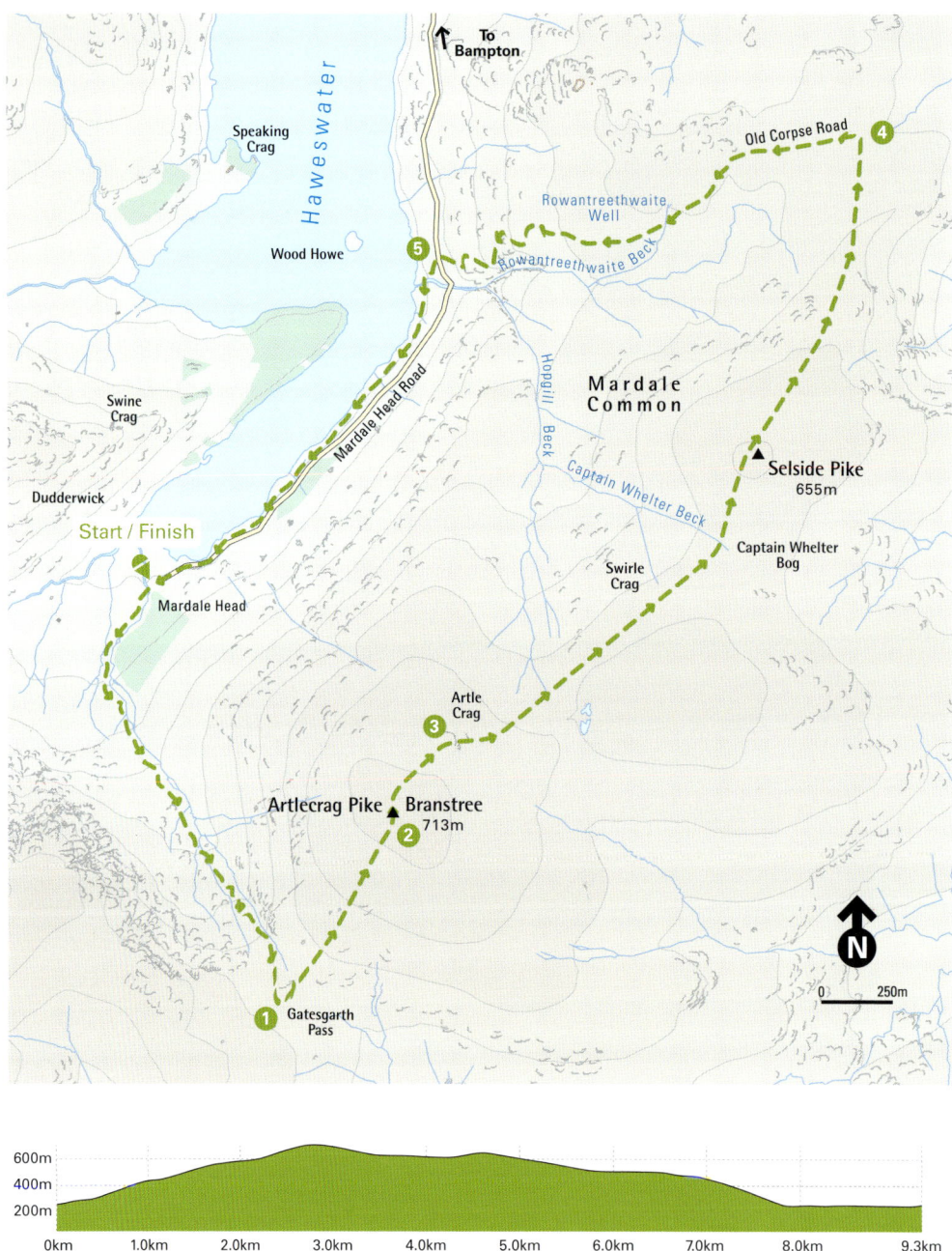

It is almost two kilometres to the top of the pass where I'll turn for Branstree; this point is not hard to spot. A fence line runs across, roughly east to west, and a fingerpost points right to Nan Bield Pass (1¾ miles), the ancient trading route from Mardale to Kentmere, and straight on to Sadgill (2½ miles). There is no arm pointing left (north-east) to Branstree but there is a path alongside the fence and this is my route. ❶ I am now on rolling moorland, bleak and desolate in winter, little visited even in the summer months. Perfect running country, which bears more resemblance to the Pennines than to typical Lakeland Fells.

Branstree and Selside Pike 18

Gatesgarth Pass – byway to Branstree

The gradient is just as severe as the packhorse byway, but the soft grass and the absence of rocks allow me to increase my pace. I follow the fence line upwards following a faint but obvious path all the way to the junction between the fence and a wall on my right. ❷ I am almost at the summit. Fifty metres to my left there is a small cairn and an unusual flat, wheel-like trig point, one of only two in in the Lake District (the other is on the top of Blencathra).

My next destination, Selside Pike, lies 1.8 kilometres across the nondescript moor. On a misty day I would keep to the fence line; today, with high clouds and perfect visibility, I follow the path angled slightly away from the wall and soon I can see the twin bee-hive-cairns that lie on the rounded summit of Artlecrag Pike just 250 metres away. ❸ On an otherwise rockless plateau, my stride is broken by a field of vertical rocks protruding from the earth, like stone Stegosaurus dermal plates. The same rocks were used to build the elegant cairns.

I head back to the fence, which I follow north-east down to a splendidly named Captain Whelter Bog and back up the other side. A path all the way, excellent running terrain when it is not too boggy, brings me to the small volcano-shaped shelter on the summit of Selside Pike.

Fingerpost at the top of the Gatesgarth Pass – turn left along the fence

Cairn on Artlecrag Pike – Branstree

18 Branstree and Selside Pike

The fence, a trusty navigation aid, turns right here in an east-southeasterly direction and I need to take some care with my path selection. One faint path follows the fence and two paths head roughly straight on; I take the path on my left which heads north-northeast down the ridge. A poor route selection would not be a disaster; it would just mean meeting the Old Corpse Road further to the east.

I pick up the pace downhill, it takes me just a few minutes to reach the Corpse Road. ❹ Here I turn left (west) back to Haweswater. Another superb running route, a wide grassy track I can bound along before the path steepens and I begin the descent to Mardale.

I contemplate the pallbearers who lugged their coffins up this slope over to Swindale Head and then on to Shap. In the depths of winter, in all weathers, they must have toiled before the tiny church in Mardale Green was given permission to bury its own dead. Few people die in Mardale these days, not since the flooding of the valley, and in a poignant twist of fate those who found rest in their valley were dug-up and shifted to Shap, where they were interred with their ancestors.

Running down the Corpse Road to Haweswater

Past the ruined peat stores, the twisting path slows me down. I soon meet the Mardale Head Road and the reservoir at its narrowest point. Left, across the road, virtually opposite, is the gate leading down to the lakeshore path. ❺

The path is an undulating, twisting, grassy jaunt all the way back to the car park.

Along the lakeshore path – the route to Mardale Head

19 Wansfell Pike and Baystones

Wansfell – a backdrop to Ambleside

19 Wansfell Pike and Baystones

Park / Start	Lake Road car park, Ambleside (NY 376 042)		
Map	OS Explorer OL7		
Exertion	●●●●		
Navigation	●		
Terrain	●		
Distance	11.3 kilometres	Time	1 hour 32 minutes
Ascent	606 metres	On road	2.7 kilometres

Ambleside's fell – an ideal place to watch the sunset over Windermere

From the centre of Ambleside, a straight up and down run to the top of Wansfell Pike is a four kilometre round trip providing one of the finest views in the Lake District. I am going further, along old drover's lanes, over grassy moors, pastures and through a varied Victorian arboretum.

START Exiting the car park east, up the steps onto Lake Road, I cross immediately and swing right up Old Lake Road. ❶ After 200 metres, I turn left up Blue Hill Road, past holiday lets and dwellings, heading for the track at the end of the lane.

I reach Gasworks Cottages and the tarmac ends. ❷ The Wansfell Pike Fell Race, and other races to the top of the fell, take the Stockghyll Lane route but this is the most straightforward way to the summit. With the gasworks long gone, Wainwright's caveat is no longer relevant.

19 Wansfell Pike and Baystones

Sixty metres along the track a fingerpost points to Wansfell Pike (1 mile). I run uphill on a rough trail hemmed in between two drystone walls. The path steepens. Ahead I spy the inn on the brow of Kirkstone Pass, and to my left cars grind up The Struggle.

After 1.4 kilometres, there is a gate ahead; this is the route up from Stockghyll Force. ❸ I turn right before the gate to climb the carefully laid erosion-resistant steps. I am now on the Fell Race route to the top of the Pike. Again, the path steepens. I have 300 metres to climb in the next 900 metres travelled; at least

Wansfell Pike and Baystones 19

Running over the summit of Wansfell Pike

the steps are smooth and there are plenty of grassy sections to protect my fell-shoe studs.

The steps end and a craggy sector of fell begins. Through the gate at the top, the summit of Wansfell Pike is revealed along with extensive views; south, the long reach of Windermere, north-west, the deep blue splashes of Rydal Water and Grasmere, reminding me why this aspect is Ambleside's favourite.

Looking back over Ambleside from the path up to Wansfell Pike

Rather than heading directly east to Nanny Lane, I turn left and run north-east along the wall towards Baystones, the highest point on Wansfell. The two sides of this triangle qualify as the most rewarding running on this loop. Two kilometres of undulating cantering over soft terrain, marshy when it rains, satisfyingly ungirded fell running.

I run close to the wall on my left for just over a kilometre. ❹ Five hundred metres beyond Wansfell Pike summit I clamber over a stone stile, before veering towards Baystones over a series of grassy hummocks. The 482-metre peak 100 metres south of the wall harbours a small cairn. Today this is my turning point. One hundred and fifty metres north of the wall, marked at 487 metres on OS maps, lies the true highest point of the fell. A detour over the wall doesn't tempt me.

At the cairn I turn, almost 180 degrees, taking the path heading just east of south with the length of Windermere directly in front of me. A vast river interrupted by Belle Isle and a flotilla of model yachts. Today, after weeks without rain, the faint path traverses straw-yellow heath, unusually dry, in the general line of the lake.

19 Wansfell Pike and Baystones

My exact line does not matter, though. Within 700 metres, I reach a wall, ❺ cross at a wooden stile and drop down onto Nanny Lane where I turn right. A green lane, an old farm track, leading down to Troutbeck. Enclosed by walls I have nowhere to go except down to the road, it is a gentle descent, 1.2 kilometres, on a runnable surface.

I turn right at the minor road, just 800 metres on a very quiet lane, looking out for the Troutbeck Institute on my right. Annie's Clock above the doorway, Robin Lane just beyond and a fingerpost for the public footpath to Ambleside (2½ miles). ❻

Annie's Clock at the Troutbeck Institute

I turn right and Robin Lane soon becomes a track, another old farm route, which I follow uphill. Just over a kilometre from the Institute, the track branches at a pair of five-barred gates, I take the left-hand fork; through the kissing gate, following the bridleway sign for Skelghyll Wood, Jenkin Crag and Ambleside. ❼

Over the footbridge above Hol Beck, I turn right, past another signpost to Ambleside (1¼ mile), and climb for the final time. Up to High Skelghyll, into the farmyard, through the gate at the end to follow the contour path towards Skelghyll Woods.

Branch of Robin Lane and Hundreds Road, Low Skelghyll

Into the woods, where wild garlic pervades, I continue to contour under a canopy of delicate young leaves. I don't want to take any of the paths to my left, which would lead me to the water's edge. I keep right at path junctions, unless this means climbing up through the trees.

❽ Exiting the woods through a gate, the track soon becomes a tarmacked road – Skelghyll Lane – which I chase down to its end. Turning right at the junction, I am back on Old Lake Road, which I follow over a small rise back to the car park.

Evening across Windermere from Skelghyll Wood

Sour Howes and Sallows **20**

Sour Howes from Troutbeck

20 Sour Howes and Sallows

Park / Start	Parking area, Troutbeck, west of Church Bridge (NY 412 026)		
Map	OS Explorer OL7		
Exertion	● ● ●		
Navigation	● ● ●		
Terrain	● ●		
Distance	8.3 kilometres	Time	1 hour 9 minutes
Ascent	440 metres	On road	250 metres

Soft, undulating fells linked by ancient Lakeland trade routes

Names redolent of rolling moorland deliver what they promise.

START Fifty metres east to Church Bridge, over the footbridge above Trout Beck then 100 metres south-west on the footpath alongside the A 592 brings me to the foot of Garburn Road. Here I cross the road. A fingerpost points to the restricted byway towards Kentmere (3¾ miles). ❶

The old packhorse route to Kentmere is rocky and climbs steeply. Ravaged by rain over the centuries, this route has been beaten into submission in places by the insertion of hundreds of irregular setts. Hard on the feet. Long sections of track mean that I favour all-terrain or trail shoes on this run. Even road shoes are sufficient in dry conditions.

20 Sour Howes and Sallows

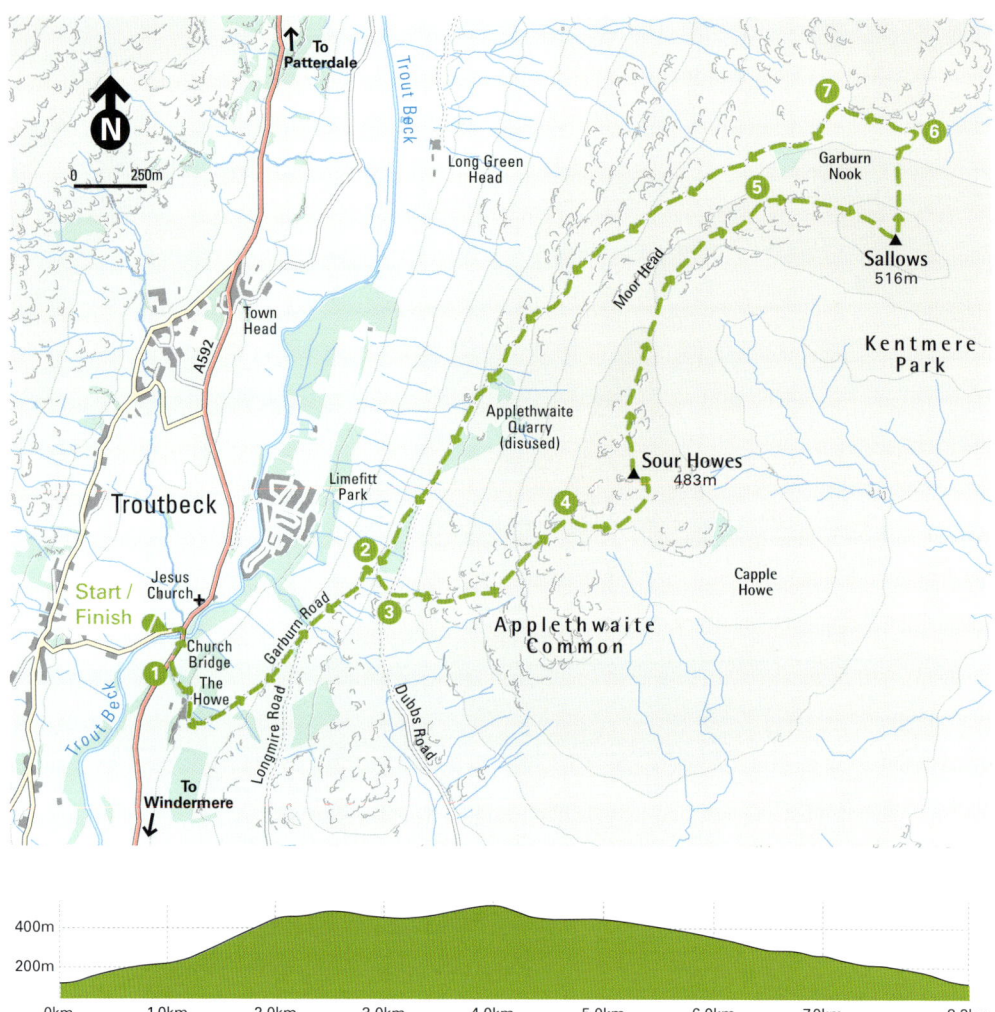

As the rocky path climbs above the lodges of Limefitt Park, the gradient steepens but I can still manage to run this segment. Longmire Road, another bygone trade route, crosses at an acute angle. I don't notice the track as it cuts in behind me over my right shoulder, but it continues on my left through a gate towards Limefitt Park. I keep right, uphill, on the Garburn Road, the terrain becoming smoother as it approaches a small plantation on my right.

Just before the plantation, 1.25 kilometres into my run, I climb the ladder stile to my right over the wall into an enclosure. ❷ Ahead, 80 metres across the pasture, another ladder stile drops me onto Dubbs Road, yet another byway. Directly across the track a third ladder stile brings me onto the open fell of Applethwaite Common. ❸

I climb on a clear path, not on the map, up a steep grassy slope. The route meanders through stony outcrops. No longer able to run, breathing hard, heading past a disinterested herd of chocolate Highland cattle, I head towards a distinctive rock, a cracked incisor, on the horizon. The gradient steepens again.

Sour Howes and Sallows 20

Following the wall from Sour Howes to Sallows

I can't breathe any harder. I slow again until I reach a wall with a step stile. ❹ Beyond here, the slope eases. Once over the wall I reach a bumpy plateau, each hillock seems to be of equal height. I follow the path north-east to a mound bearing a small cone, upon which lies a paltry pile of stones. I presume this is the summit of Sour Howes. Ill Bell dominates to the north. To my left sprawls the corrugated apex of Wansfell. South-east, a leaden Windermere stretches towards the lowland edges of the Lakelands.

Ascending Garburn Road

From this high point, I head north-east on an obvious path. My exact line is not critical; as long as I don't drift too far north I will reach the wall separating Sour Howes from Sallows. Five hundred metres beyond the top of Sour Howes I reach the wall and run with this on my right down to a depression, then up the other side.

The route up to Sour Howes

Down on the Garburn Road there were a few dog walkers, but here on a late afternoon under heavy clouds I have the damp moorland to myself. I climb up the bank looking for a step stile over the wall. ❺ As soon as I cross, I turn left then right to pick up a distinct path, again not on the map, which will take me to the summit of Sallows.

20 Sour Howes and Sallows

Route of descent from Sallows looking towards Ill Bell

Five hundred metres up a gentle incline across a moor of spiky tussocks, a field of green sea urchins, brings me to a triangular dorsal-fin bump, upon which there is another meagre pile of stones. This is Sallows summit. My route of descent is north. I take a sharp left-hand turn down the slope and it is not long before the Garburn Road comes into view. At the bottom of the col, I pick up a path heading to my right, which seems to follow a ruined wall. This brings me to a stone stile at a wall corner. ❻ Over the stile, I turn left onto the track, passing through a gate to head west, then south-west, on the Garburn byway back to Troutbeck.

Descending Garburn Road, the junction with Dubbs Road

Three hundred metres on from the gate I keep left at the turn off to Ill Bell. ❼ I follow the track through the National Trust gates, past the wooded Applethwaite Quarry. I try to pick up the pace on the gentle descent but the rough surface slows me down. Over milky-white slate slabs, I am glad I am not wearing my fell shoes.

Keeping right at the Dubbs Road fork, I am close to the ladder stile I climbed 50 minutes ago. I now retrace my steps back to the road over the pitched stone rumble strips.

Sheep on Garburn Road

The Central Fells

Within the heart of the Lakes, the Central Fells offer great variety; from rock towers and steep crags, to peaty swamps and forested glens. These runs provide views of a rosette of higher fells and vistas of a multitude of lakes and tarns. The routes include some of the most popular Lakeland rambles as well as little visited corners of immense beauty.

Thirlmere from Raven Crag (Raven Crag route)

Eden Runners descending High Rigg

High Rigg 21

High Rigg from the Old Coach Road

21 High Rigg

Park / Start	St John's Church, St John's in the Vale (NY 306 225)
Map	OS Explorer OL5
Exertion	●●
Navigation	●●
Terrain	●●
Distance	7.4 kilometres	Time	56 minutes
Ascent	310 metres	On road	250 metres

An entry-level fell offering exhilarating, undulating running

High Rigg, a small fell close to Keswick, a perfect hour.
These days I prefer to start at St John's Church to the north of the fell, partly because the parking is free but mainly because I want to get the less interesting low-level path through Low Bridge End Farm out of the way first.

START A short jog east down the road, past St John's Church, I glance through the gate at the gravestones and the slopes of the grassy fell that shield the simple stone structure and transform it into a building of immense beauty. Beyond the churchyard, on my right, a fingerpost points to a public bridleway in the direction of Sosgill Bridge (1¼ miles). ❶ Through the gate, a gentle stony descent, faster in my

21 High Rigg

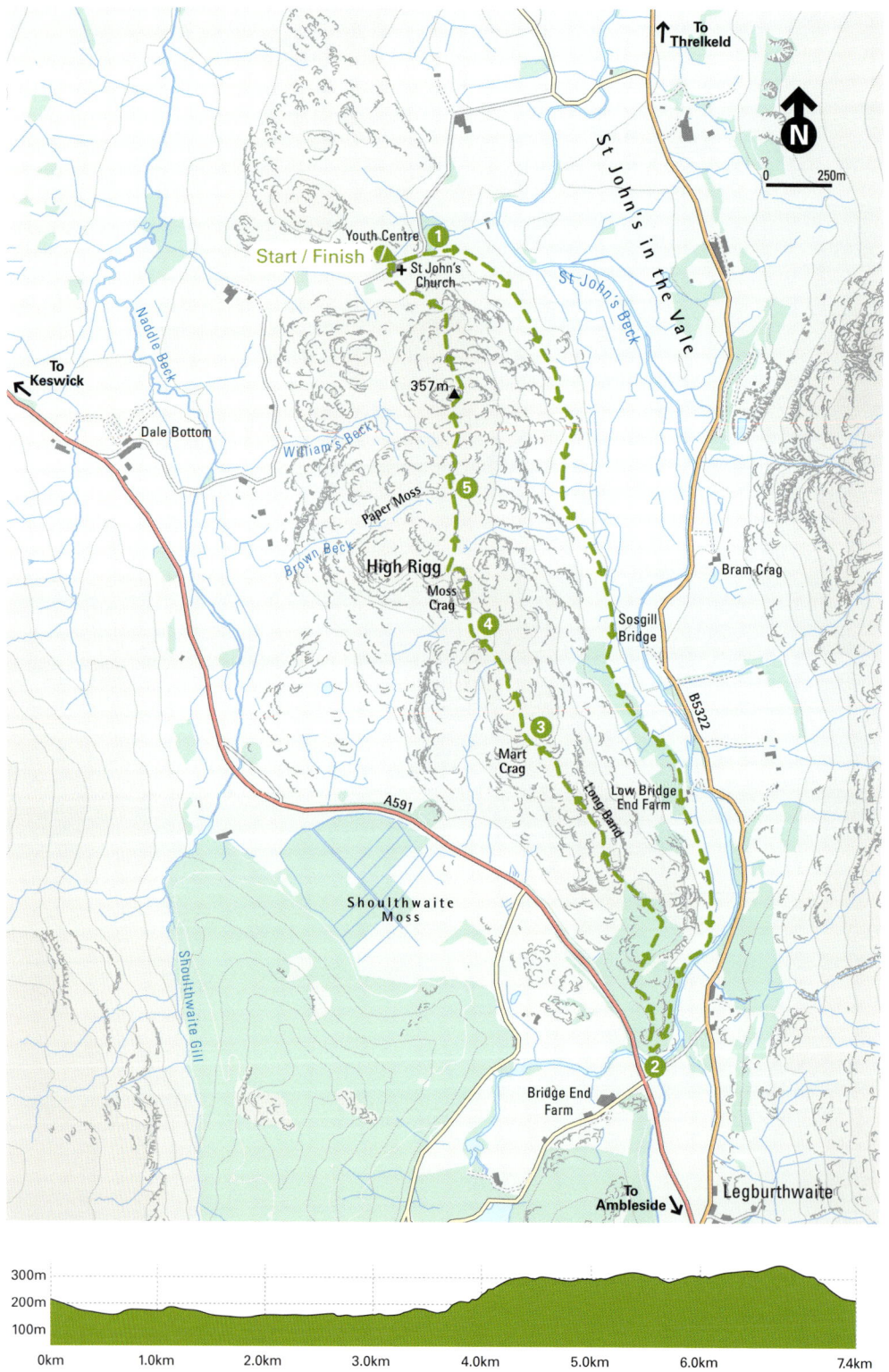

High Rigg

youth, now an easy way to flex my aging muscles. I am heading south over numerous springs, reduced to a trickle in the parched summer.

The stretch along the valley floor is a good warm-up. The path undulates, rocks and roots abound, I have to focus on where I place my feet. This level of concentration makes the time pass quickly; before I know it, I have reached the gate to the farm.

Once through the farm I have an easy stretch across pastureland, before beginning an upward scramble between the boulders alongside St John's Beck. At the southern end of the ridge, near the village of Legburthwaite, I turn right onto a storm-ravaged path through an avenue of young birch trees and start to climb. ❷ An easy turn to miss if you're not expecting it, but 100 metres further on and you reach the A591 and you know you have gone wrong.

Though relatively small – its prominence is less than 200 metres – the initial ascent of High Rigg is quite steep, past giant, fallen trees and over sharp scree. Soon I'm able to run, taking a rolling direct line north over and around the bobbles that make up the ridge. This section reminds me of a coastal way, sweeping gently up and down, like the Pembrokeshire Coast Path. I can almost imagine the Atlantic swirling into the troughs of this volcanic outcrop.

❸ Immediately over the first stile, I turn right and follow the fence north up a grassy slope. On the other side of the rise, I descend to a marshy area with a small tarn, which I pass on the left. Once around the tarn I run down another slope, dry today but usually waterlogged, following the wall on my right.

❹ Dropping down a steep grassy bank, over a ladder stile, then uphill once more with the wall again on my right. Now a bog awaits, full of water even in the height of summer, my route across this central swampy area depends on how dry it has been. Today, desiccated-moss dry, I hug the wall and climb the slope across the brittle bracken. Wet conditions advise me to keep left and seek out a meagre collection of stepping-stones to the left of the post that would seem to indicate a dry route through. I have been in the mire up to my waist here, bereft of any firm structure with which to lever myself out.

I follow the wall to the top of another small climb. ❺ The wall turns right, I continue straight ahead, due

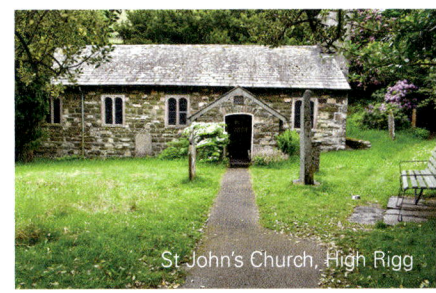
St John's Church, High Rigg

High Rigg, turn right to start the climb through the trees

Passing the small tarn on High Rigg

Eden Runners heading to High Rigg summit

21 High Rigg

Descent of High Rigg to St John's Youth Centre

north, an undulating 400 metres distance to the top. It is a short detour to the summit cairn then the path heads north again around the rocky outcrop.

A short, steep descent on soft, slippery grass brings me back to the youth centre by the church. The quick downhill strains my quads and makes my IT bands throb. I have to brake to slow before the final gate. Now I swerve around the back of the youth centre and at the road, turn right to my car.

Heading down to St John's Youth Centre

Walla Crag

Walla Crag across Derwentwater

22 Walla Crag

Park	Keswick
Start	Moot Hall, Keswick (NY 266 233)
Map	OS Explorer OL4
Exertion	•••
Navigation	••
Terrain	•

Distance	8.4 kilometres	Time	1 hour 5 minutes
Ascent	400 metres	On road	2.5 kilometres

**From the heart of Keswick, through the Great Wood
to traverse a ridge above Derwentwater**

Of the two small fells that are very easy to access from the centre of Keswick, Walla Crag is never as busy as its counterpart, Latrigg. I am not sure why. Maybe because the start is not as obvious or perhaps it is because Walla Crag is less visible to tourists from the centre of town.

START From the Moot Hall in the Market Square, I run south-east along St John's Street, past the cinema and the parish church. ❶ After 600 metres, I turn right along Springs Road; perhaps it's not apparent, but I am now on route for the fell.

113

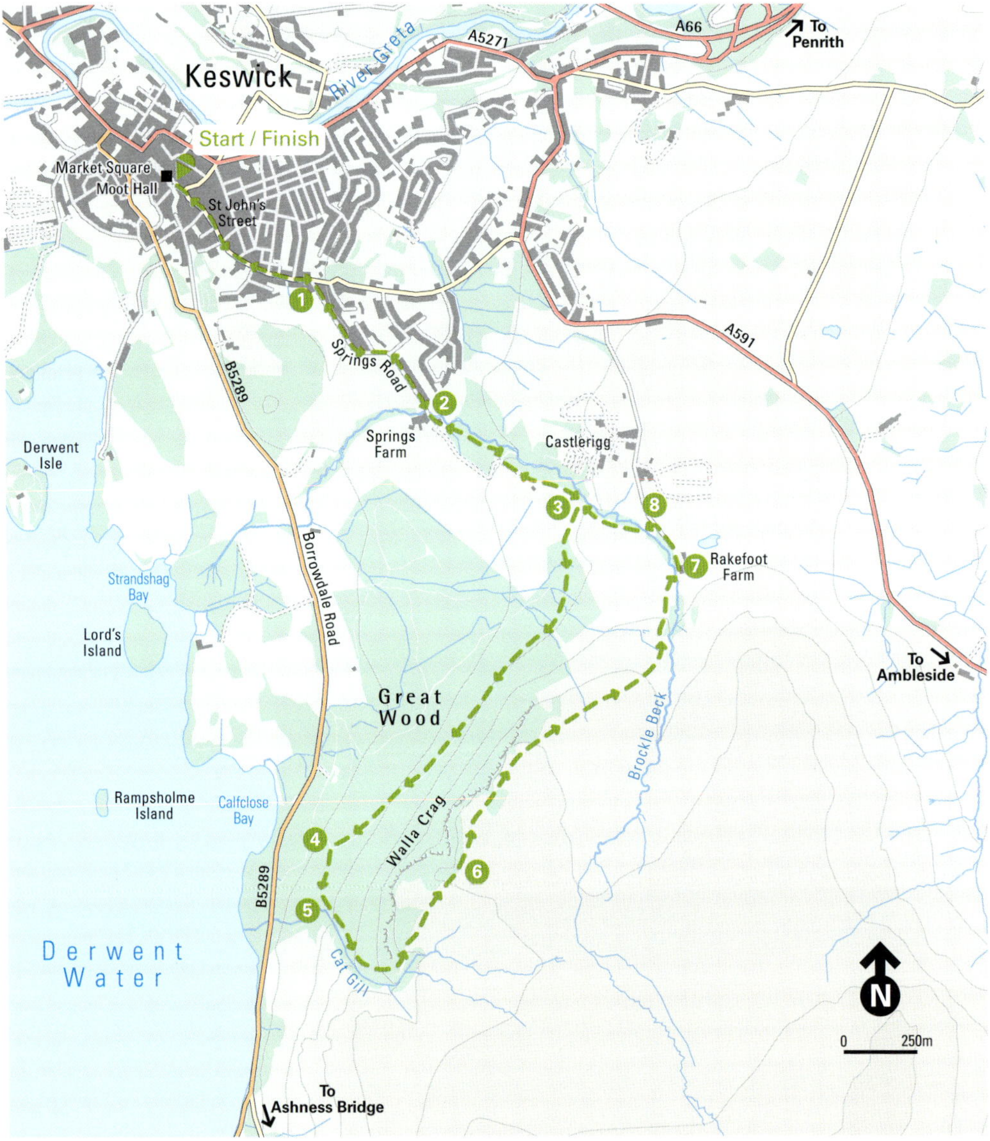

22 Walla Crag

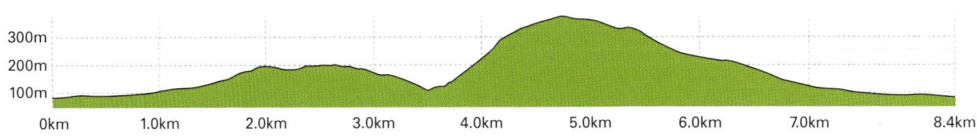

Here, still on the road, the climbing begins, gently to begin with. I'm still in the town with little to suggest that I will soon be on a craggy hillside. Over the bridge at Springs Farm, the road becomes a track and, once past the tearoom, I follow the public footpath in the direction of Rakefoot and Castlerigg. ❷

Beyond the gate into the wood, the winter sun barely penetrates through the leafless canopy. I follow the beck for a short distance. Soon a footbridge comes into view, which I don't want to cross. Instead, a small

Walla Crag

square sign on the bank ahead reminds me to go right, in the direction of Walla Crag and Rakefoot Farm.

It gets steeper now but it is still runnable. To my right I can see Walla Crag looming high over Derwentwater. I'm out of the woodland and into the sunshine, climbing alongside enclosed pastures. A little beyond the radio mast I reach a path junction. Today I am running over the crag from south to north, so I turn right at the fingerpost following the sign for Great Wood. ❸ Between a wall and a fence, up a slight incline to begin with, then down on a rocky track. It is jagged and rough so I run cautiously. A few years ago I would have blithely charged down this section; today, in fear of falling, I watch my feet.

Path junction in Springs Wood beyond Springs Farm

Into the ancient woods, I keep to the high path. The forest is being thinned and felled trees lie like fallen soldiers, row on row, perpendicular to the path. Through the leafless branches, the sun splashes down dappling the rocks and the earth. ❹ I reach a path junction, taking a left turn at the fingerpost towards Ashness Bridge (1 mile) and Walla Crag via a gradual climb (2¼ miles). I begin to ascend again and within 200 metres, another sign directs me up Cat Gill on a steep climb. ❺ This is the direct route to Walla Crag on a path of volcanic rocks, hewn with great effort into hundreds of steps alongside the cascading water of Cat Gill. This is a humid gully with swathes of mosses and lichens draped upon rocks and tree trunks. It is too steep to run, and at stages close to the top, I use my hands to hold myself as I clamber over wet slabs.

Running towards Great Wood above Derwentwater

The top of Cat Gill heading towards Walla Crag

The crag beside me, the western flank of Walla, is covered with stunted ash, oak and birch and ahead Scots pines cling to the edges of Cat Gill just below the

Running towards the summit of Walla Crag

waterfalls. Through the final gate, the path becomes grassy and more convex. I can begin to run again. I edge left, following the wall that encloses Great Wood. I'm running head-on into the cold easterly wind with the Blencathra Massif straight ahead of me and Clough Head to my right. It is well below zero here, the surface water has frozen, seemingly mid-flow, forming overlapping doilies of ice.

To reach the summit it is necessary to leave the main path and climb the stile over the wall on my left. ❻ A short distance upon rocks and through heather, the cairn is reached. I pause to look at the view.

22 Walla Crag

Derwentwater and Bassenthwaite Lake from Walla Crag

The pale sunshine illuminates the Borrowdale valley. Tiny boats sit like toys at the Marina on the far side of Derwentwater. Bassenthwaite Lake stretches away into the distance. Keswick nestles silently in the valley below. From the cairn, I continue on a rocky path that brings me out, via a gate and an enormous pile of stones, onto the main path again. Turning left, I speed-up down the bank. Keeping the wall to my left, I soon reach a gate and from here, I follow Brockle Beck down to the footbridge at Rakefoot Farm. ❼ Two hundred metres down the road I take a hairpin on my left, easy to miss, through a gate following the public footpath sign for Keswick and Great Wood. ❽

Derwentwater, Cat Bells and the Terrace path from Walla Crag

Returning to Keswick from Walla Crag, Blencathra as a backdrop

Another footbridge takes me back over the beck, which I then follow back to Springs Farm. Soon I reach the junction where I turned off earlier towards Great Wood. Now I can retrace my steps with a bit more zip, down to the tearooms, the farm and then a fast descent down Springs Road. A left-hand turn and 600 metres of running takes me back to Market Square.

23 Bleaberry Fell

Bleaberry Fell on a late summer's evening

Park / Start	Nest Brow, A591 SE of Keswick, lay-by at corner of Castle Lane (NY 287 227)
Map	OS Explorer OL4
Exertion	● ●
Navigation	● ● ●
Terrain	●
Distance	8.7 kilometres
Time	1 hour 15 minutes
Ascent	442 metres
On road	500 metres

**Bang in the middle of the Central Fells,
a heather-clad summit with panoramic views**

Despite its name Bleaberry Fell, a sea of purple in the autumn, shows little sign of bilberry bushes on its accessible slopes. And, unusually for the Central Fells, your feet can remain dry on this gradual ascent. On the way down, though, the story is different.

On the west side of the road, a sign points to Walla Crag and Keswick. **START** I cross the road and start my watch. I pass through the gate and head across the meadow. I follow the fence and wall, first south then west through several gates to Rakefoot Farm.

On my left I can see Dodd Crag and just behind that the summit of Bleaberry Fell. The clouds are high so the foothills of the Central Fells are clearly defined. Navigation will be easy.

23 Bleaberry Fell

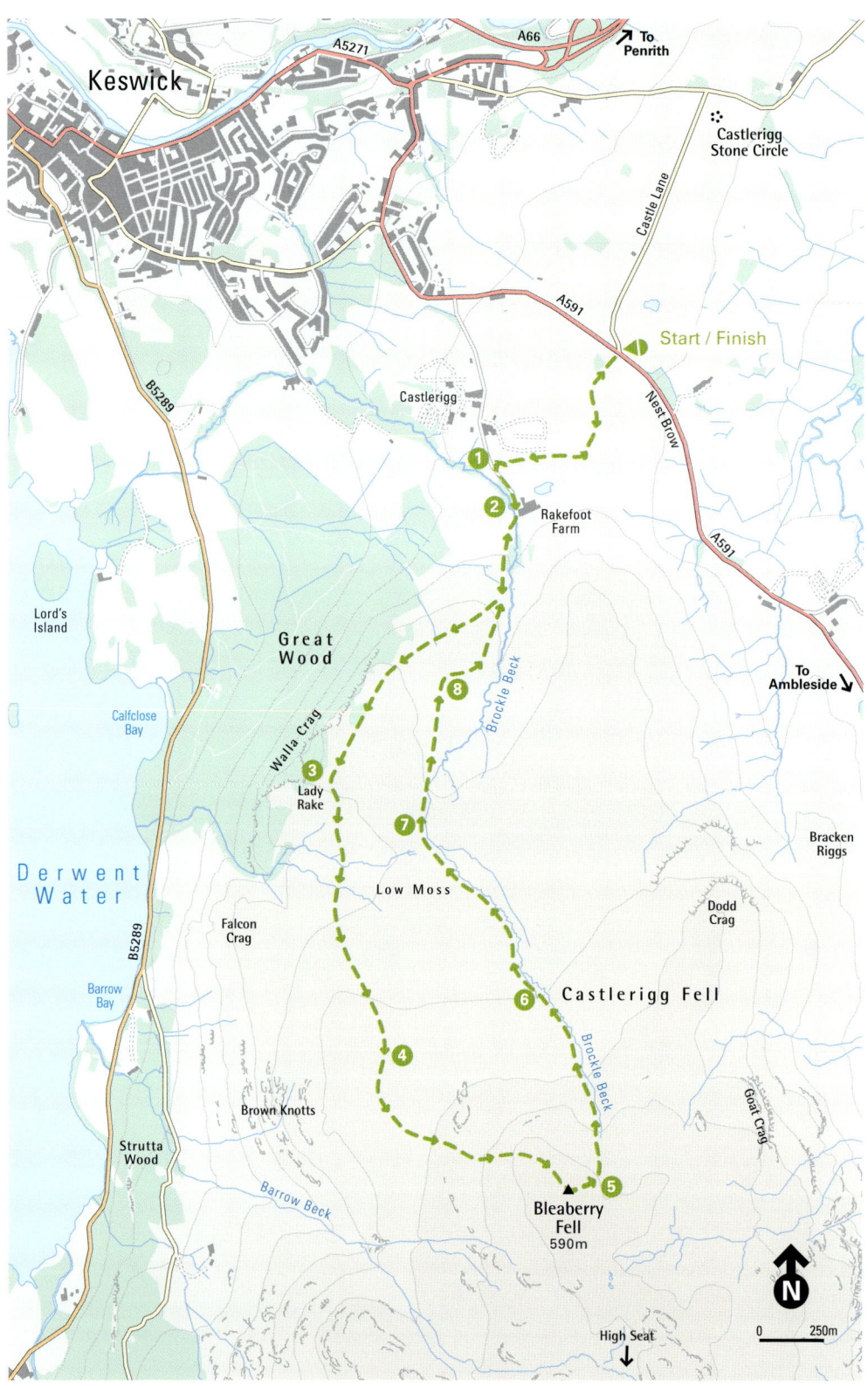

Bleaberry Fell

❶ At the road, I turn left and head past Rakefoot Farm where a faux road sign directs me towards Walla Crag. ❷ Over the footbridge I follow the track and once through the gate I begin the climb up Walla Crag. I keep close to the wall. The top of Walla Crag lies to the west of the wall but, since this is not my goal, I ignore the enormous cairn that marks the gate onto the crag. The path skirts very close to the summit though and I end up just four metres below the highest point.

Start of the Bleaberry Fell run – through the meadows to Rakefoot Farm

Just beyond the second opening to Walla summit, this time a double stile, the path branches. ❸ The left branch, south, leads to Bleaberry Fell, two kilometres of climbing on a good path. Over a couple of bubbling streams, I keep bearing left. ❹ Once I reach the sheep-fold beneath the nameless rocky knoll the gradient increases. For me at least, any pretence of running is abandoned and won't recommence until I reach the top. A bobbly peanut-brittle path gives way to well-maintained stone steps and some rotund cairns let me know that I'm approaching the summit. I'm not sure where the highest point of this heathery platform is. There is a throne-like wind shelter on what seems like the highest ground.

Follow the 'road sign' to Walla Crag

I'm reminded I am in the Central Fells when I pause a while to look at the panorama. As I face north virtually all of the Northern Fells are visible. To the east is the Helvellyn Range, topped with cotton wool clouds. South, the Langdale Fells clutter the horizon. North-westwards, Bassenthwaite Lake stretches away into the distance, and Derwentwater, visible from the north-west cairn, caresses the flank of Cat Bells.

Running towards Bleaberry Fell

Beyond the easterly cairn, rather than following the path to High Seat, I duck down to my left in a north-easterly direction to the fence corner where I pick up the fence line. I follow the fence down for 100 metres, continuing north-east. ❺ There is a small stile

The shelter on Bleaberry Fell summit

23 Bleaberry Fell

Looking back at the route down from Bleaberry Fell (Brockle Beck)

over the fence, which I don't cross, and from here, Brockle Beck emerges. At this point I head north, then north-northwest, following the stream on an indistinct path (which requires some faith and perseverance through clumps of heather) until I reach a small sheepfold, little more than a square of stones. ❻ Here a clear path begins. Wainwright describes it as intermittent but it is runnable across waterlogged, mossy fell. Brockle Beck weaves back and forth, the path forges on, crossing over the meanders. I bound like a giant, striding over the twists of the Orinoco!

❼ At a second, more intact, sheepfold I continue straight ahead (north) leaving the course of the beck for a while. ❽ After 500 metres I pick up a track that leads east, then north, back to the gate above Rakefoot, back to the banks of Brockle Beck.

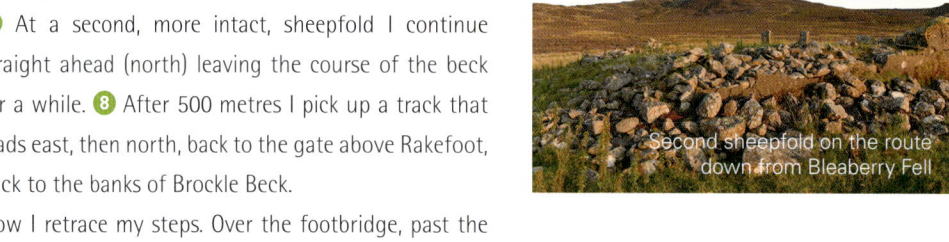
Second sheepfold on the route down from Bleaberry Fell

Now I retrace my steps. Over the footbridge, past the farm, making sure I don't miss the footpath on my right signposted to Castlerigg Stone Circle. I follow the sign for the Stone Circle across the saturated fields, back to the road and the lay-by where I'm parked. Once again, my feet are sodden and my fell shoes are caked in peaty mud. At least today, in the awakenings of spring, the water feels a little warmer.

Raven Crag from Thirlmere Dam

24 Raven Crag

Park / Start	Dam Triangle car park, west of Thirlmere Reservoir Dam (NY 306 189)		
Map	OS Explorer OL4 and OL5		
Exertion	●●●		
Navigation	●●		
Terrain	●		
Distance	6.3 kilometres	Time	50 minutes
Ascent	365 metres	On road	1.2 kilometres

The finest views of Thirlmere from a controversial viewing platform

Forests change and can be confusing. This part of Thirlmere Forest has been ravaged by storm and fire. Apparently, in 2018, ten thousand trees were destroyed and since then the owners, United Utilities, have carried out extensive work replanting trees and upgrading paths, especially the route to the summit of Raven Crag itself.

Forests may be transitory, but fells change more slowly and lend permanence and depth to a fleeting landscape. This outcrop provides a reassuring view of the ancient rolling hills and glacial scars, and casts a cynical eye upon the man-made mass of water in the valley below.

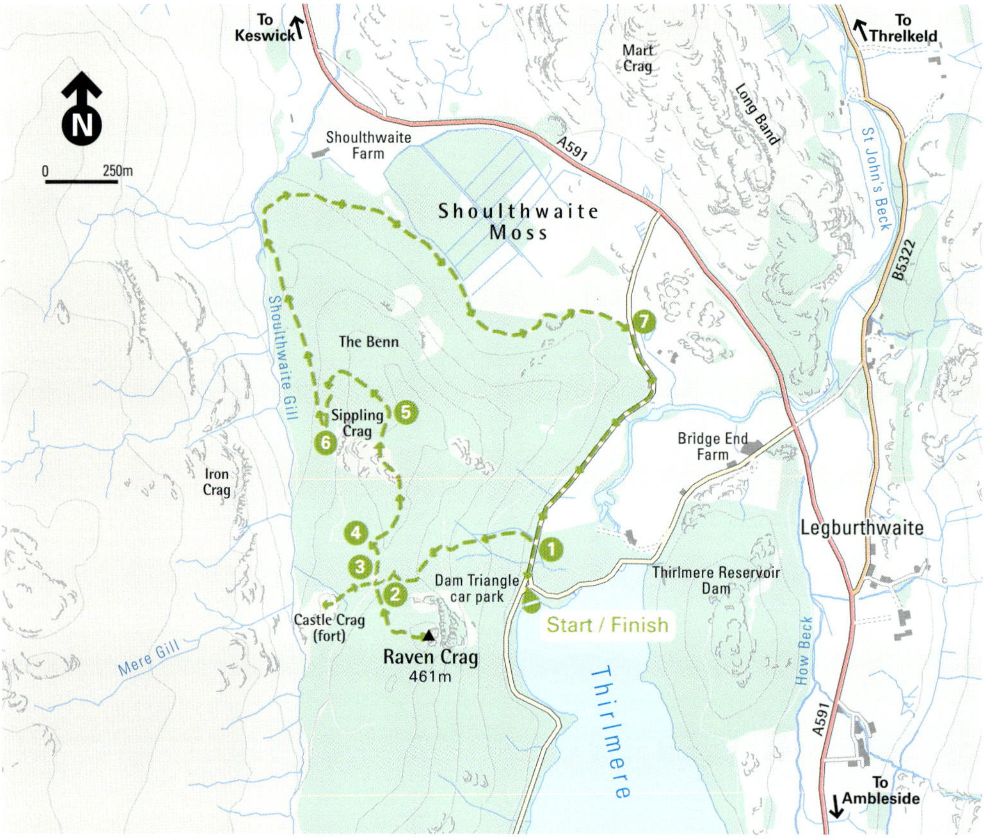

24 Raven Crag

START From the car park, I head north for 150 metres. I reach a high gate on my left. ❶ There is no sign but the path on the other side is clear. Through the gate, I head straight up through the sparse trees. I cross the winding forest track once, at 350 metres, then again at 500 metres. To the left of me is the formidable turret of Raven Crag. Ahead, a steep climb, without abatement, where I meet the forest track for a third time, at a narrow, high gate.

❷ Left now, through another narrow, high gate, up earth steps held by wooden boards, then wooden walkways and finally, beyond the highest point, a wooden platform. I don't know anywhere else in the Lakes like this! On the edge of the crag, the view down Thirlmere makes the journey worthwhile. The Blencathra Massif lurks to my left; the Helvellyn Range confronts me directly ahead.

I retrace my steps back to the gate, turn left over the forest track. Ahead a signpost points to a footpath by way of a kissing gate. ❸ Through the gate, I follow the path climbing towards Castle Crag, the site of an Iron Age hill-fort that seemed to be a disappointment to Wainwright.

Raven Crag 24

Thirlmere from the Raven Crag viewing platform

A peeling wooden sign marks the monument but tells me nothing more. I climb to the top of the rocky knoll, admire the view down the Shoulthwaite ravine, before turning to retrace my steps back to the kissing gate. Once through the gate I turn left to head north along the forest track for 100 metres, to just beyond a chained forest gate on my right. ❹ Beyond the gate, there is a faint path through the trees, which soon climbs alongside a wire fence. The path isn't convincing, but I plough on through the canopy then head to my left away from the fence. I soon pick up a clear route, the path climbs so I know I will reach the summit of The Benn, or Sippling Crag, a rocky prominence escaping through the trees.

Raven Crag from Dam Triangle car park

From the top of The Benn, I continue north on another indistinct path, but it is less than 200 metres back down to the forest track so I can't go wrong. ❺ There is a small wooden post holding a red waymarker with a white arrow telling me I am now on a permitted United Utilities footpath. I turn left down the forest track and at the track junction ❻ I keep right, soon sweeping

Raven Crag duckboards on the way to the summit

123

24 Raven Crag

Shoulthwaite valley and Skiddaw from Castle Crag

round a hairpin to head north along the valley carrying Shoulthwaite Gill.

Soon I'm running alongside the gill, at the bottom of the unfrequented, unnamed valley. Once past the weir I follow the forest trail around the base of The Benn and reach the track to Shoulthwaite Farm. Through the gate, I turn right along a muddy track, a route made messy by the construction of the Thirlmere pipeline.

Approaching Castle Crag

Easy running alongside Shoulthwaite Moss takes me back to the road. On my left, the earth has been badly damaged, temporarily, by the pipeline project, which will deliver water from Thirlmere Reservoir to West Cumbria. ❼ At the road, I turn right again and it is one kilometre back to the car park.

Brund Fell from above Watendlath

25 Brund Fell

Park / Start	Lay-by S of Leathes Head Hotel, Keswick to Borrowdale road B5289 (NY 256 176)
Map	OS Explorer OL4
Exertion	•••
Navigation	•••
Terrain	••
Distance	8.5 kilometres
Time	1 hour 22 minutes
Ascent	422 metres
On road	900 metres

An ancient woodland and an enchanting tarn

Brund Fell is one of three main summits on a table of high ground called Grange Fell. Though not the highest point on this heathery plateau of rocky outcrops and boulders, it is the one usually sought by those climbing Wainwright's fells.

START From the lay-by I cross the road and run north on the footpath past a strip of wind-battered daffodils. After 120 metres, I cross back to the east side of the road and turn right down the lane to Troutdale Lodge. There is a fingerpost pointing to a public bridleway. ❶ I am on my way.

At the end of the lane and through the gate, the path begins, taking me close to the beck across boggy ground. I then begin to climb into the narrow valley, into the woods beneath denuded trees waiting patiently for their spring buds.

25 Brund Fell

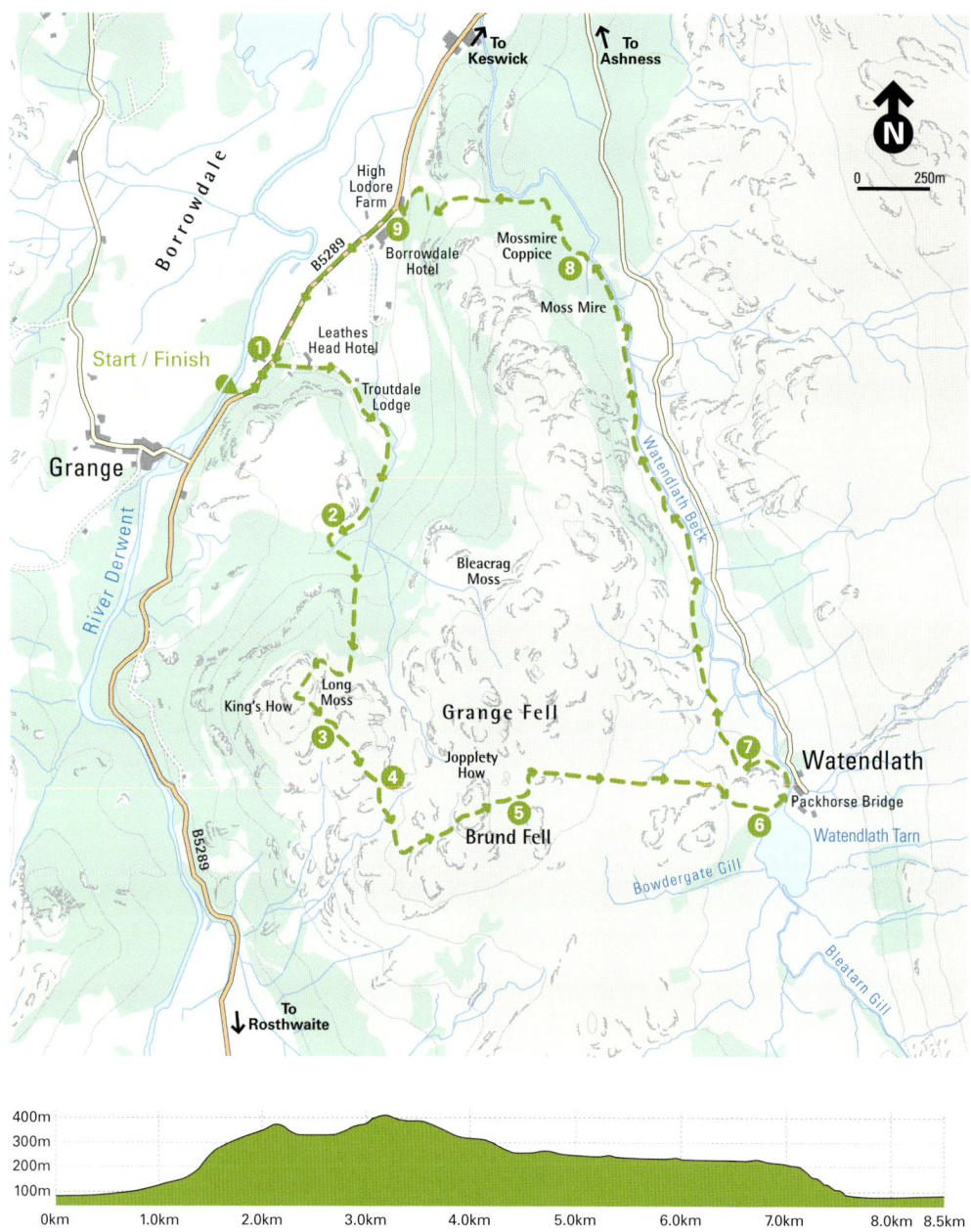

I climb by the beck; water cascades down the path over the grass and rocks. After 1.2 kilometres I reach a wall and cross the stile by the beck. ❷ My route heads south up the ravine. Soon the grass gives way to a stone-pitched path, then a steep-sided gulley of uneven rocks, tricky on a rainy day.

There is a stile over the fence to my left, which I ignore. Soon I reach a small plateau, Long Moss, and splash through the water to follow the path to my right up to King's How, one of Borrowdale's jaws. When I reach the top of the rocky tor, I stop briefly to survey the panorama. Derwentwater with a snow-capped Skiddaw at its head stretches down the valley to the north. To the west, Dale Head and High Spy stand tall,

Brund Fell

watched over menacingly by black clouds. The valley holding Stonethwaite Beck, intensely green, winds to the south. To the east, Brund Fell and the distinctive outcrop of Jopplety How show me my next destination. Coming off King's How I take the south-easterly descent. ❸ I look for the stile that takes me over the wall and follow a clear path over flat, boggy ground past a neat, square sheepfold. Ahead is another wall. ❹ Here a ladder stile takes me to the slope up Brund Fell. I climb in an east-northeasterly direction, heading for the gap between the summit of Brund Fell and Jopplety How.

Heading east off Brund Fell I run towards the corner of the wall. ❺ Here I cross another ladder stile and once on the other side I turn immediately left. In terms of navigation, it is safer to follow the wall and fence directly east all the way to Watendlath Tarn. Stray too far away from the fence and you risk a journey through acres of marshy grassland.

The magical tarn comes into view. Then, soon after, the path drops down to a major junction by the water's edge. ❻ The fingerpost points right to Rosthwaite; I go in the opposite direction, north-east, towards the gate and the farm beyond.

Through the gate I run past the tiny packhorse bridge and at the next gate a fingerpost points to a public footpath to High Lodore and Ashness (1½ m). ❼ This is the path I will follow for two kilometres all the way to the footbridge at Mossmire Coppice.

The path closely follows Watendlath Beck as it tumbles towards Derwentwater. Gradually downhill, grassy in parts but with many rocky sections, tricky to run on as the rain begins to fall.

Through the enclosure with hungry herdwick, colourfully sprayed, feeding intently on bales of hay. Back alongside the beck, swollen after days of rain, the footbridge comes into view. I don't cross here, though. Instead, I turn away from the beck and pass through the gate into Mossmire Coppice. ❽

Steps up to Long Moss

Brund Fell from King's How

Jopplety How

Watendlath water's edge

25 Brund Fell

Derwentwater from Brund Fell

There are a number of routes through the woods but it doesn't matter which I follow, as long as I keep the beck to my right. I run past the falls then begin to descend a rocky path towards the road. I can see the Borrowdale Hotel through the trees and turn south to pass behind High Lodore Farm. 9

I am on the road now and have to run 800 metres south back to my car. On the westerly side, there is a footpath for most of the way so I don't feel vulnerable to the oncoming traffic.

The rocky ground and stone steps mean that this is a route best suited to a dry, sunny day. This is the Lake District, though, and Borrowdale is the wettest place in England. For me, slippery rocks are manageable – at a leisurely pace.

The packhorse bridge at Watendlath

Footpath back to Lodore from Watendlath

Looking towards Armboth from Thirlmere Dam

26 Armboth Fell and High Tove

Park / Start	Armboth car park, west bank of Thirlmere Reservoir (NY 305 102)		
Map	OS Explorer OL4		
Exertion	•••		
Navigation	•••		
Terrain	•		
Distance	7.3 kilometres	Time	1 hour 16 minutes
Ascent	685 metres	On road	0 metres

Soft, spongy moorland affords a yielding springy run

Armboth bog. This is a notoriously marshy depression; at least I am prepared for this, which diminishes my reluctance to trudge across the spongy wasteland. I seem to spend the entire winter with soaking fell shoes and sodden socks; on the bright side once my feet are wet, they can't get any wetter.

START From the car park, I head to the road, turn right and within 50 metres I reach the fingerpost pointing to Watendlath (2 miles). I turn left up the path, entering a shady glade with the conifer plantations of Looking Stone on my right and Fishercrag on my left. Here the path is wide and cropped, climbing past large angular boulders, with Fisher Gill tumbling down to Thirlmere on the other side of the fence.

Armboth Fell and High Tove

The path becomes a little rocky as it zigzags towards the open fell but this barely impedes my progress. At the top of the clearing, I pass through a gap in the wall ❶ and on my left my first destination, the rocky outcrop of Armboth Fell, comes into view.

I continue straight ahead for a short distance to avoid dropping down into the Fisher Gill ravine. ❷ One hundred and fifty metres beyond the gap in the wall there is a faint path on my left, which I follow towards

Armboth Fell and High Tove 26

Boulders on the Armboth Fell and High Tove path

the highest point on Armboth Fell. Across a minor beck, I follow the path on a bearing of 200 degrees. The exact line is not crucial; the bog I am about to cross is bounded by fences to the south and west, a border I will reach as long as I head roughly south-southwest.

I manage to keep my feet dry as I cross the rocky, heathery ground east of Armboth Fell but, beyond the highest point, I descend into a boggy mire. I squelch across the moss and hop over a reticulation of becks.

Maintaining the same south-southwesterly line, I climb above the marsh towards the crags that form a ridge heading north towards High Tove.

Surprisingly, the higher slopes are just as waterlogged and I have to work hard to maintain even a slow running pace. I console myself by thinking this must be good strength training. At the top of the ridge, I reach the corner of the fence marked by a post, a landmark on the OS map. ❸ Blea Tarn, 400 metres ahead, on the other side of the fence, confirms my location.

Armboth car park, at the start of the Armboth and High Tove run

I turn right to follow the fence across the ridge to High Tove, first west then north, over Shivery Knott, Shivery Man and Middle Crag. The higher ground is no drier. I am running slowly over a saturated green sphagnum sponge; I expect to see 'slithy toves' and all manner of swamp creatures emerging from the marsh. I jump the

Running towards High Tove summit

26 Armboth Fell and High Tove

Path down to Armboth from the summit of High Tove

soggiest looking bogs; less to escape getting my feet wet – it is far too late for that – than to avoid being swallowed up by the quagmire.

Gradually, as I climb towards the highest point on the featureless hummock of High Tove, the terrain becomes firmer. ❹ West of the summit cairn a gate marks the way to Watendlath, just 1.5 kilometres down a gentle slope.

High Tove summit looking east

Unsurprisingly for such a central fell a multitude of peaks are visible, especially to the west and east. Unusually it is a view that lacks a single lake or tarn. I turn right, due east, back to Thirlmere on a clear path, reedy and springy but relatively dry compared to the bog I have just traversed.

Western flank of High Tove from Watendlath Tarn

Before long, I can see the conifers at the corner of Fishercrag Plantation. A kilometre down from the summit cairn I am passing through the gap in the wall, leading back into the shadowy clearing. I retrace my steps down to the reservoir, first negotiating the rocky twists then enjoying the last 400 metres of green carpet back down to the road.

My wet feet and muddy ankles are a reminder of the varied terrains of the Lakeland Fells.

27 Watendlath Tarn

A summer's evening at Watendlath Tarn

Park / Start	National Trust car park, Rosthwaite Village (NY 256 148)		
Map	OS Explorer OL4		
Exertion	●●●		
Navigation	●●		
Terrain	●●		
Distance	8.1 kilometres	Time	1 hour 15 minutes
Ascent	419 metres	On road	500 metres

Climbing through oak woodland to secluded tarns

Not all fell runs have to reach a summit. This one passes a couple of tarns and skirts by the top of Great Crag. The route could easily pass over this Wainwright with a bit of a detour, if desired.

If you want to get a PB for an 8 kilometre run, you will be disappointed. This is not a route for speed. It is a journey of peace and absorbing concentration over rocky and marshy ground, although the first two kilometres are easy and runnable.

START From the car park in Rosthwaite, I head north at the B5289 road to Keswick, then right over the stone bridge towards Hazel Bank Hotel. ❶ The signpost points to a public bridleway left to Watendlath (1½ miles) and right to Stonethwaite (1 mile). Once over the bridge I turn right to Stonethwaite and follow the beck.

27 Watendlath Tarn

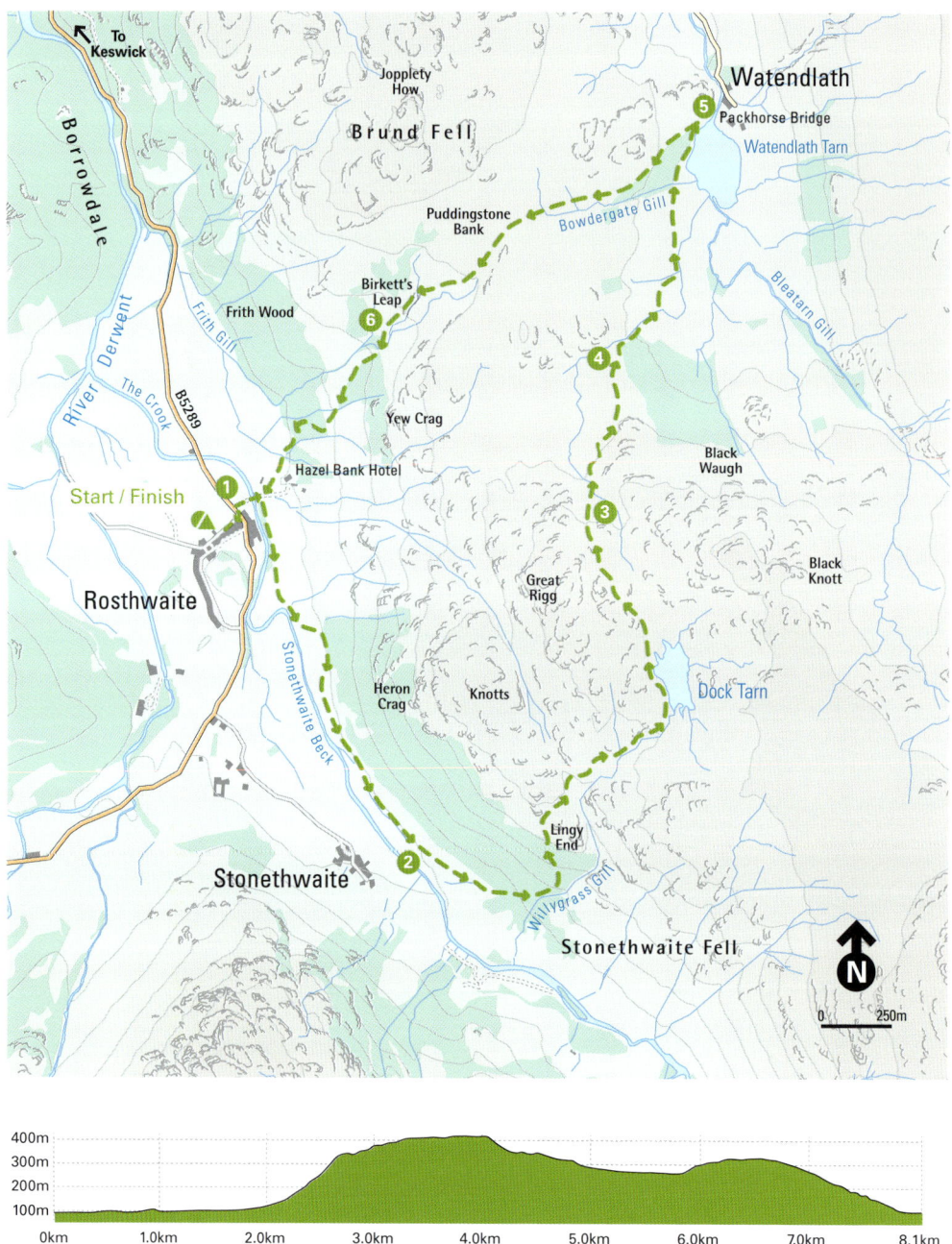

At Stonethwaite a fingerpost points onwards to Grasmere via Greenup Edge (6½ miles). I follow the sign through the gate and 200 metres beyond this a yellow footpath waymarker directs me away from the Grasmere trail upwards to the left. ❷ The climbing begins. Over a stone stile then through a gate, I pass alongside Willygrass Gill.

There is a well-maintained stone path, ascending steeply away from the gill up Lingy End. Stone after stone carefully placed to make neat steps. Eventually the path turns back towards the gurgling, tumbling

Watendlath Tarn 27

Great Crag from Rosthwaite

water of Willygrass Gill as it tumbles out of Dock Tarn. Then the tarn comes into view, 3.5 kilometres from Rosthwaite. The steep climb has been worth it. I run by the water's edge admiring a tarn of tranquillity on a late afternoon in early spring. The rocks and stones have gone; now I have reached soft, swampy ground with brilliant green sphagnum moss and bogs of unknown depth.

Today I bypass Great Crag, 200 metres to the west and 20 metres below its heathery summit. I bounce across banks of peat, jet-black puddles of viscous oil. Then I meet an area of saturated sponge where someone has kindly lain out stepping stones. The path becomes indistinct in parts, but there is really only one way to go, north to Watendlath.

Follow the bridleway to Stonethwaite

Running alongside Watendlath Tarn, Great Cragg in the background

❸ I reach a wall, pass through a kissing gate, cross a beck and follow the sodden path down. A series of wooden posts mark the route. A field gate and another kissing gate, then I follow the wall to my left.

❹ The tarn and the farm at Watendlath come into view. I reach a stone stile by a field gate and I hear someone talking. A voice from a radio. I peer over the wall but there is no one there. It is just the stream talking to me.

Watendlath Tarn

Returning to Rosthwaite

I am at Watendlath now, a remarkable place. I follow a track by the pebbly tarn. I am reminded to release any fish over 4lbs. Before I reach the farm, a fingerpost points to Rosthwaite and I turn sharply up the bridle way on my left. ❺

Up the stony track to the right of Brund Fell. Then it is downhill for nearly two kilometres all the way to Rosthwaite. Normally I would hope to pick up the pace, but the rocky path means I have to watch where I place my feet. At least the rocks are dry.

Eventually, Rosthwaite comes into view. I keep to the left where a path from Frith Wood cuts in on my right. ❻ On rare smoother sections, I try to go faster but these stretches are short lived. A number of gates slow my progress further. I reach the final sign to Rosthwaite and follow the path down to the bridge.

The gate to Watendlath Tarn

The path alongside Watendlath Tarn

For the last 250 metres, over the bridge and back to the car park, I try to stretch my legs. The slow, rocky descent seems to have worked every fibre of muscle in my legs. I jog rather than sprint back to the car.

Steel Fell 28

Looking back to Wythburn Dale

28 Steel Fell

Park / Start	Steel End car park, south of Thirlmere (NY 320 129)		
Map	OS Explorer OL5		
Exertion	●●●		
Navigation	●●●		
Terrain	●		
Distance	6.5 kilometres	Time	1 hour 8 minutes
Ascent	366 metres	On road	150 metres

A breathtaking ascent climbs above the ghosts of Wythburn

A short loop over a fell that lies on the Lake District's north and south watershed, is located virtually in the centre of the Lake District and is by the side of the A591 just a few minutes' drive away from Keswick and Ambleside. Although a minor summit, Steel Fell's accessibility makes it a compelling running route.

START From the start, on a clear day, it is easy to see the north ridge of this triangular prism, which is my way to the top. I head towards the A591 for 150 metres then take the path on my right just before West Head Farm. ❶ The fingerpost points to Grasmere via Dunmail Raise (3¾ miles); in this part of the world it feels strange to pick up a tarmacked footpath.

28 Steel Fell

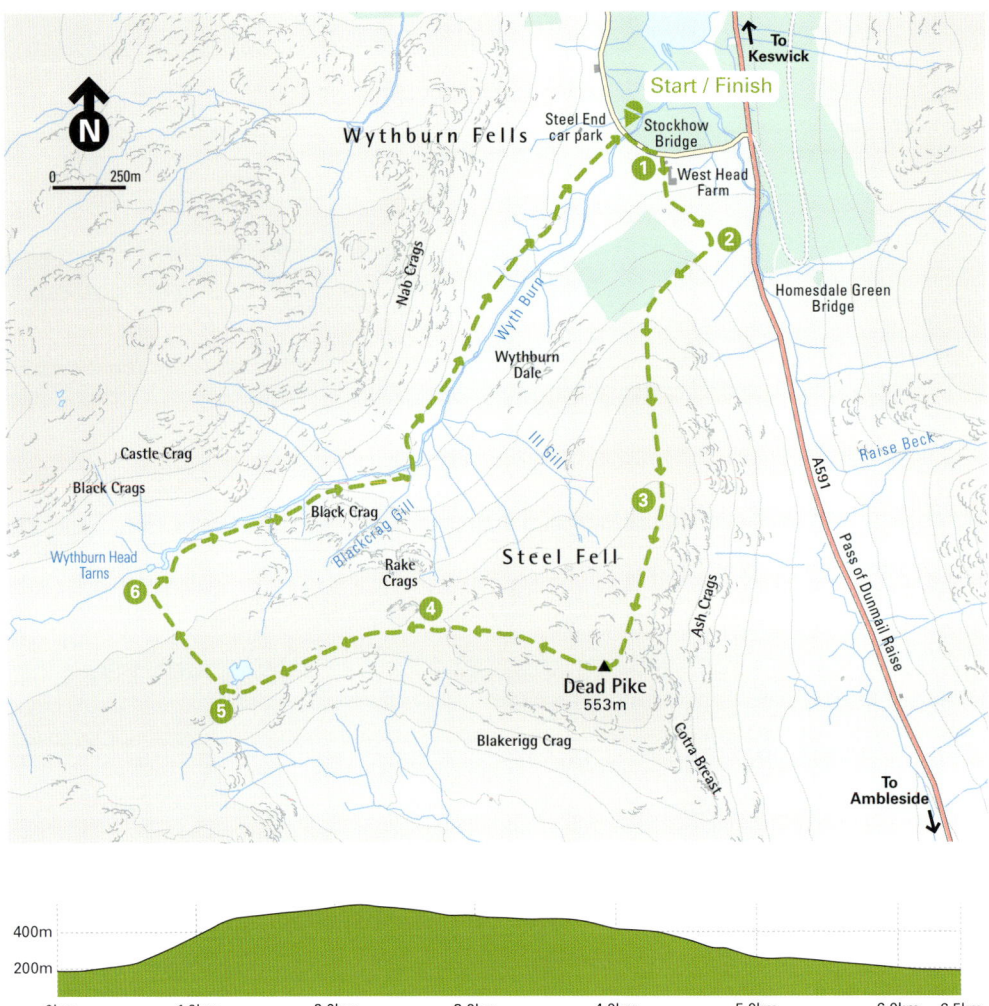

2 There is a gate after 500 metres where I leave the tarmac, turning right to follow a path up the fellside, alongside a wall and then a fence. At 880 metres, I reach a wall with an unusual sliding gate; through the gate the path leads straight ahead before veering left. I am soon climbing the ridge in a southerly direction with the grey water of Thirlmere directly behind me.

There is a steep grassy path, easy to follow, all the way up the ridge. The going is tough though, with a 40 percent gradient for a while. The slope eases and I can begin to run again, slowly towards the fence line. **3** There is a stile over the fence, and on the other side I turn right on to a path that gradually climbs towards Dead Pike, as the highest point is known. The path follows the fence all the way to the summit, a reassuring guide if the mist comes down.

The old metal boundary posts become visible towards the summit. I meander between Cumberland and Westmorland on the old county border. The summit cairn, a semi-circular shelter built of large coral-pink stones, bears a triangular boundary post on its shoulder. The fence veers right; I follow the fence away from the summit, heading just north of west.

Steel Fell 28

Looking back to Dead Pike from the Steel Fell west ridge

Six hundred metres beyond the summit the fence turns right (north). ❹ I carry straight on in a westerly direction following the old county boundary posts. The path bobbles over grassy ground with the occasional rocky step for me to negotiate.

Just ahead, I catch glimpses of the unnamed glassy tarns I am aiming for. Into the headwind on a cold spring day, with the 'feel like' temperature dipping to minus 10 degrees Celsius, I am glad that soon I will be heading down into the shelter of the valley. I am running close to the tarns, over boggy ground, and once I am beyond the last body of water I turn right to begin my descent into Wythburn Dale. ❺ I manage to pick up a faint path, more of a sheep trod, but the route I take doesn't matter as long as I am heading north. I will soon reach Wyth Burn and the path heading northeast out of the valley.

Run along the path beside West Head Farm

Looking back to Thirlmere and Wythburn from Steel Fell north ridge

It is a gentle slope and as soon as I start to descend, I spy the pools below known as Wythburn Head Tarns. The route down to the valley can be marshy, over flattened reed and bouncy moss, but it is only 500 metres to the beck and I reach the footpath in a few minutes. ❻ I turn to head east-northeast, following the water flowing towards Thirlmere.

28 Steel Fell

Wythburn Dale – the route back to Steel End

The route is easy, but I make slow progress. This valley is notoriously boggy which probably explains why it is so quiet. The water bubbles soothingly across the pebbles, snowflakes begin to fall and I squelch alone down the path. The route disappears into various mires from time to time and rocky steps interrupt me, making it hard to get into my stride. Beyond the falls, the path improves and soon I reach the footbridge beneath Rake Crags.

I have a choice here; there are two paths, one on either side of the beck, that lead directly to the car park. I decide to cross the bridge. I follow the fence to a field gate, turn right through another small gate then head back down to the beck. I know I have a soggy kilometre or so running alongside the gently flowing water.

Steel Fell, looking towards the unnamed tarns

Unnamed tarn on Steel Fell

Silver How 29

Silver How from Stone Arthur

29 Silver How

Park	Grasmere Village
Start	Corner of Langdale Road and B5287 (NY 336 075)
Map	OS Explorer OL7
Exertion	•••
Navigation	•••
Terrain	•
Distance	6.9 kilometres	Time	1 hour 15 minutes
Ascent	406 metres	On road	1.5 kilometres

Perched above Grasmere, a myriad of paths weave a route through a multitude of peaks

A brief jaunt from gingerbread Grasmere, Silver How, with its wooded slopes of conifer and juniper, has sufficient paths across its boggy summit to demand my concentration.

START I start my watch at the corner of Langdale Road and head south-west in the direction of the unseen lake. I follow the road round to the right and after 550 metres I reach a track on my right-hand side, opposite the 'world-famous' Faeryland Tea Garden, where I turn in the direction of Chapel Stile (1½ miles). ❶

141

29 Silver How

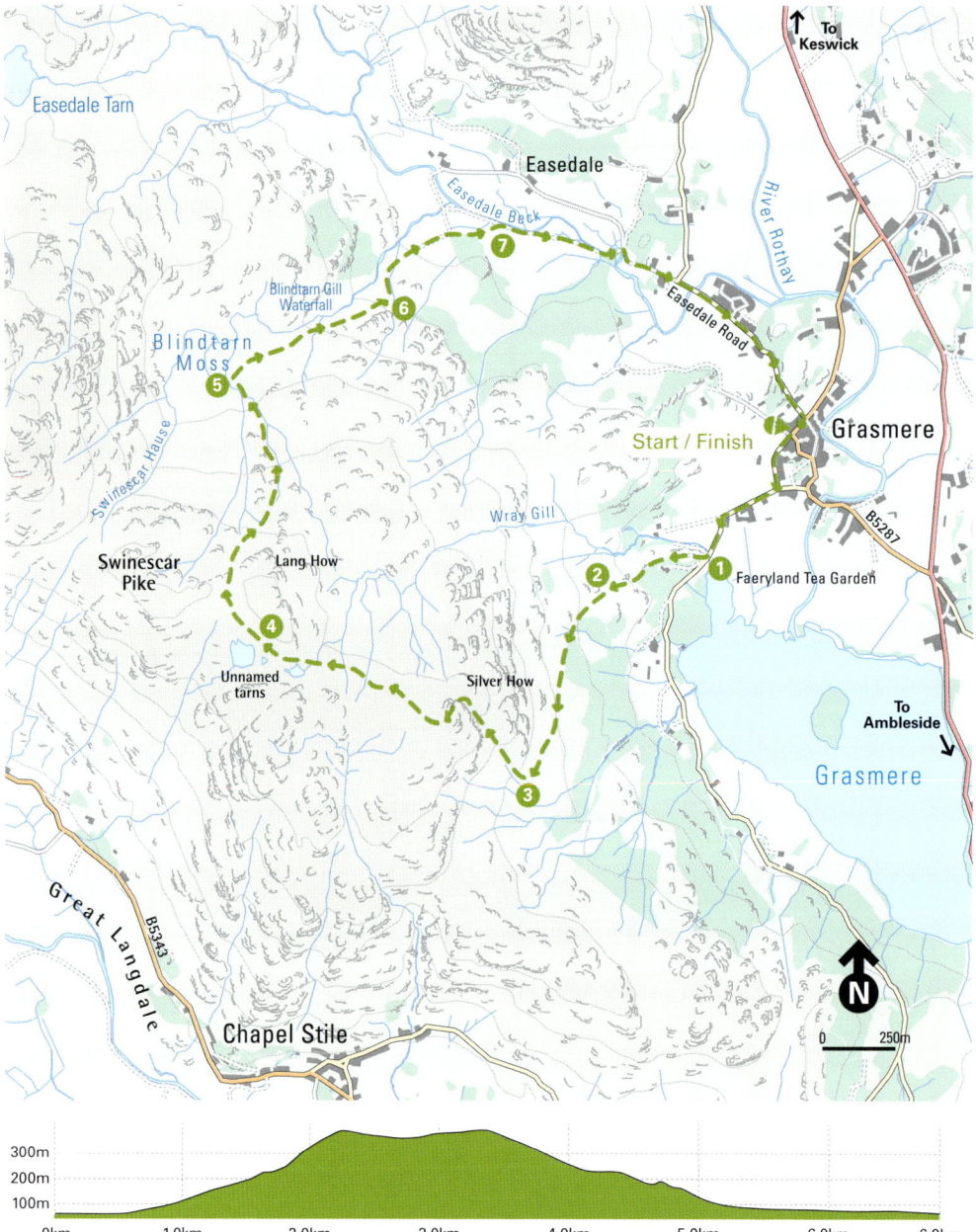

Immediately the track begins to rise. Under a grey sky, the pastures somehow look greener, the farms a starker white. Through a gate with a yellow waymarker. Across the field, I run towards another waymarked gate directly ahead. ❷ Once through the gate, at 900 metres from the start, I turn left and follow the path along the wall.

The path is rocky, not particularly easy to run on, and the persistent rain makes the stone too slippery for my trail-shoe lugs. I pass through another gate and I am on the open fell. ❸ At 1.7 kilometres the wall turns left, and at this point there is an obvious path on my right, where I turn to head up to the summit of Silver How.

Silver How

The gradient steepens but I don't have far to go. I have gained half the height and I am just 400 metres horizontal distance away from the top. I slow as the slope gets more arduous, which gives me a chance to glance back at the view that has been drawing people up this fell for hundreds of years. The clouds bring fog and mist across the water giving Grasmere a supernatural quality. I ascend a scree gulley of pink-beige rocks to a large cairn of the same colour. At the cairn, I turn left to complete the last section of the climb. By now, most of the higher fells are hidden by thick clouds but the views down to Grasmere and Rydal Water are dark and dramatic.

The routes of descent begin west-southwest of the summit cairn. There are a number of choices. I am taking the path that heads towards Blea Rigg in a west-northwesterly direction. I take a compass bearing to avoid being pulled too far south and east towards Great Langdale.

It is a marvellously knobbly fell with a number of tops higher than the summit of Silver How. Lang How, straight ahead of me, is 20 metres higher and Swinescar Pike, which I will soon skirt around, boasts a higher summit still.

There are numerous footpaths crisscrossing the top of the ridge, which can be confusing. The unnamed tarns just south of Lang How are a good navigation aid in the mist. I take the route with the tarns on my left. ❹ I follow the path to the south-west of Swinescar Pike, and 750 metres on from the northern tip of the largest tarn I reach a boggy depression with an indistinct path running across from south-west to north-east. ❺ Straight ahead and upwards is the route to Blea Rigg, left will take me down to Great Langdale. I turn right (north-east) on an indistinct path that is more like a stream.

I begin to descend, along Swinescar Hause. I am following a path but I lose it frequently under streams and down rocky steps. It doesn't really matter though – as long as I keep running north-east, I will reach the path heading out of Easedale towards Grasmere Village.

It is over two kilometres down, across Blindtarn Moss

Turn off the road at the Faeryland Tea Garden

Grasmere from the path up Silver How

The path up to Silver How

Silver How summit

Unnamed tarn northwest of Silver How

Silver How

Swinescar Hause, route of descent towards Easedale

and a myriad of streams that feed into Easedale Beck. Juniper bushes abound between the rocks and bracken. I know I am close to the Easedale path when I pass Blindtarn Gill Falls.

Goody Bridge over Easedale Beck, Easedale Road

❻ A small fingerpost points left, downhill, towards Grasmere. Down a stream. Two hundred metres on from the fingerpost I pass through a gate to the right of the farm and pick up the pace along the track to Easedale Beck. I cross a field to reach the Easedale Tarn track where I turn right. ❼ At the end of the track, I cross two footbridges and join Easedale Road. From here, I run the kilometre back to the B5287 in Grasmere. Turning right, I am 100 metres away from my starting point.

Loughrigg Fell 30

Loughrigg from across Ambleside

30 Loughrigg Fell

Park	Ambleside town centre		
Start	Corner of Millans Park and Vicarage Road, Ambleside (NY 375 044)		
Map	OS Explorer OL7		
Exertion	●●		
Navigation	●●●		
Terrain	●		
Distance	9.2 kilometres	Time	1 hour 12 minutes
Ascent	361 metres	On road	2.25 kilometres

**A well-trampled route over a knobbly summit
leading to the shores of Grasmere and Rydal Water**

An hour's run from the busy centre of Ambleside on a sunny spring evening, tame and benign. In the depths of winter with howling storms and blizzards, nature earns your respect.

START From the corner of Millans Park and Vicarage Road, opposite Zeffirellis Cinema, I start my watch and begin to run north-west along Vicarage Road towards Rothay Park. Past the school and the church with its Gothic stone spire. Through the park, across the bridge over Stock Ghyll, over the stone Miller Bridge and right at the road; ❶ pleased that I have chosen to wear my all-terrain shoes.

Loughrigg Fell

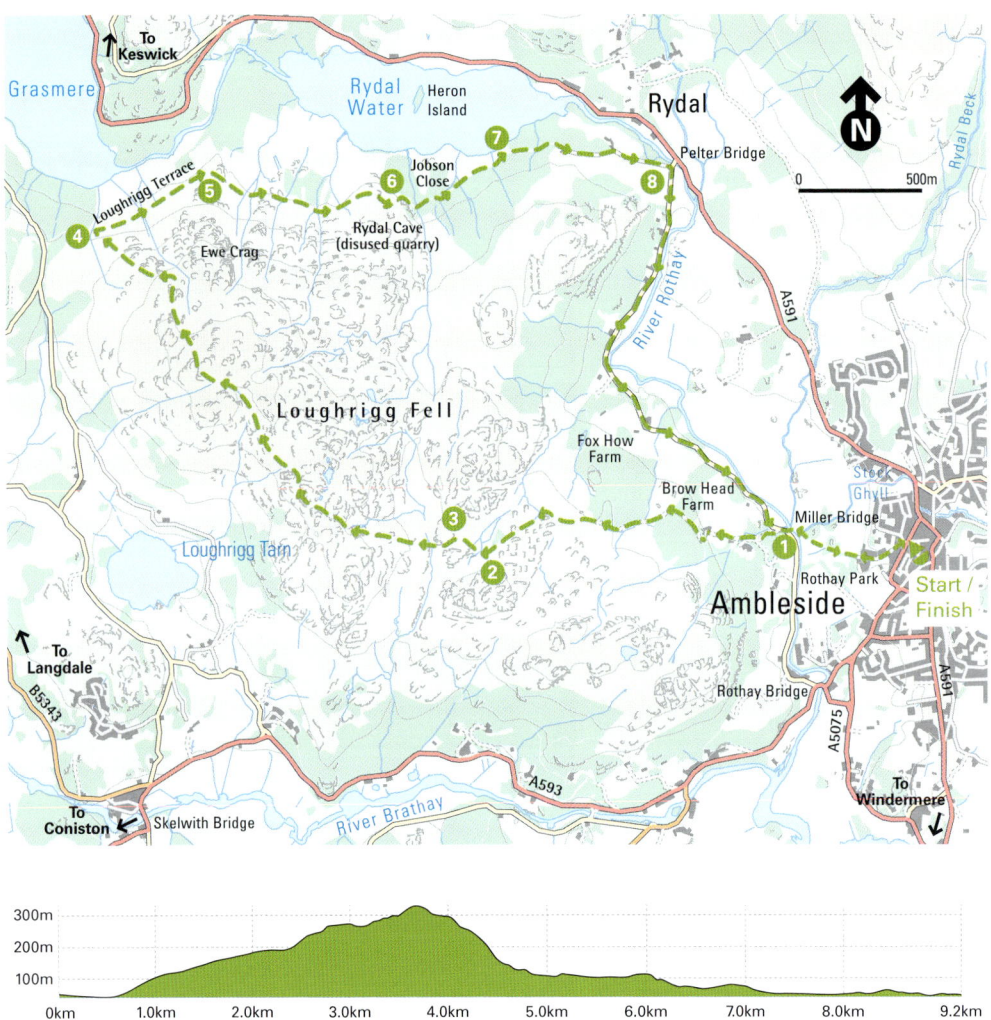

Fifty metres on from Miller Bridge, a fingerpost on my left points to a bridleway and I turn up the steep tarmacked lane. The road becomes a broad track, gradually climbing above the town. I follow the bridleway beyond the fingerpost for 1.4 kilometres, past Brow Head Farm and Pine Rigg, eventually reaching a gate opening onto the open fell. Set in the wall on the left of the gate a slate sign points to Loughrigg, Langdale and Elterwater. ❷

Once through the gate, I leave the main track to pick up the path on my right that follows the wall for 100 metres, before the wall itself turns right. ❸ I continue on the path that climbs just north of west on a barely runnable incline. This is a well-trampled fell with a multitude of paths and trods. On this clear evening, I aim for a small cleft, a nick in the craggy summit, which will lead me to the trig point. In the cloud, without the aid of this summit notch, as long as I continue to climb north-west I know I will reach the highest point.

Loughrigg Fell

I climb steadily to the top of a gnarled plateau, a slab of pistachio brittle; transitorily, Loughrigg Tarn comes into view on my left, clear and bright and heart-shaped. I reach the notch, an easy climb, and just beyond this the summit trig point appears.

A low-lying fell in a central amphitheatre of Lakeland summits, a complicated pastiche of natural patterns, an infinite variety of colour and shape. So many small mountains and valleys.

My route of descent is north-northwest and today I can head for the v-shaped groove of Dunmail Raise; in the mist, I would follow a bearing of 320 degrees. On a cloudless evening the path is obvious though, the main route to Loughrigg Terrace. A rocky route, slippery when wet, down a mixture of old and new steps and rocks, but it doesn't last long; it is only 900 metres from the trig point to the Terrace path junction. ❹

I turn right along the broad, buff trail looking down to my left at the beach and woody shores of Grasmere. I stay on the Terrace path for 650 metres then, at the next junction, I take the right branch climbing over the shoulder of Ewe Crag. ❺ Rydal Cave, marked on the map as a disused quarry, appears down the bank. At the deep slate cavern, ❻ I turn left, down the slope along the walled track south of Jobson Close.

❼ At the end of the track, through a gate onto a tarmacked lane I turn right towards Pelter Bridge. My all-terrain shoes come into their own as I follow the roads back to town; two kilometres on a quiet route alongside the River Rothay. ❽ Right at Pelter Bridge, following Under Loughrigg Road all the way back to Miller Bridge. From here, I retrace my steps through the park, past the church and back to the centre of town.

Track to Loughrigg from Ambleside

Loughrigg Tarn from Loughrigg summit looking west

Loughrigg summit trig point

Rydal Cave by Loughrigg Terrace

30 Loughrigg Fell

Path up to Loughrigg summit

The Southern Fells

England's highest peaks reside in the northerly sector of the Southern Fells, towards the centre of the National Park. These tend to be rugged, rocky and relatively inaccessible and, as such, beyond the scope of this book. To the west and south there is a softer upland landscape and it is from these fells that I chose the majority of the runs in this region. The slopes of Eskdale Valley and the hills surrounding the spectacular Hardknott and Wrynose passes provide excellent, varied running.

The boathouse at Devoke Water (Devoke Water route)

Approaching Smithymire Island alongside Langstrath Beck

Rosthwaite Fell (Bessyboot) 31

Rosthwaite Fell from Seatoller

31 Rosthwaite Fell (Bessyboot)

Park / Start	National Trust car park, Seatoller, B5289 (NY 245 138)
Map	OS Explorer OL4
Exertion	●●●●
Navigation	●●●
Terrain	●●●

Distance	10.5 kilometres	Time	1 hour 32 minutes
Ascent	452 metres	On road	2.5 kilometres

Descend from Bessyboot to the cascades and pools of the Langstrath Valley

A rocky route deep in the heart of Borrowdale, Wainwright's fairest of valleys. Once a valley yielding iron, lead, copper and the world's purest graphite and slate, on sleds careering down the fell sides of the wettest dale in England, on the darkest, coldest days in the depths of the harshest winters.

START From the car park I head east in the direction of Rosthwaite, along the narrow footpath beside the B5289. Over Strands Bridge, ignoring the footpath along the lane to Thorneythwaite Farm, I continue past Mountain View Cottages. Beyond the terrace, after 730 metres, I turn right through the gate onto the public footpath. ❶

31 Rosthwaite Fell (Bessyboot)

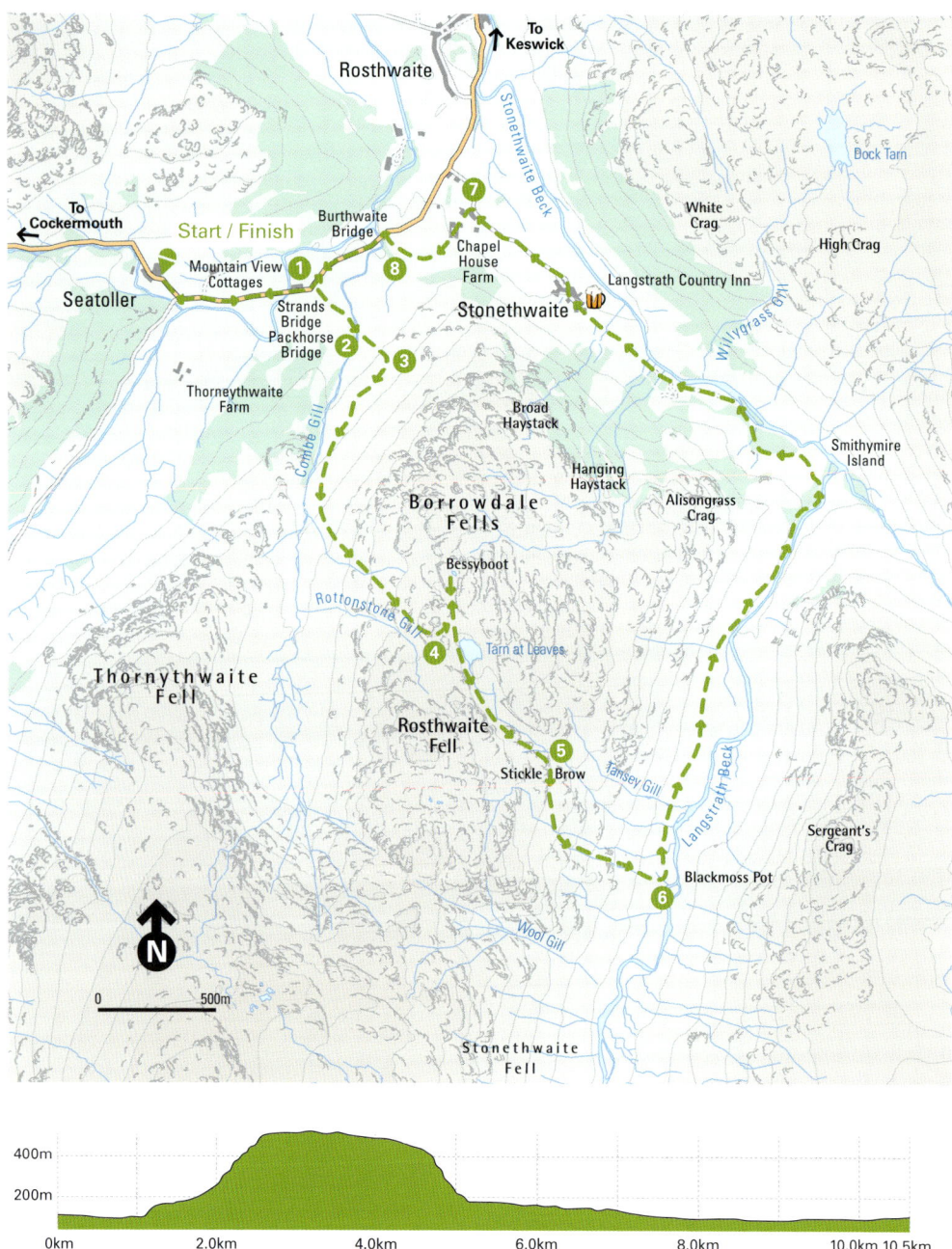

Once I've crossed the old packhorse bridge over Combe Gill I look ahead, to my right, for a faint path leading up through the rocks. ❷ A couple of yellow waymarkers point the way.

The faint path climbs steeply away from the beck between broken rocks. Within 150 metres, I meet a path cutting across the fellside and turn right to head through the first of five walls. ❸ After a brief respite, I begin to climb again.

Rosthwaite Fell (Bessyboot) 31

Below me, Combe Gill Waterfall tumbles down the hanging valley towards the River Derwent. I run parallel to the gill until I pass through the gate at the fifth wall. Beyond this point the path turns left towards Tarn at Leaves. The gradient steepens, I clamber between rocks and running water and any semblance my gait has to running vanishes.

The route draws alongside Dry Gill; I'm crawling towards a cleft in the rocky jaw bordering the Tarn at Leaves depression with gradients surpassing 40 percent in stretches. I cross Dry Gill and follow an indistinct path as it climbs by the side of Rottenstone Gill. Soon the gradient eases; I cross the rim and drop into the shallow tarn basin.

④ Before reaching the saturated reedy shore, I turn north to climb the craggy outcrop known as Bessyboot. There are higher points on Rosthwaite Fell but this is the point Wainwright took as the summit of this truncated spur. There is a clear route to the top, a 600-metre there-and-back trek from the sodden tarn.

Run past the Mountain View cottages, Seatoller

The tarn sprawls like a blue stingray in a green ocean, I run along its southern shores, following the dorsal fin of Tansey Gill towards the edge of the jagged fell top. There's a faint and boggy path, not on the map, that veers south-west over Stickle Brow. The route is not easy to follow across the marshy ground but the exact direction is not vital. I run with Tansey Gill on my left and, within 500 metres of the tarn, I reach a fence and wall. ⑤ Here I turn right following the wall south, then east down a steep, pathless slope.

Footpath to Combe Gill, Rosthwaite Fell behind

The decline is steep but not hazardous; I drop almost 250 metres in just over 500 metres distance travelled with a clear view of the Langstrath Beck below. I struggle to run and have to brake to remain on my feet. By the time I reach the valley floor my quads are screaming.

⑥ Before reaching the beck at the swimming hole of Blackmoss Pot, I turn left through the gate to pick up the broad rocky track that will take me to the hamlet of Stonethwaite. Over three kilometres of running down a gentle slope should be easy, but I struggle with legs still suffering from a steep climb and a precipitous descent. I keep to the east of the beck all the way, ignoring the footbridge at Smithymire Island where Langstrath Beck meets Greenup Gill to form Stonethwaite Beck.

The route down to Langstrath from Rosthwaite Fell

Heading to Stonethwaite along Langstrath Valley

31 Rosthwaite Fell (Bessyboot)

Rosthwaite Fell from along the Langstrath Valley

At the second footbridge, I leave the track and head through the campsite on a smoother, less demanding path. This takes me all the way to the hamlet, past the Langstrath Country Inn. Along the road for 600 metres, I turn left to run past the church following the fingerpost to Chapel House Farm. ❼ Keeping to the right of the farm, I continue on the track until I reach another fingerpost pointing to the public footpath to Burthwaite Bridge (200 yds). ❽

At the end of the path, I turn left onto the B5289 and follow the road past Mountain Cottages back to the car park in Seatoller.

Stonethwaite Hamlet

Seathwaite Fell

Seathwaite Fell behind Stockley Bridge

32 Seathwaite Fell

Park / Start	Seathwaite Farm, Seathwaite, Borrowdale (NY 235 122)		
Map	OS Explorer OL4 and OL6		
Exertion	●●●●		
Navigation	●●●		
Terrain	●●●		
Distance	8.4 kilometres	Time	1 hour 26 minutes
Ascent	525 metres	On road	0 metres

A direct route to a Wainwright summit and a vista of the Jaws of Borrowdale

A couple of kilometres south of Seatoller Bridge, at the head of the Borrowdale valley, lies the hamlet of Seathwaite. The wettest place in England. On sunny days in summer, cars are backed up on the grass verges virtually all the way to the B5289. On such days, I arrive either early or late to avoid the crowds heading for Scafell Pike and Great Gable.

START I start my watch at the entrance to the farm and head south, past the cottages towards the gate. Beyond the buildings a fingerpost points to Styhead (2½ miles), this is the route I will follow until Taylorghyll Force.

32 Seathwaite Fell

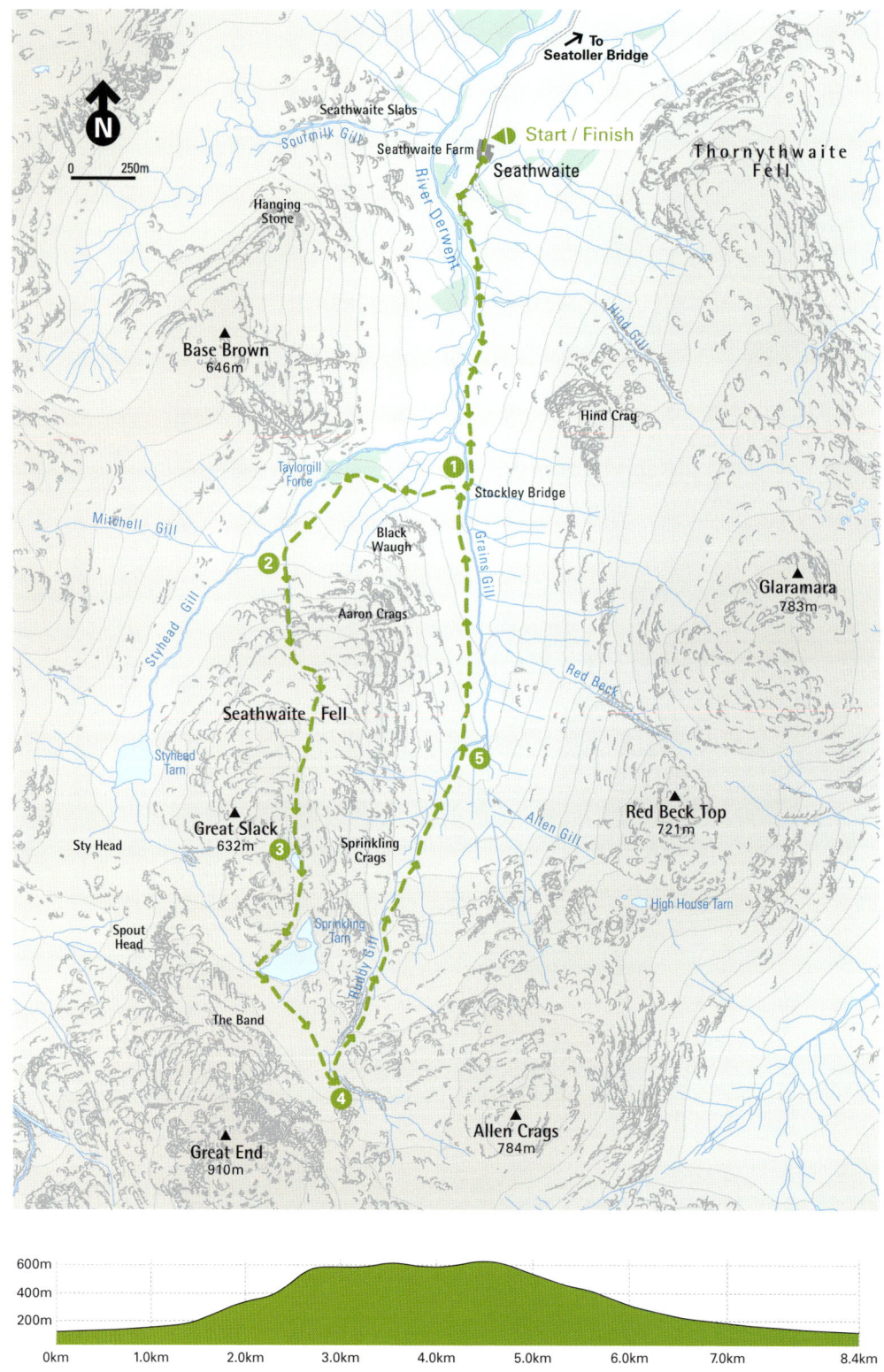

Seathwaite Fell

The start of my run follows a major hiking route alongside the nascent River Derwent. As I leave the farmyard behind, I am surrounded by fells on three sides. On my right, Sourmilk Gill plummets down the Seathwaite Slabs from the sudden rise of Base Brown, on my left craggy outcrops climb to the roof of Glaramara and ahead is Seathwaite Fell, a forgotten summit amongst more famous neighbours.

❶ I cross Stockley Bridge after 1.4 kilometres of gentle climbing up a broad, rocky track. Through the gate I head straight on – west – along the main Styhead path and from here, as I head closer to Styhead Gill and the cold shining water of Taylorghyll Force, the gradient steepens.

I am using my GPS now; 950 metres on from Stockley Bridge I reach a small stream and a metre beyond this, on my left, I find a faint path, not on the map. ❷ The path climbs south alongside the stream, towards a grassy gulley between the crags above.

The gradient steepens further; I push hard following the trod, knowing that within 500 metres distance and 200 metres ascent the slope will ease and I will reach Wainwright's summit. Occasionally the path disappears in the grass, but towards the top the terrain becomes stonier and I find a clear path littered with pebbles, pink against the green.

As soon as the gradient eases, I see the cairn upon the craggy turret. I head to my left, climb the rugged rocks, run past the cairn and drop down to join the path that runs across the ridge. I follow the path south aware of more imposing peaks around me. I run alone between outcrops that are rarely visited, on a fell that extends the beauty of solitude.

Seven hundred metres on from the northern cairn I reach a nameless tarn. ❸ I follow the path along its western bank heading towards Sprinkling Tarn, just 200 metres south. So many tents are scattered around the tarn's shore, hillocks and on its peninsula, it feels as though I have stumbled upon Everest Base Camp.

Leaving the farmyard and heading towards Stockley Bridge

The path to Styhead, with Seathwaite Fell behind

Seathwaite Fell summit

Unnamed Tarn by Great Slack

Seathwaite Fell

Footbridge over Ruddy Gill

At the southern tip of Sprinkling Tarn, in the shadow of Great End, I reach the bridleway linking Styhead and Esk Hause. I turn left to run south-east along the bridleway in the direction of Esk Pike and Angle Tarn. Within 500 metres I reach my turnoff back to Seathwaite. ❹ I drop down to the stepping stones on my left to cross Ruddy Gill.

Approaching Sprinkling Tarn

The path follows Ruddy Gill, which eventually becomes Grains Gill, all the way back to Stockley Bridge. At first, Ruddy Gill runs within a deep ravine slipping down a number of cascades towards the Grains valley floor. A steep descent down a rocky path, not hazardous, but I have to look ahead to think about my foot placement so my progress is slow.

Alongside Ruddy Gill, heading back to Seathwaite

❺ Over the footbridge then through a walled enclosure, the gradient abates and I can move with more confidence back to Stockley Bridge. I can see the bright white walls of Seathwaite's dwellings and the pastures of the glacial valley, green with summer. I pass the hordes heading up the bridleway towards more famous summits, skirting around the humble fell I traversed alone. There is only one route back to Seathwaite, down a gentle slope stony enough to demand my concentration.

Lingmoor Fell and Blea Tarn | 33

Lingmoor Fell from Blea Tarn

33 Lingmoor Fell and Blea Tarn

Park / Start	Blea Tarn car park, Little Langdale (NY 295 043)
Map	OS Explorer OL6 and OL7
Exertion	•••
Navigation	•••
Terrain	•••
Distance	7.9 kilometres
Time	1 hour 12 minutes
Ascent	425 metres
On road	1.4 kilometres

Following an undulating wall over a volcanic spine, avoiding the Fat Man's Agony

Blea Tarn, perched in a hanging valley between Little Langdale and Great Langdale, sits at the start and end of this run through the rugged heart of the English Lakes.

START From the car park I head south down Side Gates, the road linking the two Langdales. An easy start, a steep descent and then a steady decline, provides me with a kilometre warm-up before I need to look out for a path off to my left.

A low wooden barrier, like a low-slung balance beam, hangs at the start of the old quarry track. ❶ I climb up the grassy bank and follow the path along the drystone wall, past the quarry entrance, following some National Trust waymarkers.

33 Lingmoor Fell and Blea Tarn

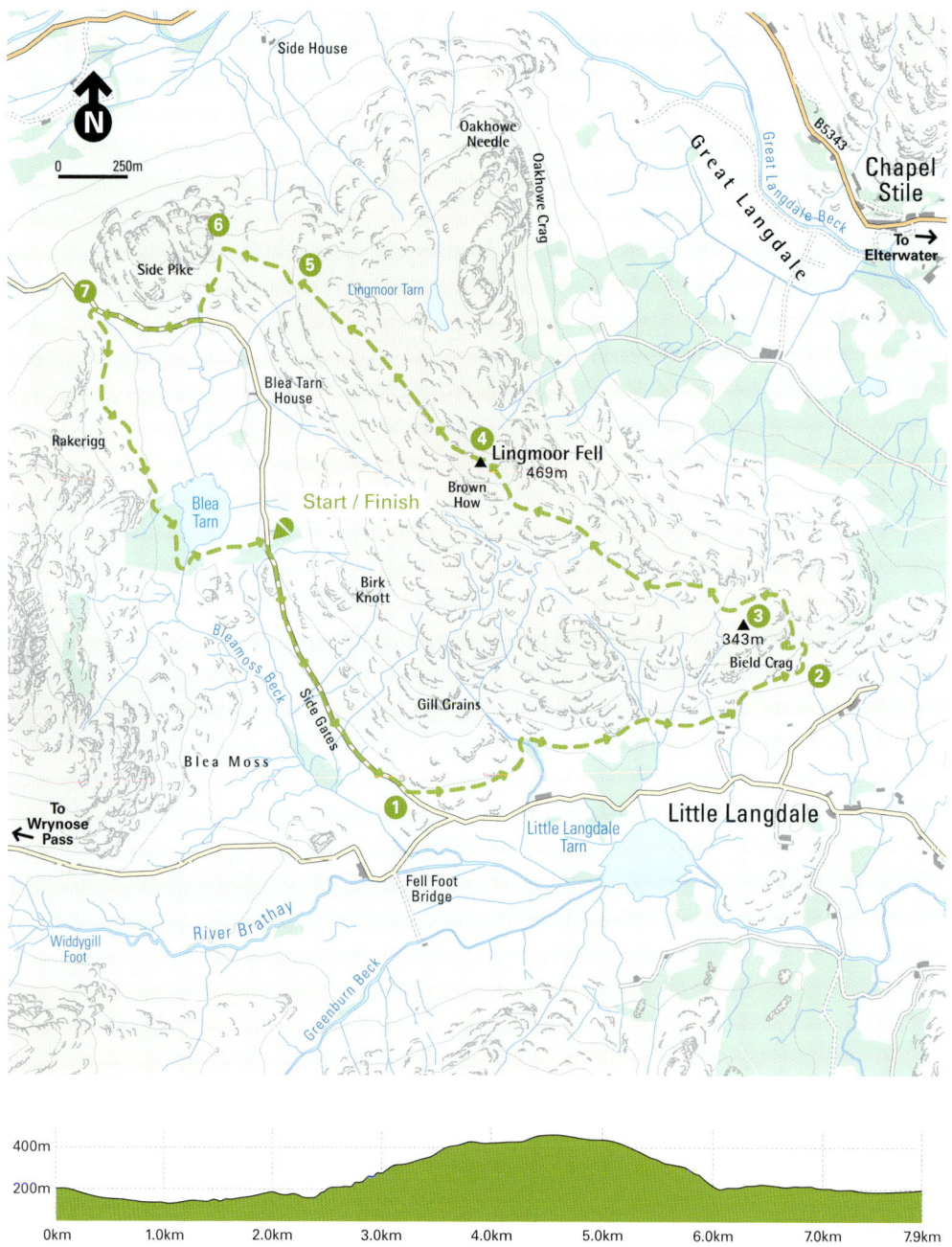

I am soon running alongside a wall on my right, a wall I will follow all the way to Bield Crag. After 1.6 kilometres I cross the beck at Gill Grains, continuing east on a rolling path through the bracken. The ferocious fern grows thick, overhanging the path, concealing the earth and slowing me down.

I climb left, then right, around an intake wall and soon, after 2.7 kilometres, I reach a wall and a gate. ❷ The path continues right through the gate, I turn left on a clear path that zigzags upwards towards a grassy gap between the crags.

Lingmoor Fell and Blea Tarn 33

I follow the wall on my right as it climbs up the fell and soon I turn west to follow another wall that traverses the summit like a roller coaster. I am now deep within the quarry area and the path to the summit is obvious. On my left, I pass a cairn perched on a rocky mound, marked on the map with a 343-metre spot height. ❸ Despite the rocks strewn around me, I keep climbing on a grassy path following the wall as it rolls along the ridge. I pass between a heap of quarried rocks and a stone sheltered seat overlooking a distant Windermere and from here, the gradient eases.

Old quarry gate – path all the way to Bield Crag

The Lingmoor Fell ridge from Little Langdale

Following the undulations towards the top of the ridge, I am able to run more freely. The wall on my right becomes a fence and I reach a step stile that delivers me to Brown How, the name given to the top of the fell. ❹ Tightly knotted grey craggy summits lie to the west, north, and east, their rugged faces chiselled by the morning sun.

From the summit, I head north-west with the fence now on my left. The route off the fell is rockier than the ascent. I follow the path alongside the fence, steadying myself occasionally down steep stone steps. The fence becomes a wall again and clings unerringly like a shackle along the spine of the fell, rising and falling over the welts and weals.

Ahead is Side Pike, a steep rock tower harbouring a multitude of climbing routes. Down to my right sits cobalt blue Lingmoor Tarn with its green pancake islets. Eight hundred metres on from the summit, I reach another wall in front of me and here, on my left, is a stepping stile that takes me back to the south side of the ridge wall. ❺

Heading down from Lingmoor Fell with Side Pike behind

Over the stile, I turn right following the path, now less rocky, westwards towards Side Pike. Again, I am following the wall, which appears to crash spectacularly into the side of the rock pile.

Three hundred metres on from the stile I reach another wall, this time with a kissing gate. The path through the kissing gate winds its way around the southern edge of Side Pike passing through Fat Man's Agony, a narrow gap between a large vertical slab of rock and the main crag face. Today I am not passing through the gate; instead, I turn left and descend on a clear path of engineered steps towards Side Gates. ❻

Lingmoor Fell and Blea Tarn

Following the path into the woods and around Blea Tarn

After a steep, short descent to the road, I turn right and run a gentle uphill slope to the cattle grid. Over the cattle grid I turn left, following the footpath signposted to Wrynose Pass (1¼ mile). ❼ From here, I have an easy run on a wide trail that takes me along the shore of Blea Tarn and back to the car park.

Into the woods, where through the summer canopy the pool glitters in the sun. At the end of the tarn, I ignore the path ahead, leading to Wrynose; instead I turn left to cross the footbridge over the outflow and back to the car park.

Great Carrs, Swirl How and Grey Friar | 34

Running towards Swirl How across the Top of Broad Slack

34 Great Carrs, Swirl How and Grey Friar

Park / Start	Off road parking close to the Three Shires Stone, summit of the Wrynose Pass (NY 277 027)		
Map	OS Explorer OL6		
Exertion	●●●●		
Navigation	●●●		
Terrain	●●●		
Distance	8.5 kilometres	**Time**	1 hour 29 minutes
Ascent	649 metres	**On road**	2.25 kilometres

Climb high above the Wrynose Pass to the roof of the Coniston Fells

On the summit of Wrynose Pass, where the old counties of Lancashire, Cumberland and Westmorland once met, there should stand a carved limestone boundary stone known as the Three Shires Stone. For the time being, the Three Shires Stone is missing, apparently being repaired.

START I start from the concrete circle that normally houses the stone and head south-west past the fingerpost pointing towards Wet Side Edge (¾ mile). Across the stepping-stones, I head in a south-westerly direction on a clear path, steep to begin with, rough in parts, but with enough grass to make this a relatively easy climb.

34 Great Carrs, Swirl How and Grey Friar

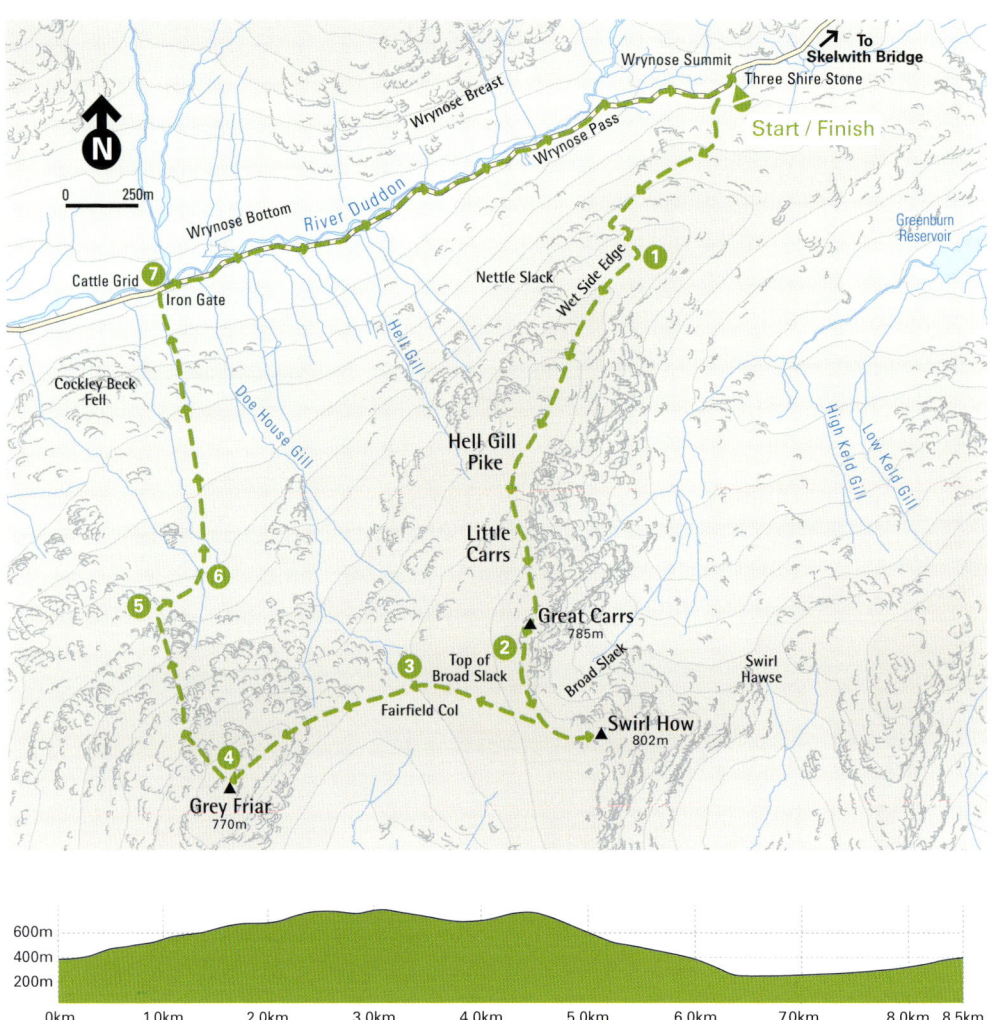

After 900 metres, I reach a path traversing the fell side from east to west, the route up from Greenburn. ❶ At the junction, marked by two large cairns, I turn right and the gradient eases. I find more of a rhythm and begin to run, slowly, towards the top of Great Carrs. On my right the summit of Grey Friar, on my left a steep precipice sweeping down to Greenburn. I skirt past Hell Gill Pike and Little Carrs. Boulders abound but there is still enough grass to make the route runnable, especially as the gradient eases towards the top of the ridge. Angular rocks – sharp edged cuboids – surround the summit cairn. ❷ On my right, I soon pass a second cairn where a cross, a wreath and pieces of rusting metal rest incongruously on the peaceful ridge, a memorial to the crash of a wartime Halifax bomber.

From the memorial, I continue south across the Top of Broad Slack, following a clear path as it sweeps southeast along the top of the steep concave escarpment. Five hundred metres from the summit of Great Carrs I approach the top of Swirl How, a boulder field of rocks protruding from the earth like truncated stalagmites. I pass a group of Herdwick who have chosen to walk to the top of this fell to graze on a thin sward of unpalatable matgrass. I join them on the summit to stand in the middle of the Coniston Fells surrounded by

Great Carrs, Swirl How and Grey Friar   34

Approaching Great Carrs summit, Swirl How is further along the edge

dramatic, grey and rugged peaks and ribbons of water. From Swirl How I turn to run back across the rocks down towards Great Carrs. After 200 metres, I reach two cairns in the dip between the two summits. From here I head left (west) picking up a grassy path towards Fairfield col. ❸

The (missing) Three Shires Stone

I welcome the easier running over soft ground, but I am soon climbing again, moving west towards Grey Friar. Seven hundred metres on from the col, with 70 metres of climbing, I reach the summit. There are two craggy mounds each bearing a substantial cairn; the outcrop on my left, to the south-east, is apparently the highest point.

I head down in front of the cairn on my right-hand side. ❹ On the map, a path is marked leading north-north-west towards Cockley Beck. Occasionally, I seem to find a faint trod but this is probably my imagination. I am not overly concerned. I know that 600 metres from the cairn, if I continue to head north-northwest, I will reach a wall and fence running west to east across the fell. ❺ I cross the wall and turn right, running east alongside

River Duddon from Wet Side Edge, on the way up to Great Carrs

34 Great Carrs, Swirl How and Grey Friar

Fairfield col, between Great Carrs and Grey Friar

the fence. Within three hundred metres, the fence turns north heading down the fell side towards the Wrynose Pass. ❻ I follow the fence, descending steeply over ground that is mainly soft tussocky grass. A kilometre down to the road with a 260-metre drop, too steep and clumpy to run on with any freedom. Then I reach a field of rough boulders and slow even more.

The fence line meets the road at the cattle grid by Iron Gate, at Wrynose Bottom. ❼ Since I am parked at Wrynose summit I now have some climbing to do – one hundred and fifty metres of ascent in the 2 kilometres back to the absent Three Shires Stone. A steady slog that feels easy on a smooth surface.

Herdwick on Great Carrs

Halifax bomber memorial, Great Carrs

Black Fell and Tarn Hows 35

Running alongside The Tarns on a summer's morning

35 Black Fell and Tarn Hows

Park / Start	Glen Mary Bridge National Trust car park, A593 Coniston (SD 321 998)		
Map	OS Explorer OL7		
Exertion	●●		
Navigation	●●●		
Terrain	●		
Distance	8.7 kilometres	Time	1 hour 11 minutes
Ascent	294 metres	On road	1 kilometre

Climb beyond Tarn Hows arboretum for a stunning view of Windermere

I venture into a park of manufactured beauty that annually draws hundreds of thousands of visitors, few of who will roam onto the fell that forms a rolling backdrop to the passive tarn.

START A large sign at the north side of the car park welcomes me to Glen Mary; this is my start. I cross the footbridge ahead and turn right to Tarn Hows following the sign. It is a rocky path alongside the beck, Tom Gill, reinvented as Glen Mary by the 19th century writer Ruskin.

Past the waterfall, I emerge at The Tarns (once there were three) and turn right over the footbridge above the outflow dam. ❶ I run on the Access for All path keeping to the water's edge along the southern shore. ❷ At 1.7 kilometres, I reach a path junction where I keep left following the fingerpost to Skelwith Bridge and The Langdales.

167

35 Black Fell and Tarn Hows

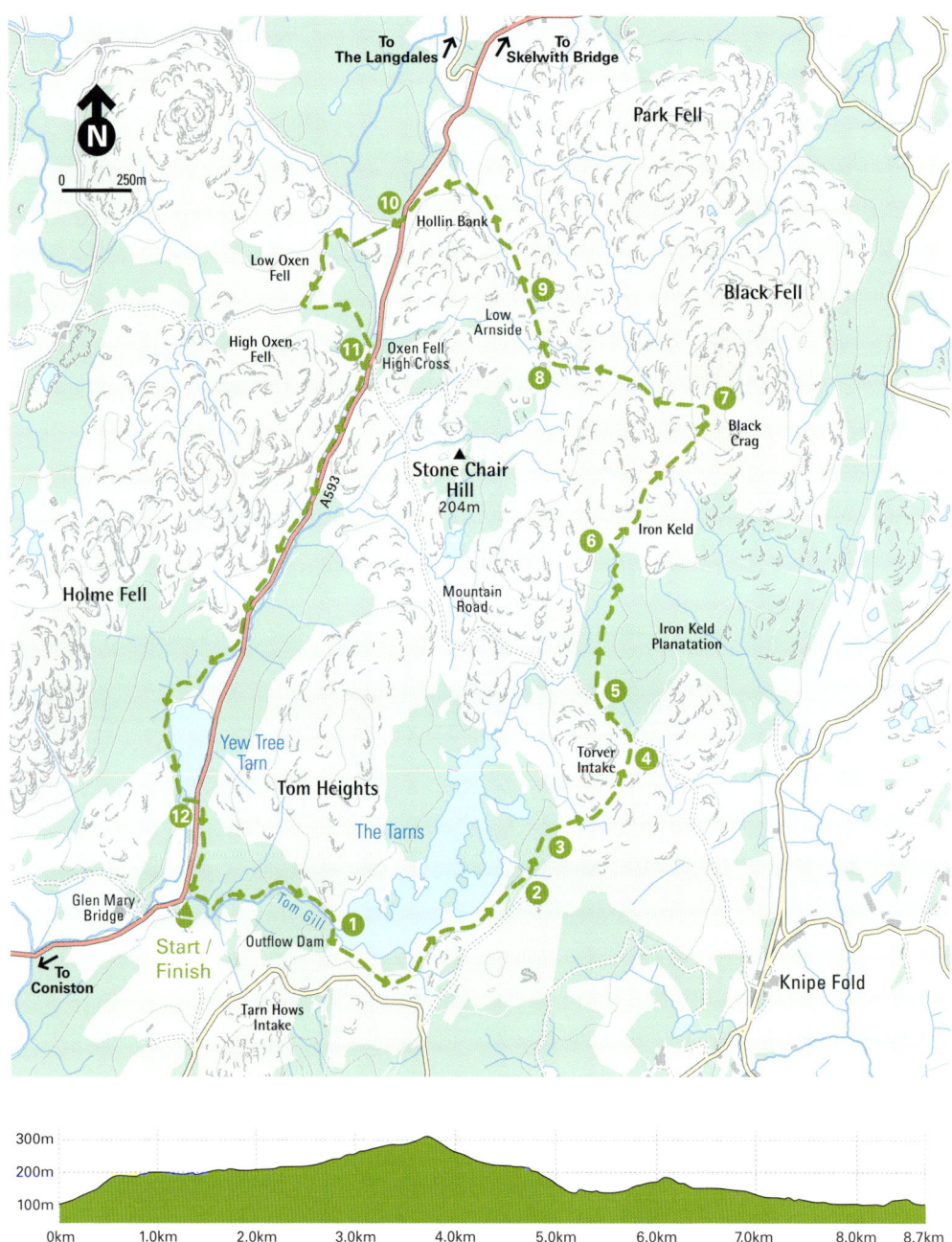

A further 250 metres up the track there is a step stile on my right over the fence. ③ I cross onto terrain that feels more like open fell and run across a squelching path, skirting to the south-east of Torver Intake. Within 500 metres I meet another fence with a step stile and climb over onto a broad rough lane. ④ Locally this is known as the Mountain Road, a byway crossing the western slopes of Black Fell between Knipe Fold and Oxen Fell High Cross.

Black Fell and Tarn Hows

Ignoring the entrance to Iron Keld directly ahead, I turn left up the byway following the sign to Oxen Fell. One hundred and fifty metres north-west there is another entrance to Iron Keld on my right, along a public bridleway. ❺

I pass through the gate and cross a sparsely populated conifer plantation. The gradient steepens but the path is still runnable. This is one of the lowest of Wainwright's fells, a gentle lope across bracken-draped rises.

❻ Five hundred and fifty metres on, I leave the plantation via a gate and immediately turn sharp right onto the path that will take me to the top of Black Fell. A clear route, not on the map, marked with cairns over a ruffled duvet of greening moor grass and delicate bracken.

Soon I can see the summit of the fell with the trig point visible on my left and the bell-shaped cairn on the lower south-eastern peak. I head for the trig point, an almost effortless climb meandering between the folds until the final sharp rise to the top.

The summit is marked on OS maps as Black Crag, a National Trust plaque pinned to the pillar labels the peak as Black Crag, Wainwright calls it Black Fell. Whatever its name, for such a minor fell, the views it offers are stunning. The hanging, rugged peaks of the Langdales, the soft slopes embracing Windermere and an abundance of lakes and tarns.

North from the summit, I don't climb the ladder stile ahead; instead, I turn left and follow the path, not on the map, alongside the wall in a westerly direction.

❼ The wall turns right; I carry straight on down the fell, across marshy ground heading directly west along a path that disappears. My exact route is not vital as long as I keep west; I am aiming for a broad track, a bridleway, which will take me through Low Arnside.

Three hundred and fifty metres from the summit I cross a wall through a gate and follow a faint path across a boggy enclosure. ❽ When I reach the track I turn right, picking up the pace on a clear path

Heading to The Tarns at Tarn Hows

The path alongside the tarns

The stile leading into Torver Intake

Black Fell summit, Black Crag

From the summit of Black Fell, follow the wall west

35 Black Fell and Tarn Hows

The path alongside Yew Tree Tarn

descending easily over moorland with few obstacles. Beyond Low Arnside, through a gap in the wall, the path forks and a blue waymarker points right along the bridleway. ❾ I take the left branch, the footpath contouring Hollin Bank.

I follow the path along the wall ignoring the gate into the enclosure on my right. Round the bank, through the gate ahead, I reach the A593. ❿ I cross the road and take the quiet lane ahead to Low Oxen Fell. At the road junction I turn left, following the fingerpost directing me to the A593 along a bridleway.

⓫ Before the road, I turn right at the four-way signpost to take the footpath running south towards Yew Tree Tarn. Over a kilometre on an undulating path, through meadows strewn with bluebells and unfurling fern fronds, with enough rocks and roots to keep me alert.

Belted Galloways on the path to Black Fell summit

Descending from Black Fell summit to Low Arnside

At the National Trust Holme Fell sign, I run straight on towards the tarn, picking up the path close to the reedy water's edge. ⓬ Over the small dam at the southern end, I reach the A593 again, cross the road and head right through the trees on a path back to Glen Mary Bridge.

Wetherlam summit from Birk Fell Hawse

36 Wetherlam

Park / Start	Low Tilberthwaite car park, Tilberthwaite (NY 306 010)		
Map	OS Explorer OL6		
Exertion	●●●●●		
Navigation	●●●		
Terrain	●●●●●		
Distance	8.4 kilometres	Time	1 hour 32 minutes
Ascent	620 metres	On road	0 metres

Following the routes of miners and quarrymen to the roof of a formidable mountain

The Coniston Fells, rugged, rocky, and industrial. A hundred quarrymen eked out a living in the quarries on these mountains. A tough workplace providing a strenuous fell run.

START Facing the car park the steps on the left by the honesty box are easy to spot. I start to climb on slate slabs lifted from the spoils that litter the slopes around Yewdale Beck. A short flight of steps, then a slate-strewn path take me past entrances to quarry halls and more heaps of rock. After 300 metres, I reach the remains of a small stone building on my right. ❶ Here the path splits; I take the right branch dropping down to the ravine.

36 Wetherlam

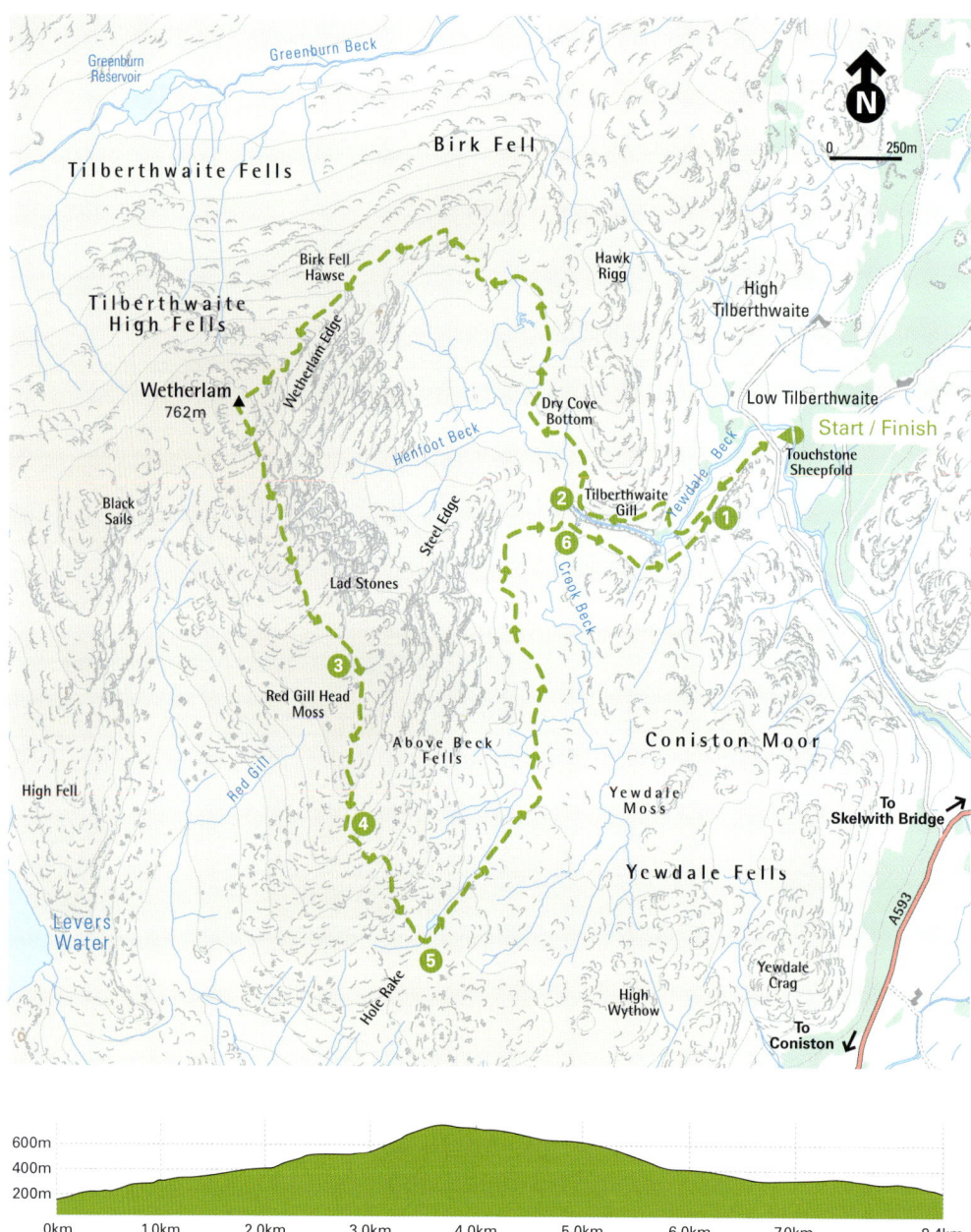

Across the footbridge, I climb the bank out of Tilberthwaite Gill, pass through a gate and soon reach the footpath emerging from the cottages at Low Tilberthwaite. Here I turn left towards the old copper mines at Dry Cove Bottom. Yewdale Beck, hidden beneath the larch and rowan canopy, gushes through the ravine on my left.

❷ After 950 metres, I reach a path junction at the top of the ravine, where I turn left (north) to begin the climb towards Birk Fell. I am on a clear path running up a gentle incline past numerous fenced-off shafts, levels and tumbled down mine buildings.

Wetherlam 36

On a good path, runnable to begin with, I continue north towards Birk Fell Hawse. On my left, the water-soaked moss of Dry Cove shimmers under the bright morning sun, to my right the crags of Hawk Rigg cast dark shadows, and ahead the steepening path edges left towards the Hawse. Once I reach the Hawse I turn away from Birk Fell and the path soon begins its relentless, rocky ascent of Wetherlam Edge. Craggy and steep, the path restricts me to a lung-busting, quad-pounding struggle. I toil up an ever-steepening gradient; I'm reduced to little more than a crawl. Reassuringly though, I know this rough, arduous section is short lived. It is steep and I have to stretch up big stone steps, but it is safe and there's no point where I feel exposed.

The gradient eases and within 500 metres, with the worst of the climbing over, I begin to move more freely. I am greeted by the smile of a solitary Herdwick, whose disdainful face seems to ask me what all my huffing and puffing is about. I soon spy a recklessly balanced cairn on a large mound that marks the highest point of the fell. The climb was worth the effort; on a clear day a host of tarns sparkle and tightly gnarled peaks play with the sunlight.

The lunar landscape obscures my route off the fell; as a precaution, I set a bearing of 150 degrees to run on, soon picking up the path down the Lad Stones ridge that eventually leads to Coniston. Now on a clear path, I leave the rocks behind and pick up the pace on grassy terrain down a gentle slope. Free of the craggy ground I bound south. Ahead, like a bright blue streak across a green canvas, the expanse of Coniston Water stretches away into the distance.

A kilometre from the summit I pass two small tarns on my left, ❸ which signal that within 600 metres I will take a less distinct route left towards Crook Beck and the miners' track from Coppermines Valley to Tilberthwaite. ❹ Finding this path on my left is not essential; if I miss the turning, I will simply meet the track 250 metres further south at Hole Rake.

Low Tilberthwaite Quarry hall

Footbridge over Yewdale Beck

Dry Cove Moss from Wetherlam Edge

Climbing Wetherlam Edge

36 Wetherlam

Andy Goldsworthy's Touchstone Sheepfold, angled slates

Down a grassy bank, a small tarn soon becomes visible on my left and ahead is the grassy route to Tilberthwaite. I cross Crook Beck via a pavement of stepping-stones, climb up to the path and turn left.

❺ Less than two kilometres along a valley floor, a gentle descent of unshackled running on soft terrain lies before me.

Soon I am back at Tilberthwaite Gill. ❻ I follow the path right, keeping the ravine to my left, descending gently at first and then more steeply towards the old slate quarries. There is an occasional band of sharp stone but the route is easy, rough but runnable.

I pass the point where I descended down into the ravine 90 minutes earlier and follow the path to the spoil heaps. Ahead, over the road, I spy the Touchstone Sheepfold and I drop down the steps back to the car park.

A demanding run to begin with, reduced to a slug's pace up the steep Wetherlam Edge. I console myself that the climb was good for my lungs and heart, and great for my glutes.

Herdwick on the slopes of Wetherlam

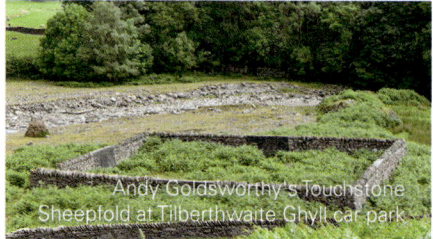
Andy Goldsworthy's Touchstone Sheepfold at Tilberthwaite Ghyll car park

Holme Fell from the Mountain Road on the way to Oxen Fell High Cross

37 Holme Fell and Tarn Hows

Park / Start	Lay-by on the A593, Oxen Fell High Cross, Coniston (NY 328 018)
Map	OS Explorer OL7
Exertion	●●
Navigation	●●
Terrain	●●
Distance	7.5 kilometres
Time	1 hour 9 minutes
Ascent	354 metres
On road	300 metres

An entry-level run revealing the ribbon of Coniston Water

Fell runs should be judged by how much you enjoy them, not by the height gained or the distance covered. Early morning in Yewdale, a cuckoo calls from across the valley. The sun is not yet high; a broad moon is still visible against the deep blue sky. This is a perfect way to begin a run.

START I start from the four-way fingerpost and follow the road north-west in the direction of Hodge Close (¾ mile), past the High Oxen Fell National Trust sign. The lane climbs quite steeply beneath the trees. After 300 metres, I turn left through a six-barred field gate onto the open fell. ❶ There is no signpost but there is a path, not marked on the map.

I cross the lumpy moor, sometimes on a distinct grass path, sometimes on faint trods, sometimes on no path at all. This does not really matter as long as I run south-west and continue to gain height.

37 Holme Fell and Tarn Hows

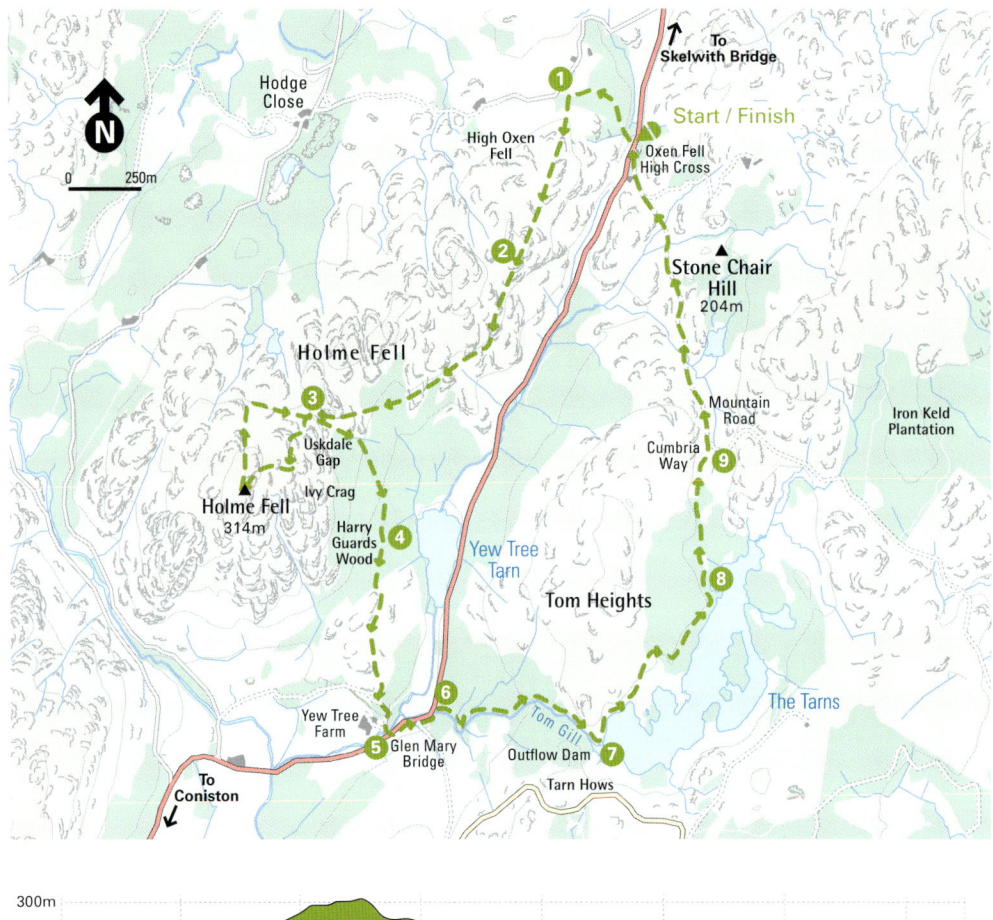

After a kilometre, I meet an ugly, rusting metal fence that runs east to west across the fell. ❷ I cross via a step stile and make sure I maintain a high line, still heading south-west, trying to avoid drifting left and down towards Harry Guards Wood.

All paths meet at Uskdale Gap. ❸ The pass is marked by a large cairn and a fragment of broken wall running north to south. The gap provides a window west to Wetherlam and east to Black Fell. A clear path ahead (south) is my route of ascent to the summit of Ivy Crag.

It is an easy climb, with only 50 metres of height gained from the gap but the final section to the top is a minor scramble. Standing by the robust cairn, I look back at the crags I have traversed, protruding like the bruised knuckles of the quarrymen who once eked out a living on this fell.

In the hollow below are the reservoirs that provided the waterpower for the stone-lowering funicular. To the north-west, quarries, together with the artefacts of tramways and the aerial ropeways used to shift tonnes of green slate, scar the lower flanks of Wetherlam.

I bound down to a boggy depression to the west, then climb the short distance to the summit of Holme

Holme Fell and Tarn Hows 37

Fell. I linger to gaze south along the length of Coniston Water, stretching to the southern edge of the national park. Exhilarated by the bright bare sky, I leap inflexibly back down to the gap. ❸

At the gap, I turn right (east) down a rocky path, focusing on my footfall, picking out the easiest line. Descending steeply on a jagged trail I soon reach Harry Guards Wood. My progress is slow but the route is not hazardous.

Following the lane uphill towards Holme Fell

❹ Four hundred and fifty metres from the cairn at the gap I meet a path on my left rising from Yew Tree Tarn. I keep right and follow the footpath south towards Yew Tree Farm. I leave the wood via a gate on my left, run through a rough pasture to a kissing gate and from here I follow the track alongside the wall down to the A593. I cross the road with care, turning right in front of Yew Tree Farm. ❺ Within twenty metres, I turn left into a field and immediately turn left again to cross the meadow and head towards the car park at Glen Mary Bridge. To the north of the car park, I pass the *Welcome to Glen Mary* board, cross the footbridge and follow the Tarn Hows sign through the gate. ❻. Another climb awaits, through woodland and alongside the waterfall tumbling down Tom Gill. A short, steep ascent on rocksteps through a mixed wood, I soon reach the dam at the top of the gill. ❼

Uskdale Gap, Holme Fell

Ivy Crag cairn, Holme Fell

I emerge at the water's edge where I turn left onto the smooth Access for All path, a section of the Cumbria Way. Rhythmically I run alongside the tarn on a peaceful morning. A flat mirror lake, red-petalled water lilies and a celeste sky with spruce, larch and pine filtering the rising sun.

I have an easy route back to where I am parked. Eight hundred metres on from the dam, at the head of the tarn, the path branches. ❽ I follow the signpost left towards Skelwith Bridge and Langdales. After a further 440 metres, I pass through a gate onto a byway known locally as the Mountain Road. ❾ I turn left again following the fingerpost to Oxenfell and Langdales, on a rougher track, all the way back to the A593 at Oxen Fell High Cross.

The spinning house at Yew Tree Farm

The Tarns, by the path to the Mountain Road

37 Holme Fell and Tarn Hows

Coniston Water from Ivy Crag, Holme Fell

Harter Fell (Eskdale) 38

Harter Fell from Hardknott Fort

38 Harter Fell (Eskdale)

Park / Start	Off-road parking, Jubilee Bridge, Hardknott Pass (NY 213 011)		
Map	OS Explorer OL6		
Exertion	●●●		
Navigation	●●●		
Terrain	●●		
Distance	7.2 kilometres	Time	1 hour 19 minutes
Ascent	546 metres	On road	750 metres

In the footsteps of Roman infantry soldiers on Hardknott's height

Over the centuries foot soldiers, packhorse drivers, coachmen and cyclists have all approached Hardknott Pass with some apprehension. I have a mountain to climb before I reach the summit of the pass.

START At the western base of the Hardknott Pass, just by the cattle grid, a fingerpost points to a Public Bridleway to Dunnerdale (3 miles). This is where I start my watch. I cross the elegant Jubilee Bridge to follow a clear path that contours around Dod Knott and then climbs towards Dodknott Gill.

For 900 metres, I run with a wall on my right, then I pass through a gate to run with the wall on my left. Within 300 metres, I pass through another gate returning to the east side of the wall and here, close to the gurgling Spothow Gill, I have to watch my navigation. On my right, at the wall corner, there is a stile; I ignore this. After 80 metres, the bridleway crosses a small beck and continues beside the wall towards Dunnerdale

179

38 Harter Fell (Eskdale)

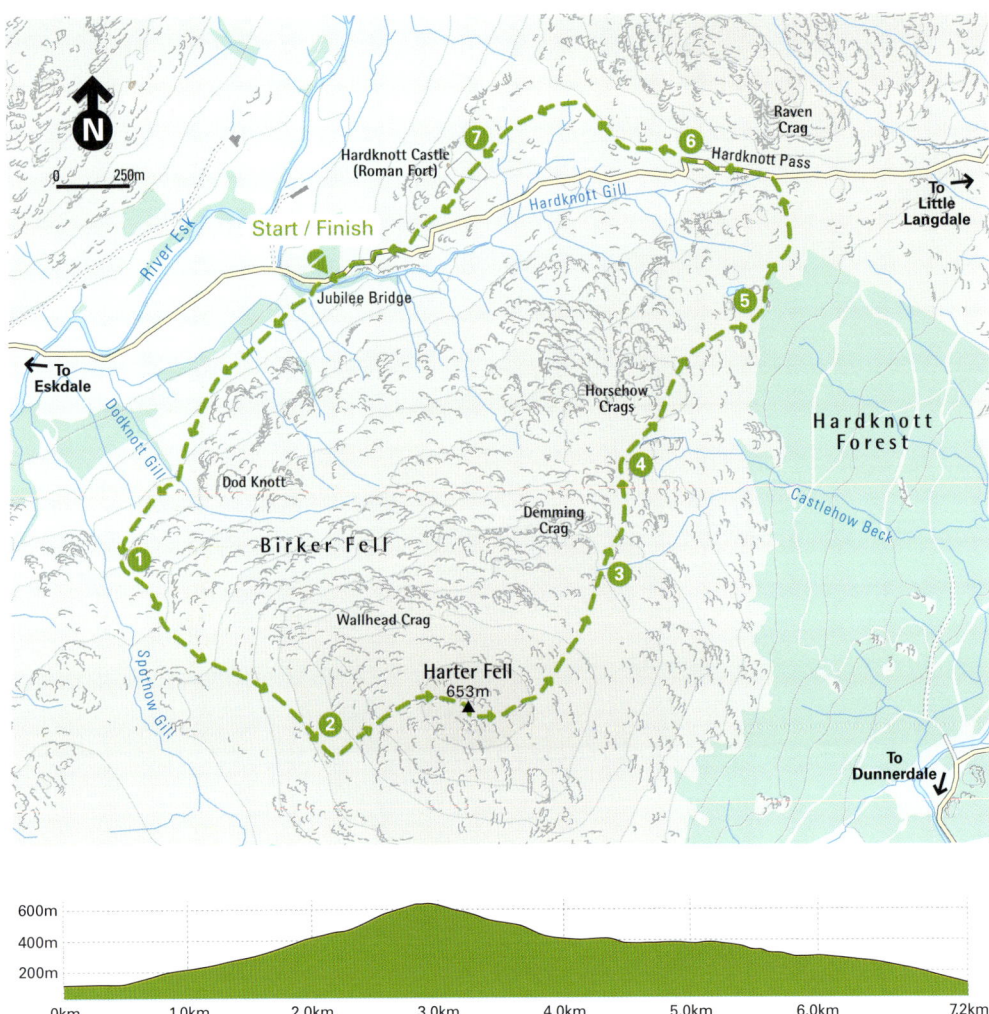

Forest. ❶ Here I look to my left; there is a faint path and a cairn, this is my route up to the summit of Harter Fell. The rest of this run is easy to follow. The route becomes more distinct; to begin with, it is an easy climb through ferns on a rock free path. At 2.2 kilometres, I cross a broken wall that follows the parish boundary. ❷ This tells me the path I am on is lower (further south) to the one indicated on the map. I'm not concerned though: I'm still climbing and within 50 metres, I reach a path junction marked by a cairn. Here I turn left onto a clear trail, heading up into the mist.

The path continues to climb towards the highest point of the fell. Ascent is always easier than descent in the clag; as long as I am climbing, I will reach the summit. Soft earth gives way to a rocky pinnacle comprised of three distinctive jagged cusps. I take a circuitous route to the south of the summit emerging at the trig point, an elongated frustum, which appears beneath a shifting veil of cloud. There is nothing to see. Despite the conditions, my route of descent isn't hard to find. As a precaution, I set my compass on an easterly bearing and immediately see a distinct path, which I follow around the eastern tor, the true high point on the fell.

Harter Fell (Eskdale) 38

Jubilee Bridge by Hardknott Pass

Beneath the craggy outcrop, I follow a beautiful grassy path that veers north-east towards the Hardknott Pass. Despite the swirling mist, the route down the ridge is easy to follow. ❸ I lope out of the clouds down the turfy trail, drop down a ravine at 4 kilometres, follow the path below Demming Crag before crossing a fence through a gate into a swampy meadow. ❹

I cross the pasture, easy running across a bog left dry after weeks without rain, to come alongside a wall. ❺ I ignore the gate leading into Hardknott Forest; instead, I pick up the bridleway heading north towards the pass. Over a stile, down a grass slope to the notorious byway where I turn left.

Hardknott Pass, described as Britain's most outrageous road, the route taken by Hadrian's army from Ravenglass to Ambleside. Instead of running directly to Jubilee Bridge I run 300 metres down the steep pass, hard on my quads, before taking the footpath on my right towards the Roman fort. ❻

❼ I run past the parade ground then through the eastern gate into the fort, along the main street in

Start of the Harter Fell run, following the bridleway to Spothow Gill

From Harter Fell, descend the Hardknott Pass to the Fort

38 Harter Fell (Eskdale)

Hardknott Fort – along the main street

front of the commandant's house, contemplating the life of the soldiers in this harsh, far-flung outpost of the Roman Empire. A hardship posting. On a bitter winter's day, sheltering in leather tents as the wind whips down the pass; soldiers longing for the shores of the Adriatic must have counted down the days.

Exhilarated by a sense of history and the wildness of the fells I pass through the western gate and descend towards the road. A right-hand turn takes me back to Jubilee Bridge.

A perfect loop around a perfectly situated mountain in the south-west fringes of the Cumbrian Mountains; a run undiminished by dank air and oppressive clouds.

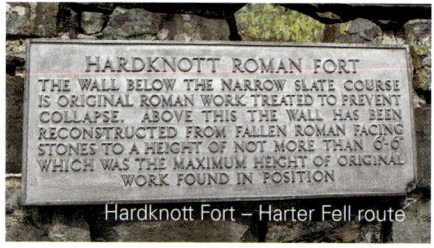
Hardknott Fort – Harter Fell route

Hardknott Fort looking west

Green Crag from the Birker Fell road

39 Green Crag

Park / Start	The Woolpack, Hardknott Pass, Eskdale (NY 190 009)		
Map	OS Explorer OL6		
Exertion	•••		
Navigation	•••		
Terrain	••		
Distance	7.9 kilometres	Time	1 hour 23 minutes
Ascent	459 metres	On road	700 metres

A crenellated plateau accessed by spongy peat roads

Proud of the Birker Fell moorland, a line of tors, like the back plates of a giant Stegosaurus, protrude black and dramatic through the peat and matgrass. Green Crag, the highest of the rocky out-thrusts, lies to the south of the ridge at the boundary of Wainwright's fell-walking country.

START From The Woolpack I head west along the road towards Boot for 150 metres, turn left down the lane signposted to St Catherine's Church (1½ mile) and within 350 metres, I reach Doctor Bridge. ❶ Over the bridge, I turn right at the slate sign for Low Birker following the bridleway to Dalegarth (1½ mile). The path passes in front of Low Birker then, at the end of the buildings, I immediately turn sharp left onto a footpath that follows a wall. ❷ Through the gate, I climb through a field of ferns towards the

39 Green Crag

wall-corner, where another gate takes me out of the enclosure onto a clear path that zigzags up the fell.
❸ From here, the climbing begins.

I am now on the Low Birker peat 'road', as evidenced by the collapsing Low Birker peat hut I pass after 1.6 kilometres. ❹ The path continues to climb towards Low Birker Tarn, a gentle gradient to accommodate the peat sleds.

Green Crag

The graded track winds essentially south, easy to follow until beyond the tarn. South of the tarn, the route becomes less distinct. I skirt around Tarn Crag avoiding any paths attempting to lure me on to higher ground, heading just east of south on a faint path to the left of the swampy Foxbield Moss.

Gradually the path climbs east out of the swamp and I head for the col between Crook Crag and Green Crag. I am now above the grassy slopes and into the rocky prominences. The route climbs south-east then grinds south towards Green Crag's jagged turret, it is a bit of a scramble to the top but nothing perilous. A pile of stones marks the highest point; in the low cloud, I can see little else.

However, I know, to begin with, that my route of descent is the way I ascended, towards the col between Crook and Green Crags. As I scramble down from the crown, I veer to my right heading for the crest of the col. ❺ Here there is a distinctive standing stone, marked on my map as a boundary stone, and beyond this a path leads directly north up to The Pike and then Crook Crag.

As I descend Crook Crag, I head just east of north down to a swampy plateau, along a faint path keeping the rocky outcrops to my left. In front of me is Kepple Crag, the key landmark for finding the route of descent. I run towards the southern edge of the crag looking for the Penny Hill peat 'road' that will deliver me to the intake land in the Eskdale Valley.

I head for the door between the unnamed crag on my left and the distinctive face of Kepple Crag. I enter through the door from the east, keeping to the left of a cotton-grass swamp. ❻ The peat road begins at the base of the Kepple Crag, hugging the slabs as they contour north.

The path, a wide, clear route, swings around the western perimeter of Kepple Crag then zigzags down the fell side. Stone buttresses support the edges of a path smooth enough to allow ponies to haul peat-laden sleds.

The Woolpack, Eskdale

Zigzag path to Low Birker Tarn – Low Birker Peat Road

Peat hut on the way to Low Birker Tarn

Low Birker Tarn from Tarn Crag

Approaching Kepple Crag

39 Green Crag

Penny Hill Farm detour

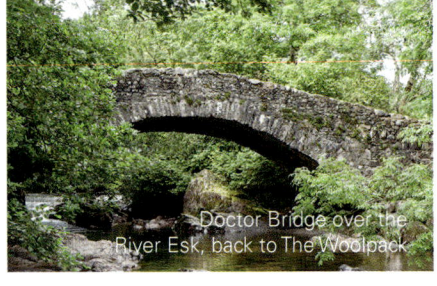
Doctor Bridge over the River Esk, back to The Woolpack

Past three dilapidated peat huts, the track swings east towards a wall where it meets the path descending from Spothow Gill. ❼ I follow the wall down to a gate alongside a sheepfold, cross a field of ancient of oak trees, pass through another gate and drop down to the bridleway leading up from Wha Bridge.

I turn left, follow the detour around Penny Hill Farm then rejoin the bridleway that delivers me back to Doctor Bridge. ❶ From here, I follow the lane north and I retrace my steps back to The Woolpack.

I return from a tranquil outpost of Wainwright country on a dank morning under iron skies, invigorated by the wind, the mizzle and a sense of history. Few venture onto this fell, perhaps deterred by the serrated profile and unaware that the routes largely avoid the rocks and boulders.

Devoke Water Circuit 40

Looking across Devoke Water, Green Crag and Harter Fell in the background

40 Devoke Water Circuit

Park / Start	Off road parking, Birker Fell Road Summit (SD 170 977)
Map	OS Explorer OL6
Exertion	●●
Navigation	●●●●
Terrain	●
Distance	7.6 kilometres
Time	1 hour 19 minutes
Ascent	396 metres
On road	0 metres

**In the western reaches of the Lake District
lies the wilderness of Birker Fell**

Like a scene from Wuthering Heights, dense, gloomy, graphite clouds lurk moodily above the bleak moor. I zip up my Gore-Tex jacket.

Eastwards the corrugated profile of the Green Crag ridge lies poised like a black dragon across the shrouded moss. Devoke Water, to the west, is hidden behind the ground rising to the peaks of Rough Crag and Seat How. **START** I start my watch by the rusty road sign and follow the bridleway west to the water (½ mile).

Within 200 metres, I pass through a wooden gate, just 20 metres beyond this a faint path leads up the fell side on my right. ❶ The path rises gradually across the moor grass towards my first summit, Rough Crag.

40 Devoke Water Circuit

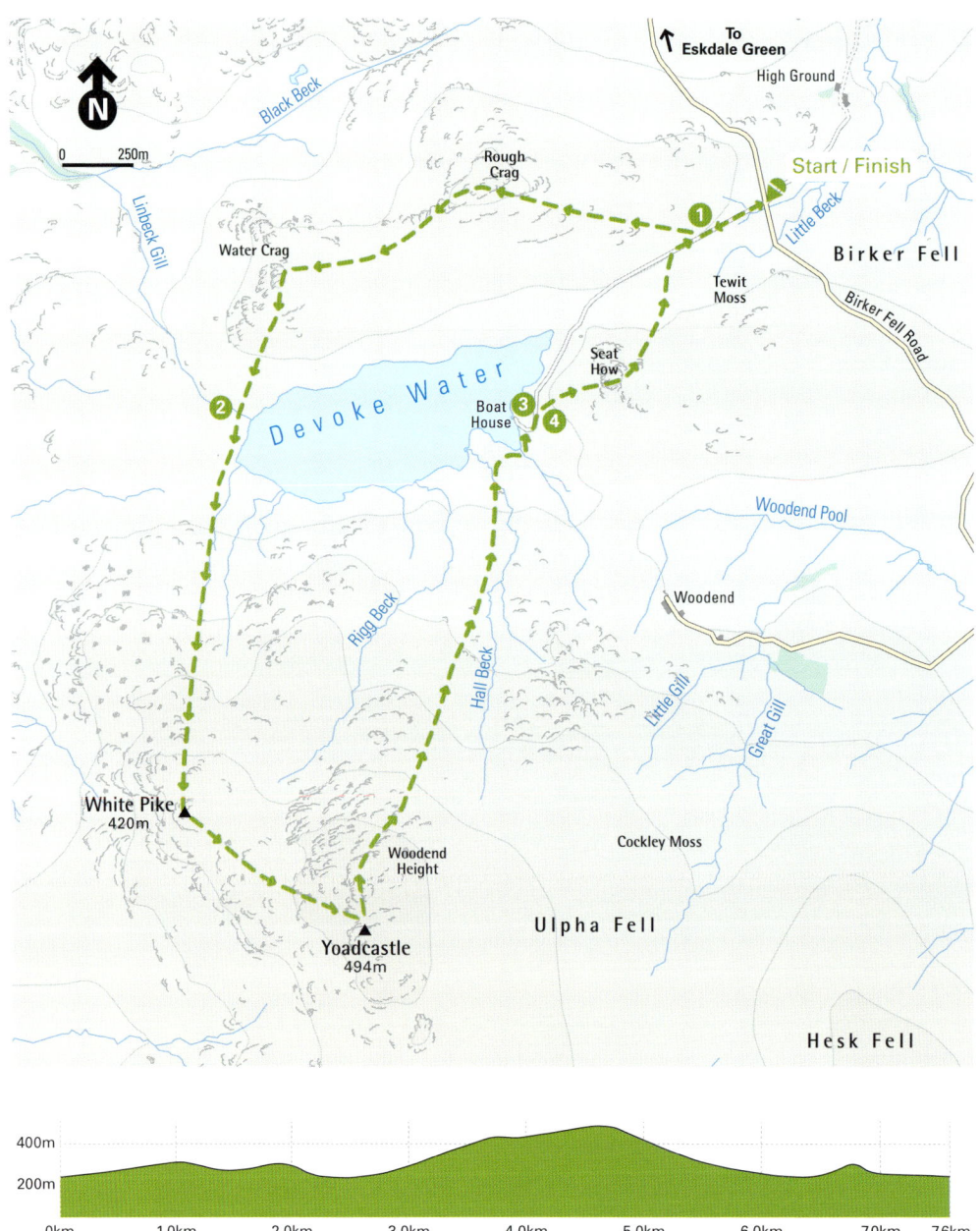

A small pile of stones marks the top, 1.15 kilometres from the start on easy ground.
Devoke Water, on my left, sparkling beneath a brief break in the clouds. Ahead (west) is Water Crag, 800 metres on a clear path, effortless running, a gentle slope down and a gentle slope up to another cairn. From the top of Water Crag I look south towards the distinctive cairn on White Pike, my next destination. I run on a bearing just west of south. There is a path down but this disappears within the boggy depression west of the water's edge. I keep running south through the marshes, squelching across the peat, jumping the outflow of Linbeck Gill. ❷

Devoke Water Circuit 40

A flock of geese scatter skywards from the cover of the cotton grass. I keep south, eventually meeting drier ground, climbing over tussocks and through numerous trickling streams. There is no path out of the swampy hollow. This is a good run to practise your compass skills if running on a bearing is not part of your usual repertoire. Devoke Water provides a handy navigation aid. Three flat, blue-grey hectares – the biggest tarn in the Lake District according to some – surrounded by a ring of crags and summits, visible over most of the circuit except in the foulest conditions.

The summit of White Pike lies on a bearing of 190 degrees from the most westerly point of the tarn, with no obstacles to bar your way if you don't mind getting your feet wet. An impressive prism-shaped cairn at the south-west corner of the crag marks the highest point. The sands of Ravenglass and the Sellafield nuclear site at Seascale are just about visible, but lead-black clouds roll in from across the Irish Sea and I need to move quickly to avoid a soaking.

There is a clear path south-east to the top of Yoadcastle, a brief descent and a short climb, just 800 metres from White Pike. I head up to the rocky mound on top of Yoadcastle with the rainclouds chasing me down. From here the tarn is obscured from view, but a 200-metre hop north takes me to the top of Woodend Height, and from the cairn on the top of this summit the water appears once again.

I run over pathless terrain towards the boathouse, clearly visible on the eastern shore, on a bearing of 20 degrees. I ignore any faint trods, bounding in a straight line, prancing over tussocks, avoiding any rocky tracts, unshackled by paths, gates or stiles.

The boathouse, 1.5 kilometres from Woodend Height, draws closer. I approach the bridleway that runs east to west along the southern shore. Clouds oppress the moorland and the water, black behind the boathouse.

❸ It begins to rain as I turn right onto the bridleway, heavy globules.

The bridleway to Devoke Water

Looking down on Devoke Water from Roughcrag

Crossing Linbeck Gill with the geese

Devoke Water and the Boathouse

Devoke Water Circuit

Looking back at Seat How across Tewit Moss

④ Directly east of the boathouse a faint path rises towards Seat How. I could carry on along the bridleway, but I opt to climb the rough rocky tor. I edge around the southern slope and once over the top pick up a faint trod that disappears across Tewit Moss. More pathless running. Soon I reach the bridleway where I turn right for the final run back to Birker Fell Road.

Heading towards Seat How from Devoke Water

The Northern Fells

The independent north, peaceful, rolling upland with undivided expanses of yielding turf, provides some of the best running terrain in the English Lakelands. From the entry-level gems of Latrigg and the Glenderaterra valley to the imposing arc of the Blencathra Massif, each of these runs takes you across heather and fern-clad slopes up to soft grass summits, largely avoiding roads and hard trails.

The Northern Fells across Derwentwater

Path from Binsey to the A591

Binsey from Longlands

41 Binsey Double

Park / Start	Binsey Lodge (NY 236 351)		
Map	OS Explorer OL4		
Exertion	● ● ●		
Navigation	● ● ●		
Terrain	●		
Distance	7.7 kilometres	Time	1 hour 5 minutes
Ascent	464 metres	On road	2.1 kilometres

A double helping of plum pudding

Binsey is a great little mountain to run up and down, with the summit a mere 1.2 kilometres and less than 200 metres of ascent from the start at Binsey Lodge. This route passes over the summit twice, making it more of a challenge.

START I leave the car on the corner by Binsey Lodge. Along the road leading to Bewaldeth there is a gate on the right that opens onto one of the broadest grassland fell paths you will find.

It is just over a kilometre from the gate to the summit; crunching frost and vestiges of snow all the way to the top. A milky mist lingers, obscuring views of Bassenthwaite Lake's northern fringes over my left shoulder and tear-shaped Over Water to my right.

41 Binsey Double

It's a tough slope because it is runnable all the way, even for me. The grass is yielding and the gradient lessens as I near the summit. Then the mist magically clears. A pale winter light from behind illuminates the tumulus, highlighting the cairn and the trig point upon the top.

For a small pudding-shaped dome, the panorama is spectacular. North, the coastal plain stretches away to the Solway Firth and beyond to the offshore wind turbines and the hills of Galloway. East, across Over Water, lies the little frequented Northern Fells: Longlands, Great Sca and Knott. South, the flanks of Skiddaw, sparkling silver, covered in deep snow. West, the tip of Bassenthwaite Lake and the white caps of the Western Fells. Straight over the summit at the cairn, I return to the main path heading north-west, descending with a small protuberance – West Crag – on my left. I clamber down the fell taking the left path at the fork. ❶ Arcing west, around West Crag, I follow the sodden path alongside a stream, with one wall to my right and another straight ahead of me. I head for the wall straight ahead, beneath West Crag. On my left, I spot the large metal gate I am looking for and run towards it over tussocks of matgrass and mossy bogs. ❷

Binsey Double

Once through the gate I pick up the pace on a clear path through farm pasture. A second gate leads to a farm track thick with cloying mud; I try to keep on the grass all the way to the A591, the Keswick to Carlisle road. Once at the road, I turn left and run on the verge for a few hundred metres before I reach the turning to the settlement of Bewaldeth.

Left again, now on a narrow lane that rises gently, winding up to Fell End Farm. I could head straight along the road back to where I am parked; a better route, though, is back over Binsey. At the farm, I take the footpath on my left, through a field gate, ❸ across an enclosed field to the small gate in the wall. ❹ Once through the gate I am back on open fell. I continue straight on, up the fell in a north-northeasterly direction, following an indistinct path through clumps of heather; brown, woody and gnarled by the ravages of winter. It is a steep slope up the southern side of Binsey. I resist the temptation to take any of the paths (a variety of sheep trods) that crisscross my vague route to the top. If I keep heading upwards, I will reach the summit.

I feel the warmth of the sun on my back. Behind me Bassenthwaite Lake, a cool, clean knife blade, mirror flat, separates the Northern and Western Fells, pointing all the way to the Coniston Fells. Few people see this view. Today I am the only one.

The tumulus mound and the trig point are revealed from a different angle. I turn right when I reach the main path. A fast kilometre down on smooth, cropped, grass. My studs sink into the soft ground. In places, though, I feel myself sliding down the greasy surface. I hold back. On a dry day, this must be one of the fastest descents in the Cumbrian Mountains. A slope where a fast runner could break the world kilometre record.

Suddenly the wall is approaching. I head for the gate – the finish line.

Binsey Lodge parking area

The gate near Binsey Lodge, the start of the Binsey run

Running up the broad path to Binsey

Cairn and trig point on the Binsey tumulus

Turning to Bewaldeth, a short road section

41 Binsey Double

A fast kilometre back to Binsey Lodge

West Fell, High Pike – from Haltcliff View

42 High Pike (Caldbeck)

Park / Start	Calebreck, Hesket Newmarket (NY 345 358)		
Map	OS Explorer OL5		
Exertion	●●		
Navigation	●●●●		
Terrain	●		
Distance	8.1 kilometres	Time	1 hour 8 minutes
Ascent	380 metres	On road	0 metres

**Away from the madding crowds, a traverse
of a halcyon fell under stirring skies**

I can still hear the miners hewing with their oak shovels, cursing in German and Cumberland dialect. Heave-ho into the wooden tubs hauled by hund wagons. Wagons yapping on the wooden rails as they travel to the smelting sites. In the dark of a winter's afternoon with the rain lashing and the wind howling, carrying copper and silver ores extracted from a harsh earth. There were no tourists, no hikers, boulderers or paragliders. This was an unforgiving industrial landscape. A fell crisscrossed with mining tracks and old wagonway rails, scarred by adits and shafts and tumbled down stone dwellings and washhouses.

42 High Pike (Caldbeck)

START I park at Calebreck, an old lead-smelting site to the east of High Pike. The sky is glacier blue – it doesn't always rain here – and there is a cold breath of wind. A wooden fingerpost points to Fellside, three miles along the bridleway, but almost immediately my path veers off to the left (south-west) across the boggy common in the direction of Miton Hill (1½ miles). ❶ I expect to get my feet wet, but the sub-zero temperature means the ground is rock-hard and the springs are frozen, so I can crunch across the frosty grass running in the shadow of Carrock Fell.

The path, broad and grassy, skirts westwards and soon joins the track that runs up from the ford across Carrock Beck. I follow the track west, running gently uphill, still chilly in the shade, but warming up. After 1.5 kilometres there is an obvious path to my left towards the beck. ❷ I take this route, leaving the track and the slopes of West Fell behind. Easy running on soft grass by the edge of the path. Easy running by the fast flowing water, few come this way. Not in the winter. After a further 300 metres, I jump across the beck and begin to climb on a good path up the north-western slope of Carrock Fell.

High Pike (Caldbeck) 42

High Pike, a broad ridge for running

It's tough going here, not really runnable for me. I shuffle upwards until, just over a kilometre from the beck, I meet the path descending from Carrock summit and turn right, across Drygill Head towards the Cumbria Way. ❸ A broad track gouged through stiff sedge and sheep's fescue, a byway from another era. After 600 metres I turn due north onto a path that heads directly to the top of High Pike. ❹ Straight across the track, a convex climb, more runnable, leads me to the summit.

Four kilometres into the run I come to a cluttered summit with a stone bench, trig point and a huge pile of stones, the remains of a shepherd's shelter. I stop and listen; a faint murmur suffocates the silence – a farm vehicle, a drone, a distant aircraft? A jet-black raven caws. The low winter sun warms me. Blencathra and Skiddaw Massifs to the south and west, to the north the Solway Firth and Scotland beyond, on a raw day with drifts of snow and white translucent ice.

Climbing to Miton Hill alongside Drygill Mine

I can pick up the pace, travelling north on a clear route towards a large stone shelter and then north-northeast beyond the next pile of stones on another distinct path. It is easy on a cloudless day; I can see Caldbeck village ahead. In the clag and driving rain, the route off this featureless fell is less obvious. Past the shelter, I head north-northeast, ignoring paths to my left and right.

High Pike summit looking south

High Pike (Caldbeck)

The path past the old mine workings towards Woodhall Park

5 Seven hundred metres on from the trig point, I reach a small cairn; beyond this point, the path begins to curve right (north-east) heading to the right of a group of fenced-off mine shafts. **6** I cross a track and continue straight ahead on a grassy path, more of a sheep trod, heading east now, past the old mine workings with West Fell on my right.

I reach the bridleway; I could go right but I prefer the yielding, grassy earth to the hard compacted track, so I carry on towards the wall at Woodhall Park. **7** Right at the wall, across the beck, on the sodden path south; the ice is melting here in the sun. As I run towards the low winter sun, flashes of red and orange force me to bow my head.

An effortless run across a sloping grassy fell. I didn't see another soul.

Following the Woodhall Park wall back to Calebreck

Uldale Fells

Longlands Fell, the last of five moorland summits

43 Uldale Fells

Park / Start	Parking area by the bridge over Longlands Beck (NY 266 358)		
Map	OS Explorer OL4		
Exertion	•••		
Navigation	••••		
Terrain	•		
Distance	9.2 kilometres	Time	1 hour 12 minutes
Ascent	592 metres	On road	0 metres

Tremendous running over undulating moorland pasture

A refuge of serenity at the Back o'Skiddaw, the Uldale Fells are far from the crowds that throng the central Lakeland peaks.

START There is room for a dozen or so cars by the roadside, a convenient parking place for the start of a circuit over some of the Uldale Fells – Meal Fell, Great Sca Fell, Little Sca Fell, Lowthwaite Fell and Longlands Fell.

Just north of the road bridge a wooden gate opens onto the old road to Green Head. A fingerpost indicates that Green Head is 1½ miles along the green lane. This is part of the alternative back route of the Cumbria Way.

Uldale Fells

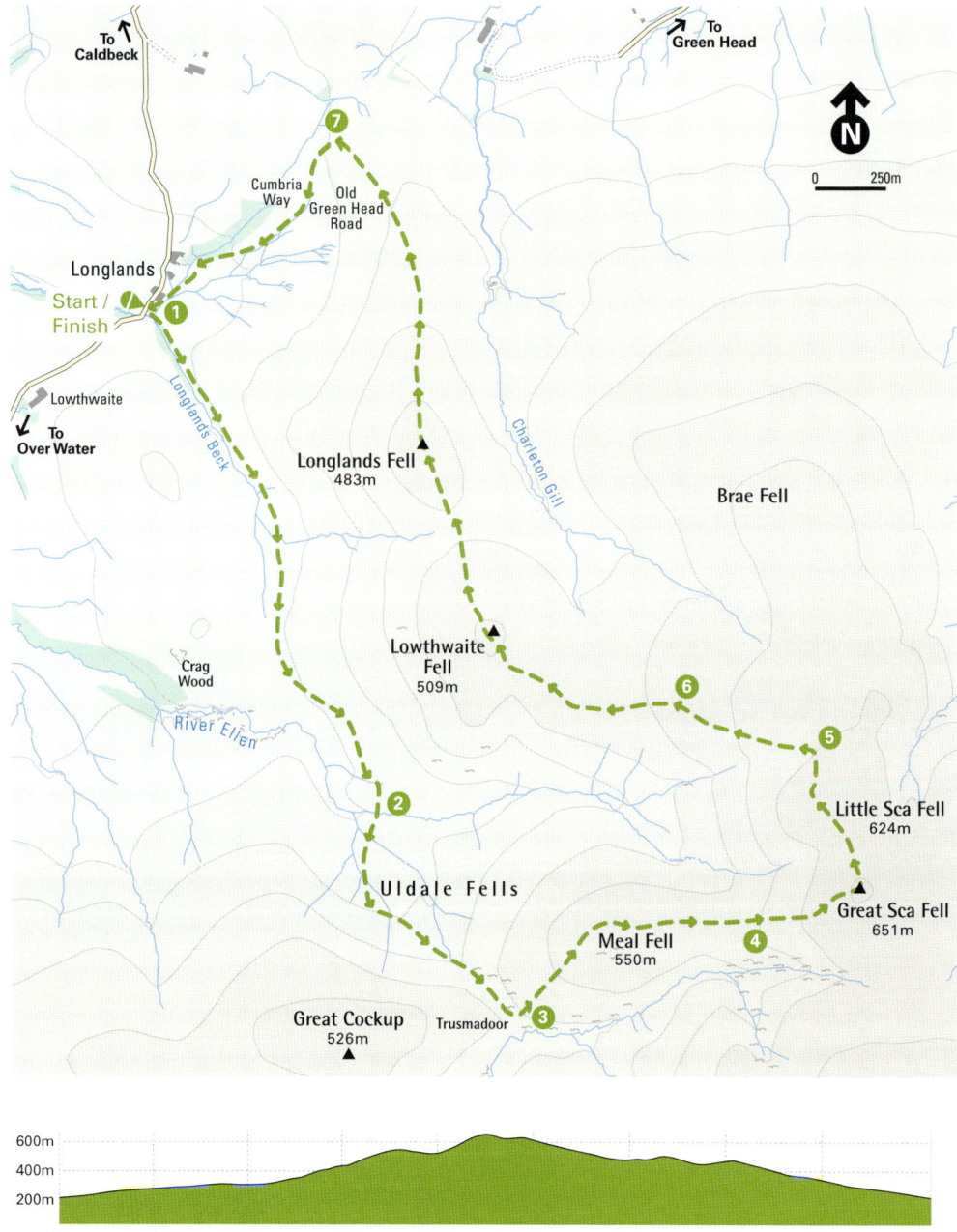

1 Through the gate, I immediately leave the lane, turning right to follow the wall and the beck south-southeast. After a muddy section, a clear track follows the wall for a kilometre. The wall then turns right and the path now follows the River Ellen.

Ahead I can see the distinctive outline of Trusmadoor – Wainwright's natural railway cutting. A strong jawline, an angular geological corridor, a strangely evocative window into a timeless world.

2 I cross the River Ellen at a small ford and the path enters the v-shaped cut between the slopes of Great

Uldale Fells

Crossing the River Ellen

Cockup and Meal Fell. I have run exactly 3 kilometres to the head of the pass where the path divides. ❸ I take the left-hand branch, north-east, up the side of Meal Fell. After a further 500 metres, I reach the circular summit shelter and continue past the small tarns heading directly east to descend to a small col. Ahead, there is a clear path up to Great Sca Fell. After 500 metres of climbing the path splits, with the left-hand branch heading to the depression between Great Sca Fell and Little Sca Fell. ❹ I head straight on.

The fells around here are notoriously indistinct. You can easily get confused even if the clouds are high. It can take many hours of running before the individual fells become recognisable. If the clag comes down you have to beware. Knowing distances and compass directions can be very useful.

Follow Longlands Beck towards Trusmador

On the plus side, these grassy rolling hills are eminently runnable. The slopes are soft and gentle, rocks are few and far between and the depressions between the summits are shallow enough to enjoy.

On the summit of Great Sca Fell is a sad-looking pile of stones. I turn left (directly north) and there is an obvious path. Four hundred metres of down and up brings me to the top of Little Sca Fell with its large, untidy cairn and its neat, sunken wind-shelter.

The path continues past the cairn, veering slightly right,

The clear path up Great Sca Fell, Little Sca Fell to the left

43 Uldale Fells

A grassy run from Great Sca Fell to Little Sca Fell

and within 100 metres I reach the old bridle road, a grassy track with deep grooves. ❺ I turn left onto the track and continue down a gentle slope. I have to concentrate here – otherwise I will end up running towards Charlton Gill. ❻ My branch to Lowthwaite Fell begins just 500 metres down the bridleway on my left. I turn to run north-west with Over Water straight ahead and the isolated dome of Binsey beyond.

I am soon climbing the easy slope towards the summit of Lowthwaite Fell; I then have one last dip before the summit of Longlands Fell. From the final summit cairn, I have two kilometres of easy running back to hamlet of Longlands. I run directly north towards the Old Green Head Road. A superb kilometre of moorland running, a gentle descent to the green lane. ❼ At the lane, I turn left and follow the furrowed track back to the gate by Longlands Beck.

This is so unlike a typical Lakeland journey. There are no rocky paths or craggy outcrops, and the becks tumble gently into grassy valleys. Yet the running is unbridled and kind to the joints, muscles and sinews. Just be careful in the mist.

Little Sca Fell summit

An easy climb to Lowthwaite Fell

Bowscale Fell

Sunset in the Mosedale Valley

44 Bowscale Fell

Park / Start	Car park in the hamlet of Bowscale (NY 359 316)
Map	OS Explorer OL5
Exertion	•••
Navigation	•••
Terrain	••
Distance	7.3 kilometres
Time	57 minutes
Ascent	484 metres
On road	200 metres

Sweeping across fell-grass slopes high above a jewel of a glacial tarn

Bowscale is a capricious fell. From winter's icy runnels and becks, and a bitter wind that has travelled all the way from Siberia, to a parched summer of dry, fragile moss and springs that offer the sheep some respite, this run to Bowscale Tarn, then up the corrie wall to the top of the fell, offers a variety of challenges.

START From the car park I run north-west to where the road bends right at Home Farm, and carry straight on along the bridleway signposted to Bowscale Tarn. It's a straightforward 2.5 kilometre run to the water's edge with no choice of route; runnable all the way.

Today, unusually, there is a very gentle breeze, so my ascent to the tarn is unimpeded. When the prevailing westerly wind blows, it comes straight down the valley hitting you head-on as you ascend the bridleway to the tarn. On some days, the gusts are so severe it becomes impossible to make any progress.

44 Bowscale Fell

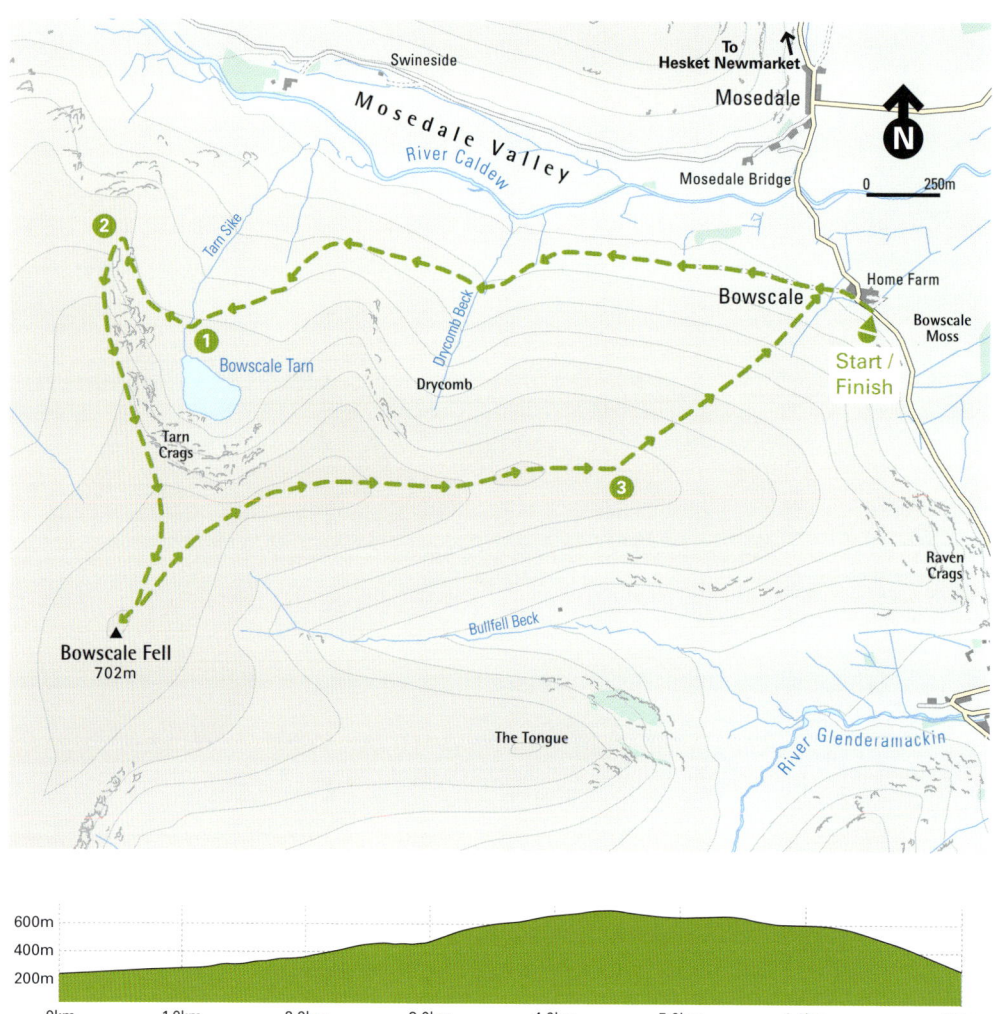

The bridleway, a pony track popular with Victorian tourists lured by tales of immortal fish, runs alongside the Mosedale Valley. Down to my right, the River Caldew meanders beneath the steep southern face of Carrock Fell, already turning purple, pink, mauve as the heather blooms. High on my left, brown and olive-green grasses swathe the northern flank of the great rounded mound of Bowscale Fell.

Halfway up the track, I cross Drycomb Beck and from here, the gradient steepens. I am soon running beneath the head wall of the classic cirque towards a location beloved by geologists.

Utterly calm under the pure blue sky, the tarn looks like a sheet of blue glass. Despite it being a sublime day in the height of summer, I am alone, in a silent cauldron. ❶ I cross the stream, Tarn Sike, just at the point where it pours over the lip of the cirque and head west, aiming for the zigzag path up the steep cirque wall. The route up through the rocks onto the shoulder of Bowscale Fell ascends more than 100 metres in a horizontal distance of 250 metres, so this is not running terrain; it is hands-on-quads calf-busting tramping.

❷ At the top of the climb I reach a small pile of stones; here I turn left on a path that heads south above Tarn Crags. It takes a while to adjust back to anything resembling a running gait, but I am soon trudging

Bowscale Fell

Along the edge of Bowscale Tarn

across the tussocks towards Bowscale's rounded crest. The path edges around the top of the cirque wall offering vertiginous views of the tarn below. Today under a cloudless sky, I can clearly see the pile of stones to the east of the summit.

Gradually I run more freely across the grassy moor, a kilometre traverse from where I emerged at the top of the bank to the fell summit. The path delivers me to the pile of stones and from here the summit shelter is visible, 80 metres to the south-east.

I am on my own, surrounded by the Northern Fells with vast horizons stretching north to Scotland and east to the Pennines. Even in the summer, this feels like a remote location. In the winter, this is a wild and restless place and on cloudy days, I use my compass to check my line of descent.

I turn swiftly, retracing my steps to the pile of stones. Beyond this cairn, however, I take the north-easterly path leading over the ridge towards Raven Crags. Running down two dips and over two rises, I keep the several cairns along the ridge-route to my left. A more

The climb up to the shoulder of Bowscale Fell from the tarn

Leading to the summit shelter on Bowscale Fell

44 Bowscale Fell

Returning from Bowscale summit

northerly line would have me running too close to the top of Tarn Crags, directly above the tarn.

③ One hundred and ninety metres east of a small cairn, at end of the second rise, I leave the ridge path. Less than two kilometres on from the summit I head left to begin my descent towards the hamlet of Bowscale. I take a north-easterly course, following the line of the track across Bowscale Moss in the distance. In misty conditions, I run on a 45-degree compass bearing.

It is a steep descent across clusters of heath rush and clumps of soft bog-moss. I bounce over the spongy peat hags, disturbing the meadow pipits. The chimneystacks of the Bowscale cottages appear; I am on a good line, heading straight for the gate at the bottom of the bridleway.

Dropping down onto the track, I turn right, pass through the gate and retrace my steps back to the car park.

The route down Bowscale Fell to Bowscale

Bannerdale Crags

Bannerdale Crags from The Tongue

45 Bannerdale Crags

Park / Start	Mungrisdale Village Hall (NY 368 302)		
Map	OS Explorer OL5		
Exertion	•••		
Navigation	•••		
Terrain	•		
Distance	11.5 kilometres	**Time**	1 hour 45 minutes
Ascent	630 metres	**On road**	440 metres

Tranquil steep-sided crags with a fine grassy ridge route

You have to go out of your way to cross Bannerdale Crags, so it is a route less travelled.

START From the car park opposite Mungrisdale Village Hall I follow the road north, then west, alongside the river. I turn left after the bridge, following the fingerpost pointing in the direction of Mungrisdale Common.

I don't bother trying to keep my feet dry as I cross the first of many becks. I can predict what lies ahead. The great gritstone slabs, like giants' gravestones, laid when the path was diverted in the aftermath of Storm Desmond in 2015, are already festooned with moss. Water perpetually flows across these slabs and when this freezes, they become mini ice rinks, amusing or perilous.

45 Bannerdale Crags

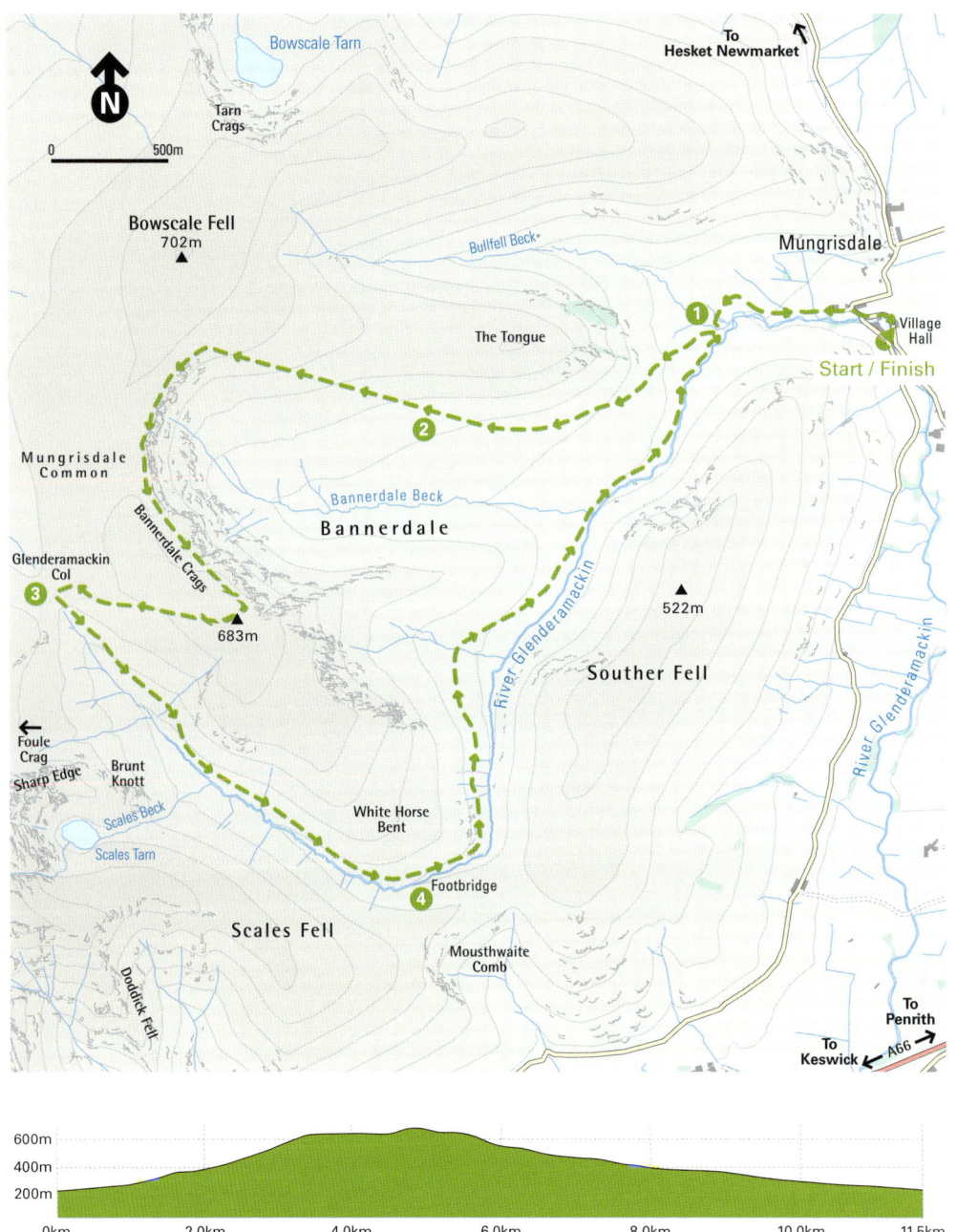

In the gap between Souther Fell on my left and The Tongue directly ahead, I see the face of the Bannerdale escarpment, today a white wall. I wasn't expecting this.

① Immediately after the footbridge, I take the right-hand fork and begin to climb the broad path that runs west, beneath the southern slope of The Tongue. I prefer to run up this route rather than down. Deep runnels lurk, often hidden by overhanging tufts of matgrass. Ankle twisters if you are trying to descend at speed.

Bannerdale Crags

Soon I reach the snowline. Deep snow has drifted across the path, filling and hiding the trenches and crevices. Pristine snow. The whitest of white, dazzling, makes it hard to see. Then it starts to hail. Tiny splinters of ice pummel my cheeks. I am running against a stiff sub-zero breeze. It is tough going. After 2.3 kilometres, the path splits. I take the less distinct, steeper right-hand fork. ❷ The going gets tougher. I collapse into a cleft up to my thighs. At best, the snow is ankle deep.

It seems to take me an age to reach the ridge at the depression between Bowscale Fell and Bannerdale Crags. I turn left (south-west) and the full force of the wind blasts me head on. The hail scours my face. The snow is smooth and thick, obscuring the paths. The elements are raw and wild, so close to home. To run in the fells means embracing the weather, the cold and the wet, enjoying its ferocity and taking some satisfaction in not yielding.

The top of Souther Fell has disappeared, masked by a veil of slate-grey cloud. I run higher onto the ridge, away from the steep eastern crags, avoiding potential cornices. To the north-east, anthracite clouds hang above the plain at the end of the Cumbrian Mountains. At the base of the cloud, great swinging hooks hang and swirl menacingly. Beneath the darkness, I glimpse into another world; green fields, blue sky and splashes of sunshine are revealed through an open shutter.

High to my right is the saddle of Blencathra, hanging between Hall's Fell Top and Sharp Edge summit, somehow even whiter than the snow I trudge across. On my left, on the ridge path from Bannerdale summit, a lone runner, a red streak, edges close to the top of the crags. I find this reassuring – affirming, I am not the only person enjoying this fell in these conditions.

Close to the summit there a small cairn, with a slate on its edge, like a dorsal fin, pointing the way. Beyond the summit, I head just north of west down to the Glenderamackin col. Despite the deep snow, the path to my left is easy to spot.

Route to Bannerdale Crags through Mungrisdale

Crossing the giant slabs towards the River Glenderamackin

Path up to the depression between Bannerdale Crags and Bowscale Fell

The route to the summit of Bannerdale Crags

Residents of Bannerdale Crags summit

45 Bannerdale Crags

Within 800 metres of the summit, I reach the head of the Glenderamackin valley. If I go any further, I will start to climb out of the col and up Foule Crag towards Blencathra. ❸ Here I turn left (south-east) dropping down into a channel of blown snow. Patches of the gravelly path have been exposed, cleared by surface water. Normally this is an easy descent alongside the nascent River Glenderamackin around the base of White Horse Bent. ❹ In the heavy snow, however, much of the path is concealed, so I move slowly, tentatively.

The river flows in a double hairpin, south to the end of Bannerdale Crags, north between the east face of Bannerdale and the western slopes of Souther Fell, through Mungrisdale, and then south once more towards the A66. I am following the river all the way to Mungrisdale. Beyond the footbridge directly south of White Horse Bent, I too sweep north again, staying on the left bank. The snow recedes. This path is always wet; today, after weeks of rain, the path is a river. Squelching moss, gushing springs, shifting stones. A path being reshaped in real-time.

The banks of the river are being further undercut. The collapsing earth and shifting black-peat leave me floundering like an eel. I splash through Bannerdale Beck, wide and deep and flowing fast, before clambering down the bank to the edge of the river. The path has gone here, ravaged by the deluge precipitated by Storm Desmond. Through more bog and anaerobic mud, until I reach the footbridge at the base of The Tongue that I crossed an hour ago. Less than a kilometre now back to Mungrisdale, over the colossal tombstones.

Route around Bannerdale Crags to White Horse Bent

River Glenderamackin flowing towards Mungrisdale

River Glenderamackin, real-time erosion

Route back to Mungrisdale

Longside Edge from Bassenthwaite Lake

46 Longside Edge

Park / Start	Dodd Wood car park, A591 (NY 234 281)		
Map	OS Explorer OL4		
Exertion	●●●●		
Navigation	●●		
Terrain	●●		
Distance	8.25 kilometres	Time	1 hour 23 minutes
Ascent	710 metres	On road	0 metres

An invigorating ascent of Skiddaw's north-west ridge along the length of Bassenthwaite Lake

One of the tougher, shorter fell runs, and not one to do if you are wanting some speed work. The climb is good cardiovascular training though, and useful for strengthening both calfs and quads.

START From the Old Saw Mill tearoom, I take the footbridge north over Skill Beck then follow the yellow waymarkers for the Dodd Wood Sandbeds Gill trail.

The climbing begins straight away on a broad forest track. Soon the red, blue and green trails turn off to the right. The yellow route carries straight on. ❶ A path through a dense conifer and broadleaf plantation rises gently towards the footbridge over Sandbeds Gill and continues, subdued and sheltered, with views of Bassenthwaite Lake flashing through the precipitous tree trunks.

46 Longside Edge

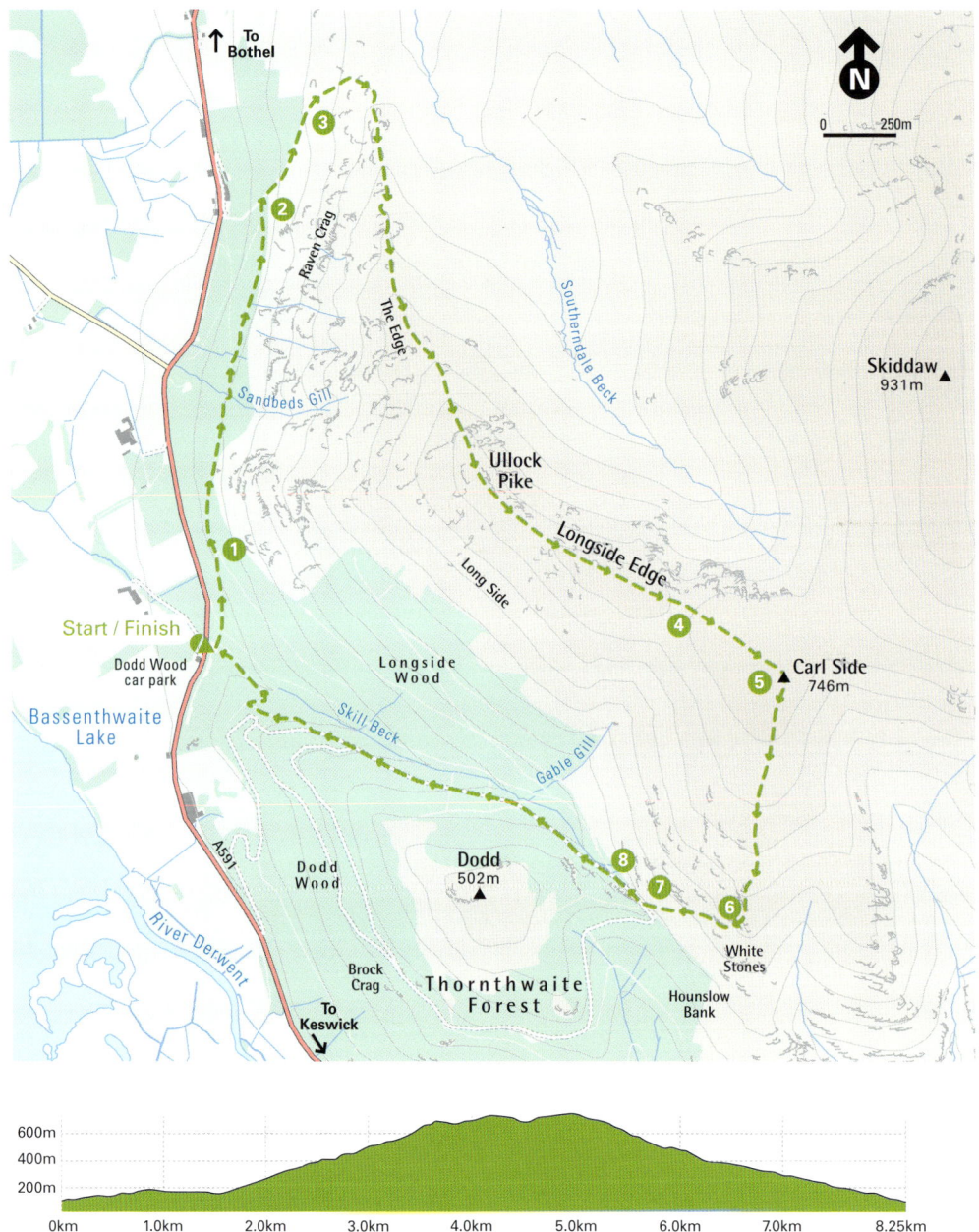

I keep high, following the yellow waymarkers for 1.5 kilometres, until the junction where the forest trail sweeps left and back to the car park. Here I go right, and keep right until I reach a wooden gate that leads through the fence out of the plantation onto the open fell. ❷

Running gets harder here, through the heather on a clear footpath. ❸ At the junction of the fence and wall, I take an obvious route that cuts across the fell. In minutes, I reach the path leading up The Edge from Barkbeth. I follow this to the right to begin the hardest section of the route. I am now on The Edge heading south with Bassenthwaite Lake on my right. Only now, on this exposed arête, is it apparent how cold the

Longside Edge 46

easterly wind is. I keep climbing steeply. It is not runnable for me here, it is tough going; I am breathing hard and my heart rate is high.

Once I reach the top of Ullock Pike, the most arduous ascent is behind me. I am on Longside Edge, buffeted by a biting head wind. It is minus 10 degrees Celsius and gusts of up to 65 kilometres per hour slow me down. I pull up my buff. The views are dramatic. On my left, I have a steep slope that falls away to Southerndale Beck, rising on the other side to the precipitous western face of Skiddaw. To my right the River Derwent flows into Bassenthwaite Lake, and a multitude of becks crisscross the flood plain between the lakes of Derwentwater and Bassenthwaite.

There is little water on the rocky edge but occasionally I crunch spicules of ice beneath my fell shoes and have to negotiate tracts of refrozen snow. I scramble over Long Side, the highest point of Longside Edge, without really noticing the summit. Dodd comes into view on my right and Skiddaw Little Man is straight ahead. I am nearing the end of my climb.

❹ I descend 50 metres to a small depression and take the grassy right-hand path (south-east) that takes me directly to the summit of Carl Side, an indistinct turfy mound. With five kilometres of climbing behind me, I now start to descend. After a couple of cairns, I pick up the wide, straight path heading south through a corridor of heather. ❺ It is a broad steep descent, upon which I make slow progress, held up by loose stones.

❻ At White Stones, a large and obvious craggy outcrop, I take the path to my right, which is tricky, rocky and unrunnable. In only a few minutes, though, I reach a wall and climb the stile that brings me onto a forest track. ❼ A sharp turn right and I can begin to run again.

Any descent north-west will bring me out at the car park. I decide to take the track that keeps Skill Beck on my right. ❽ Firstly, I follow the green and then the red forest trail signs back down to the tearoom. I can move freely now on cinder tracks all the way to the footbridge I crossed at the start.

Over Skill Beck towards Sandbeds Gill

Looking back on the trail from Sandbeds Gill

The steep climb to Ullock Pike

Looking down on Bassenthwaite Lake from Longside Edge

46 Longside Edge

Looking back at The Edge

47 Souther Fell

Souther Fell from Low Beckside Farm

Park / Start	Scales, Threlkeld (NY 343 269)		
Map	OS Explorer OL5		
Exertion	●●●		
Navigation	●●●		
Terrain	●		
Distance	9.1 kilometres	Time	1 hour 31 minutes
Ascent	559 metres	On road	1.2 kilometres

A peaceful fell, moated by the River Glenderamackin, giving uninterrupted views of the Pennines

Souther Fell is more famous for its phantom army than its challenge as a mountain. On Midsummer's Eve 1745 more than a score of witnesses testified on oath to what they had seen. Infantry, mounted troops and carriages traversed this tabletop summit.

START From the car park in Scales I take the road north-east, part of the Coast-to-Coast (C2C) cycle route (71), known locally as the *gated road*.

Six hundred metres of tarmac allows me to get into my stride and gives my breathing a chance to stabilize. It also allows me to contemplate the run ahead. An eye of a needle route, with a large eye, and a double peaked loop, like the back of a Mongolian camel.

47 Souther Fell

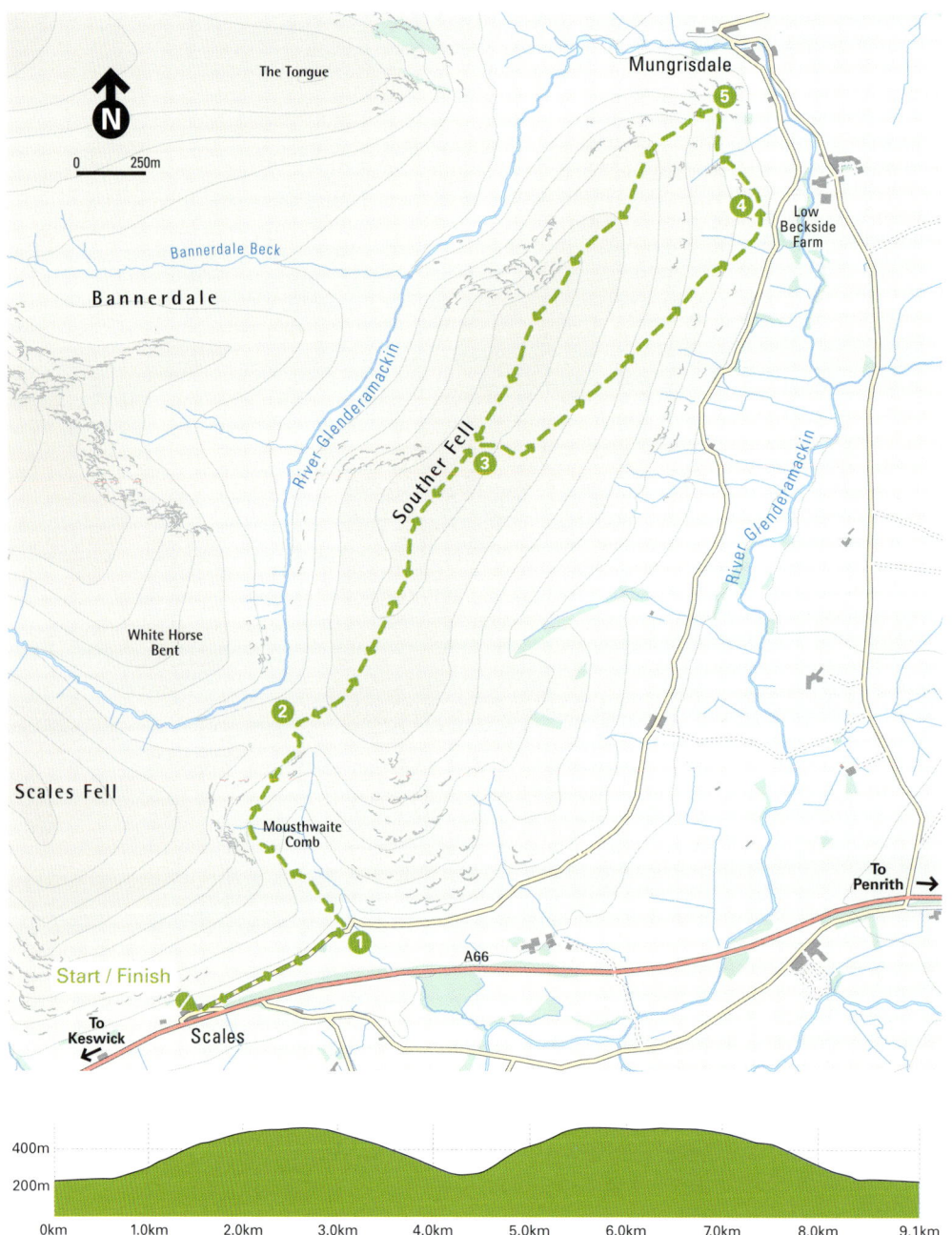

It is more than breezy, that much I learnt from my journey here. I could feel the car being buffeted by the wind. Now the sky darkens, suddenly, like a light being switched off. The rain, cold and nearly horizontal, is getting heavier.

❶ After 600 metres there is a fingerpost pointing to Blackhazel Beck 2¾ miles away, a strange location to warrant a sign. I turn left at the post, pass through the gate and my climb up to Mousthwaite Comb begins. Steep and relentless, a kilometre in length with 200 metres of ascent.

Souther Fell

Around a rocky buttress near the top of the col, I veer right as the slope eases. ❷ The wind smacks me head on, sweeping across Bannerdale Crags; it knocks me back. I was not expecting this. I brace myself and take the north-easterly path across a carpet of sodden moss. A brief respite before the climb up Souther begins.

At these heights, it is hailing. The frozen rain pits my face painfully, abrasively, like a sand blaster.

The wind, now battering my left side, evokes memories of physics lessons on vectors. How much force do I need to counter the hammering I am enduring on my left flank? Then the hail stops. A gentle limelight illuminates me from behind. Smudges of blue sky appear as the grizzly grey clouds race across from west to east.

Trudging upwards, north-east, towards the summit. The gale hinders my progress, flapping my Gore-Tex jacket and pushing my exhaled air back into my lungs. I stride across the kowtowing moor grass, my feet already soaked by the snowmelt; water that has filled the bogs and formed impromptu streams across the dull green carpet. Patches of pristine snow remain, knee-deep and melting, between floats of brown sludge.

I will leave the summit path soon. I check my GPS, I will turn off this path before the three kilometre point and skirt down the fellside towards Mungrisdale. ❸ I reach a soft hollow, take the path to the right, directly east, which soon sweeps north-east down the eastern flank of Souther.

Shielded from the wind, I have entered another country. Slipping on the strips of wet snow, skating on the smooth well-trampled grass as I descend. On a dry day, it is possible to stride out here, confidently, down the grassy slope.

Directly ahead, Low Beckside Farm comes into view. The gated road is beside me. I splash through the springs and I drag my shoes out of the mires until I reach a walled enclosure.

❹ I keep high of the wall rather than dropping down to the road, and after a few metres the climbing starts

Footpath to Mousthwaite Comb

The top of Mousthwaite Comb, Souther ahead

The top of Mousthwaite Comb and the path to Souther Fell

Running over Souther Fell

The east flank of Souther Fell towards Low Beckside Farm

47 Souther Fell

Dropping down the edge of Mousthwaite Comb back to Scales

again – the second hump of the camel. The path is a stream at first, but there is good contact with the cloying earth. ❺ As I begin to head west, I start to climb the north end of the fell and the path becomes unrunnable – for me.

I turn away from Mungrisdale and suddenly the wind is back. It clobbers me, head on, surprisingly strong. At times, in gusts, I cannot move forward. It is cold, too. I am losing the feeling in my toes and fingers.

I endure two kilometres of great struggle back to the top of Mousthwaite Comb. South-west, across the fell top, the path is clear but the wind howls like a hammer. I am blown towards the slope, away from the hang gliding site, in the direction of the oblique path I jogged down minutes earlier.

Keeping high of the fence to start the second ascent of Souther

It takes great effort to stay on my feet; I certainly didn't anticipate this. The bogs lure me in, saturated now that the snow has melted, and I repeatedly lose my footing. Inwardly laughing I fall, blown around like a straw dog. Eventually I reach the col above Mousthwaite Comb, a full circle of Souther Fell across its blustery summit. I drop down to my left over the edge of the comb. The wind has gone. I am numb with cold. I move warily around the rocks, then more easily through the stream that pours down the path.

I reach the road on tired legs, turn right and jog back to Scales. I can't feel my feet; I am running on senseless stumps.

A surprisingly arduous nine kilometres over a gentle fell, quite an adventure in these conditions.

Blencathra | 48

The Blencathra saddle from Scales Fell

48 Blencathra

Park / Start	Car park, Blease Road, Threlkeld (NY 318 256)		
Map	OS Explorer OL5		
Exertion	●●●●●		
Navigation	●●		
Terrain	●		
Distance	11 kilometres	**Time**	1 hour 38 minutes
Ascent	783 metres	**On road**	0 metres

A majestic mountain with a broad sweeping racecourse ridge of gentle descent

According to Alfred Wainwright, Blencathra is one of the grandest objects in the English Lake District, a mountaineers' mountain, a mountain that demands attention.

A runnable mountain, and a compelling mountain, the Blencathra Massif is more of a small range of fells rather than a single top, with three steep spurs, Gategill Fell, Hall's Fell and Doddick Fell, leading sharply up the southern face.

START I take the path leading north out of the car park alongside Blease Gill, cross the footbridge at the waterfall and climb the steps beside the wall, leading up to the open fell. After 500 metres, I go

Blencathra

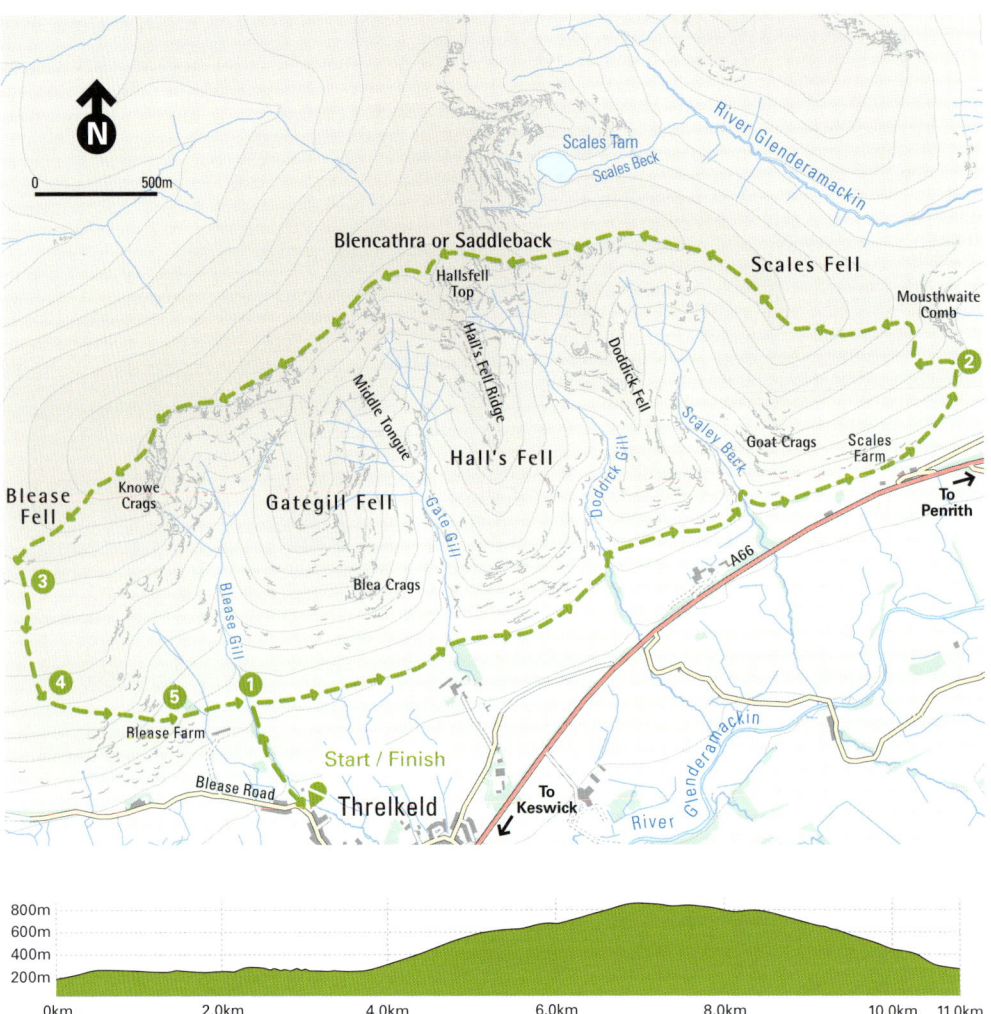

through a five-barred gate and turn right to pass through another gate into a walled enclosure. ❶ A slate sign by the gate points to Gate Ghyll.

The path clings to the wall all the way to Scales Fell, traversing three ravines, each carrying water down to the River Glenderamackin. About 1.2 kilometres into the run, I climb a stone stile and pass through a gate perched on the top of the wall. Two hundred metres further on I cross Gate Gill at the old lead mine. Down the beck, at the kennels, the Blencathra hounds are barking. Over Doddick Gill, I climb left up the bank then veer right to follow the wall east again. At Scaley Beck, I take care down the polished rocky outcrop, using my hands to ease myself into the ravine. I climb up the other side and within 800 metres of the ravine, I reach the stile leading down to the White Horse Bunkhouse in Scales. ❷ It is possible to turn left here and go straight up the fellside but this is an unrelenting, lactate-inducing climb, so I elect to follow the path and ascend Scales Fell from the east. The route is obvious with the path doubling back west before the climbing begins in earnest. I focus on the changing vegetation; damp bracken gives way to bilberry shrubs, which are replaced by hard mountain matgrass.

Blencathra

The tough climb up Scales Fell

Soon I reach the path leading up from Mousthwaite Comb, a well-worn hiker's freeway. Through the swirling mist, I am welcomed by views of Scaley Beck to my left and Scales Tarn to my right. Once I am at the top of Doddick Fell, the ridge stretches away before me. I still have a kilometre to Hallsfell Top, the highest point on Blencathra, but I am running more freely now, pushing hard up the final zigzags to get to the summit.

Blease Road car park, the route to Blease Gill

At Hallsfell Top my work is done; at the unusual concrete-ring trig point, I turn right to head west over the undulating ridge, gradually descending. I can coast along the fell chain with rugged cliffs and buttresses above Threlkeld to the south, and the soft rolling moorland of Mungrisdale Common to the north. Kilometres of soft ground and broad shaley paths allow me to run with childlike abandon towards Blease Fell.

Looking back on Mousthwaite Comb on the route up to Blencathra

Soon I am descending abruptly, freewheeling, snaking back and forth down a stony path. Once I am beyond Knowe Crags, 2.5 kilometres from Hallsfell Top, I reach a path junction marked by a pile of stones. ❸ Here I take the left branch heading directly south down a grassy slope. Steep to begin, my quads now take a pounding as I brake, wary of the smooth surface. ❹ Then, 500 metres down from the pile of stones, I meet another path junction where I again turn left, proceeding east back to Threlkeld.

Blencathra

At the top of Doddick Fell, approaching the zigzags

The descent is gentler now; I pick up the pace and follow the path down to the south side of a walled enclosure ahead. ❺ Through the gate behind Blease Farm, I run along a corridor enclosed by two drystone walls. This takes me back to Blease Gill. I cross the gill and turn right towards the gate I passed through 90 minutes earlier. Now I retrace my route down the steps beside the waterfall, back to the car park.

The ring trig point on Hallsfell Top, the highest point on Blencathra

Running across the entire ridge, either from Scales Fell in the east or from Blease Fell in the west is a tough run, but one that can't be replicated on any of the other big Lakeland mountains.

Glenderaterra Valley

Looking down the Glenderaterra valley towards Great Calva

49 Glenderaterra Valley

Park / Start	Blencathra Field Studies Centre, Threlkeld (NY 302 256)		
Map	OS Explorer OL4		
Exertion	●●		
Navigation	●		
Terrain	●●		
Distance	9.8 kilometres	**Time**	1 hour 10 minutes
Ascent	448 metres	**On road**	200 metres

An entry-level trip along a secluded valley to the Back O'Skiddaw

A runnable, undulating loop, as hard as you want to make it. Heather, fern, fountains, falls, fords, mountains and valleys made vast by their proximity. And a run worth doing for the ancient Brittonic name of the valley.

START I leave the Blencathra Field Studies Centre behind. Climbing gently, the rocks soon give way to gravel. The beck meanders, unseeing, through the V-shaped valley bottom. Ghosts of the mineworkers, heaving and hewing, stooped and beaten by the wind and the rain, lugging at their lode, ignore me too. On a wide track high above the Glenderaterra Beck, a vision from the *Misty Mountains*, high above the old Brundholme lead mine on a winter's afternoon, I am heading north.

49 Glenderaterra Valley

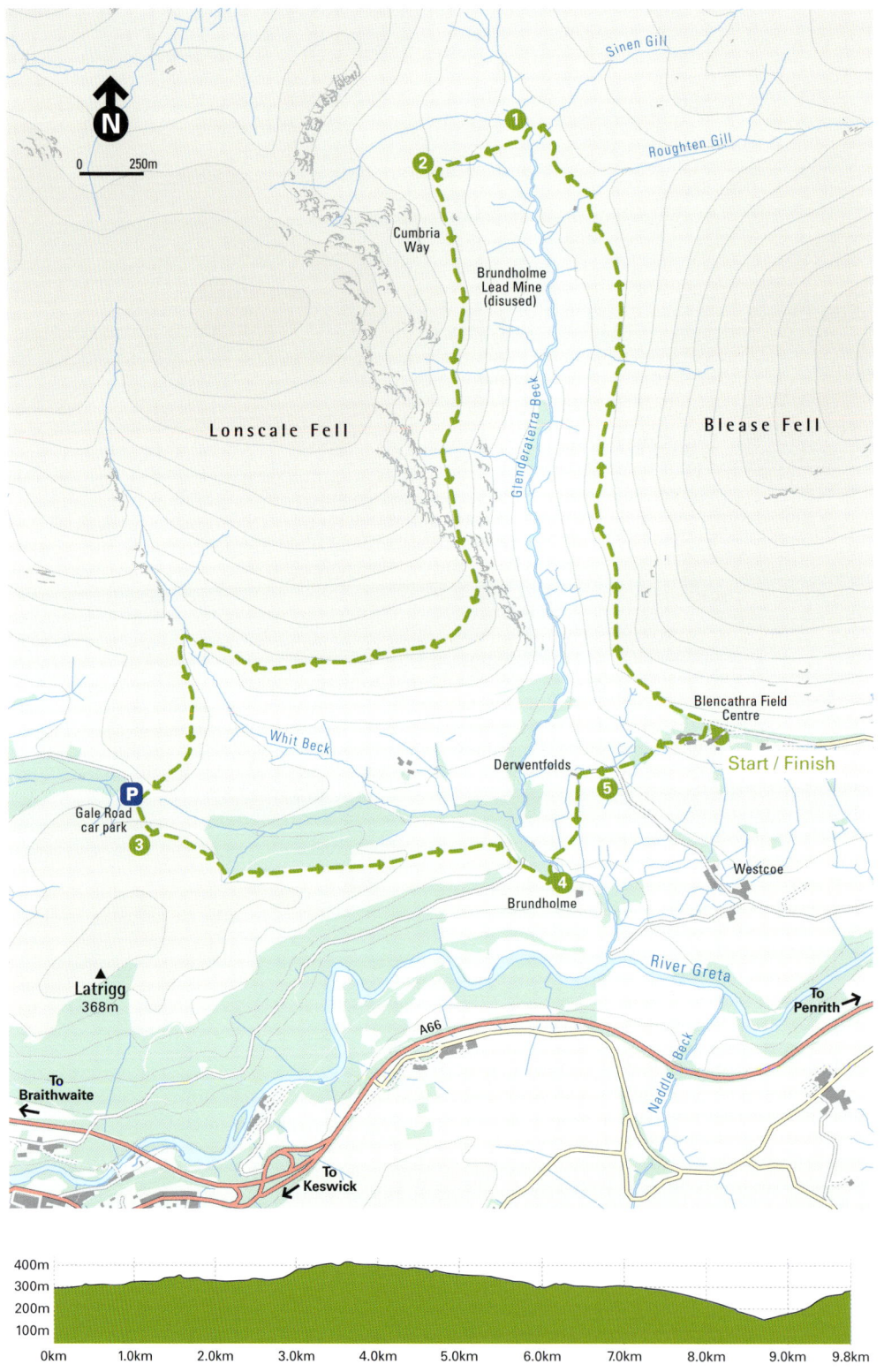

Glenderaterra Valley

Soon I hear the first mountain cascade crashing down Blencathra's western buttress and smell the scents of the wet fells and mosses diffusing through the fine aerosol that fills the perfect valley.

On some days, I've seen the mist swirling low along the valley floor, poking into the gullies and creeping over the spurs on the flanks of Blease and Lonscale fells. I've run this loop through deep snow and on summer's afternoons when the sky forms a bleached blue ceiling between the fern green walls. Today the clouds above the valley skate past, blown by the stiff westerly breeze. Across the ford at Roughten Gill at an easy pace, cutting over the corner by the hidden sheep fold, I have two wooden footbridges to cross, one over Sinen Gill and the other over Glenderaterra Beck itself, before reaching the gate that marks the head of the valley. ❶ Eighteen minutes for the 2.5 kilometres from the car park is conversational pace. ❷ A few metres through the gate I take the left fork and follow a grassy, boggy path to the Cumbria Way. Left along the Cumbria Way, the path is a stream here and stony, on an upward journey to the highest part of the run at 415 metres, 200 metres above the beck.

High above the valley the view is strangely soothing. A stream snaking across a green carpet, white water crashing down a grey-green, sheep-nibbled fell, the white snow-capped wall of the Helvellyn range ahead. Rocky outcrops tell me I will soon be out of the valley. The path arcs west, revealing glimpses of Keswick and Derwent Water lit by shafts of light piercing the graphite-grey shroud. Through the gate, down the slope to Whit Beck. Splash through the swollen water, I don't look for stepping stones. My wet feet, instantly cold, soon warm as I climb gently out of the ravine towards the tourist path up to Skiddaw.

I travel south veering south-west to Gale Road car park, then left along the public way to Brundholme (1¼ miles). ❸ Soon, a fast descent east down the soft pastures of Latrigg, and I cut right across the

The start of the path around the Glenderaterra valley

Running above the Glenderaterra Beck

The Cumbria Way, crossing the eastern side of Lonscale Fell

The Cumbria Way, leaving the Glenderaterra valley

The turn-off to Derwent Folds and the Blencathra Centre

49 Glenderaterra Valley

Over the footbridge, following the beck to Derwent Folds

fell down to the stile leading to Brundholme Road. Over the stile, left down a short, fast road section to Brundholme, being careful not to miss the turn-off.
❹ A fingerpost points to my left (Derwent Folds and Blencathra), down to the footbridge over the beck, then up to Derwent Folds.
I run alongside the beck. The beck talks, babbling onwards towards the River Greta. Once I get to the farm at Derwent Folds I can see the woods surrounding the Blencathra Centre. I turn right along the road and then, after a hundred and fifty metres, left over a stile (Blencathra Centre ¼ mile). ❺ From here I follow the yellow arrows to the centre, up the steps, first wooden then stone, cutting through the buildings to the footpath that brings me back to the car park.

Derwent Folds, beneath the Blencathra Centre

The path through the Blencathra Centre

Latrigg 50

Latrigg across Derwentwater

50 Latrigg

Park / Start	Entrance to Spooney Green Lane, Briar Rigg, Keswick (NY 267 241)
Map	OS Explorer OL4
Exertion	●●
Navigation	●●
Terrain	●
Distance	8.8 kilometres
Time	57 minutes
Ascent	381 metres
On road	0 metres

An entry-level route with dazzling views of Keswick and Borrowdale

Spooney Green Lane, a busy route on a sunny day. Hard to believe that less than 140 years ago this was the site of one of the largest mass-trespass protests on these shores.

START The fingerpost at the start of the lane points to Skiddaw (4 miles) and straight away I begin to climb. For such a small fell, the rise is quite arduous, mainly because it is runnable, even for me.

After 370 metres, at Spooney Green House, I reach the first gate and a slate sign on the ground confirms the route. The gradient steepens up a wide path, a section of the Cumbria Way.

The first path junction signals a respite; the steepest section is behind me. By huge stone gateposts, a legacy from when the landowners closed this old lane to the public, I head left and try to increase my pace. The path twists over becks and through a kissing gate then climbs north-east with expansive views across

50 Latrigg

the flood plain between Derwentwater and Bassenthwaite Lake.

After 1.7 kilometres, I leave the main Skiddaw track. A fingerpost points to Latrigg Summit (¾ mile) and I turn sharp right onto what the locals call the zigzag path. ❶ This fell belongs to Keswick. It is a hill upon which to walk the dog in the evening and a quick up-and-down lunchtime run from the centre of town. This snaking route means the kilometre up to bench beneath the summit is a runnable incline, even on a tempestuous winter's afternoon with a brutal westerly wind with which to do battle.

At the bench, I sweep left up a broad fairway towards the bumpy summit ridge. Keswick, to my right, nestles snugly in the valley, like a model village. Derwentwater stretches southwards towards Borrowdale, like a model lake. This land can be harsh; the rain and wind are never far away, but it is real, barely tamed and still shaped by natural forces.

Just 300 metres east of the bench is the highest grassy hillock; I know that one natural force will soon be my ally. I chase down a gently rolling path that flows off the summit, letting gravity help me.

An unfettered mile down a gradient gradual enough to run pell-mell, I am on soft pasture; my arms are flailing like windmill blades. I can't explain how good it feels to be running as fast as I can through the chilled air, running for the sheer joy of it; like a dog chasing a stick, like a horse galloping across a paddock, like spring lambs romping through a pasture.

Beyond the first gate, I stay close to the edge of the east ridge, delaying the descent to the track on my left until I see the next gate at the fence corner. Through the gate, I run flat-out, keeping to the grass on the right of the path, deluding myself that I am travelling fast.

As the track veers slightly left, I run across the fellside edging right towards the fence. This brings me to a gate and a step-stile. ❷ I turn almost 180 degrees to my right and climb the stile so that I am now running west on a permissive path through Brundholme Wood. A deciduous wood of oak, ash and sycamore, leaves of intense lime-green, flush with springtime chlorophyll, undulating along the southern flank of Latrigg – a route these days little used. Vivid lemon gorse flowers blanket the borders of a path that soon leads into a working conifer plantation.

After 5.5 kilometres I reach a gate that I can skirt around through a broken fence. Five hundred metres beyond this I cross a beck and I reach the conifer stand. ❸ Here the permissive path has been concealed by a forest track but 700 metres beyond the gate, I pick the contour route up again on my right.

Forests are shapeshifters and can be confusing but within this small woodland, it is hard to get lost. If I keep running west, any path I take will lead me to Spooney Green Lane and here I will turn left. If I head too far south I will reach Brundholme Road, the back route to Keswick.

Onwards through the woodland via a tract of freshly felled spruce, rich resins and camphors pervade the afternoon breeze as I follow the rollercoaster path. I ignore turn-offs to my left, keeping high until I reach the monolithic gateposts I ran past on my way up to the summit. ❹ I turn left and head back down Spooney Green Lane to Briar Rigg.

Spooney Green Lane, heading towards Latrigg

Route to Latrigg, left at the path junction

On the zigzag path to the top of Latrigg

View across Keswick and Derwentwater from Latrigg summit

Turn left at the gateposts back to Keswick

50 Latrigg

A fast descent off Latrigg

The North Western Fells

The North Western Fells contain some of the Lakelands most distinctive peaks, many of which are steep-sided with runnable ridges. Bordered by lakes that are often in view, they rise from some of the region's best-known villages. Across all of these runs, rocky terrain is rare and most offer long, marvellously grassy descents.

Rowling End (Causey Pike and Scar Crags route)

Descending Sale Fell

Sale Fell and Ling Fell 51

Sale Fell from Ling Fell

51 Sale Fell and Ling Fell

Park / Start	Brumston Bridge, Wythop Mill (NY 185 293)
Map	OS Explorer OL4
Exertion	●●
Navigation	●●●
Terrain	●
Distance	7.9 kilometres
Time	59 minutes
Ascent	437 metres
On road	1.7 kilometres

A figure of eight loop through heather and gorse on beautiful, soft pasture

At Brumston Bridge, a single arch bridge over Wythop Beck, I'm in a valley between Sale Fell and Ling Fell. This is a figure of eight loop with a number of options: clockwise or anticlockwise, Ling Fell first or Sale Fell first. This is splendid running country. Gentle rolling moors on wide dry paths of short clipped grass. Many sections can be run at a canter – some at an all-out sprint.

I decide on Sale Fell to begin with, heading through Chapel Wood first and up the eastern slope to the summit. **START** East on the road towards Kelswick Farm following Wythop Beck, running into an easterly wind, which is not really strong enough to account for my slow pace.

51 Sale Fell and Ling Fell

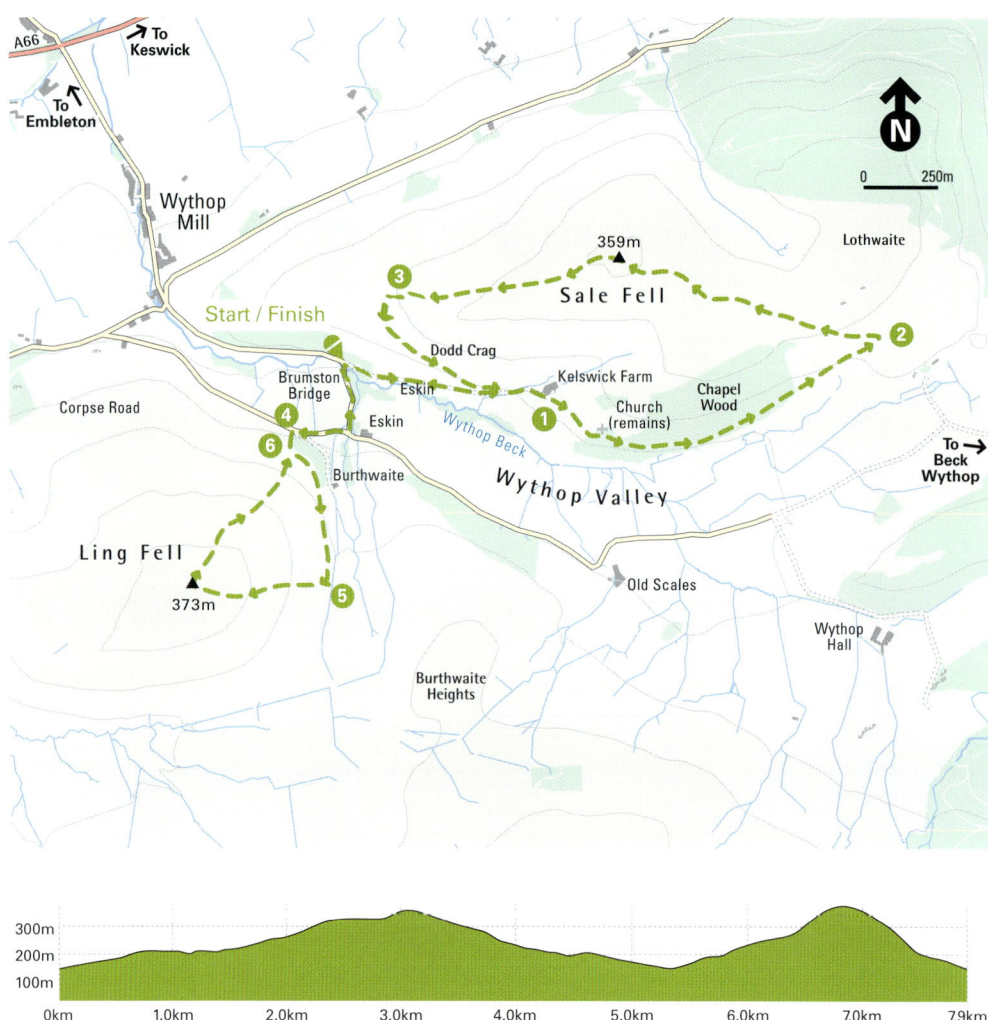

At Kelswick, there is a route up the fell, which I ignore. Instead, I take the bridleway through the gate following the fingerpost pointing the way to Beck Wythop (2 miles). ❶ The bridleway is a glorious track, which allows some faster running, especially when it is dry. Today the going is heavy. Greasy mud clings to my shoes, clogging my lugs and lessening my grip.

The old ruined Wythop Church is in a gloomy place. Apparently used as a chapel of ease for coffins, a temporary resting place for corpses before they were taken to the mother church. Immediately beyond the chapel I enter through a tall wooden gate into Chapel Wood, half a kilometre on flat ground beneath ancient oaks, I've hardly done any climbing yet.

Out of the wood, through another tall gate, I keep an eye out for my route up the fell. Three hundred and forty metres from the gate. ❷ If I go beyond a wall that cuts in on my right, I know I have gone too far. The path I take on my left is at an acute angle, taking me west-northwest directly to the top of the fell. One kilometre to the summit. To begin with, I cut through encroaching stunted gorse bushes before reaching a broad racecourse of a path, a golf-fairway up a steady slope all the way to the crest of the moor.

Sale Fell and Ling Fell 51

The route up Sale Fell from the Beck Wythop bridleway

I don't hang around on the top. The easterly wind brings in icy air. Anvil clouds loiter ominously over Longside Edge on the far side of Bassenthwaite Lake. I continue west on an earth and grass descent it's possible to charge down. I head for the wall. There are several routes off; it doesn't really matter which I take as long as I turn left when I get to the wall.

❸ On reaching the wall, I pick up the path heading left beneath Dodd Crag, which takes me back to the road to Kelswick Farm. Once on the road a right turn and half a kilometre of downhill running returns me to Brumston Bridge. My first loop is over.

Over the bridge, I run up the hill towards Eskin. At the top of the rise, I turn right and immediately see the metal gate that opens onto the Corpse Road. ❹ Through the gate, I decide to take a clockwise loop over Ling Fell so I turn directly left running alongside the short wooded section above Burthwaite.

Bridleway at Kelswick Farm to the old chapel

The remains of the Wythop Old Church

There are several paths off to my left up the fellside. I continue on the track until I reach a fence cutting in on my left and a small gate with a *no path* sign. ❺ Then it's straight up the fell, due west, through clumps of stunted heather. This is the steepest climb of my run, just 490 metres of distance to the trig point but with 120 metres of ascent.

51 Sale Fell and Ling Fell

The trig point on Ling Fell

Sleet then hail on my back with the wind behind me. I am warm enough though as I struggle towards the summit. As the slope eases and the trig point comes into view, there's a break in the clouds and the fell is flooded with light from a weak February sun. Once again, the natural elements combine to produce a spectacular display. A vivid rainbow arcs across my field of view from the village of Embleton on my left to the Wythop Valley on my right.

Over the summit, I take the north-easterly path down the soft yielding grass towards the Corpse Road. Braver runners than me will career out of control down here. On the steeper sections, I find myself braking, wary of the gradient and a lack of grip. ❻ The gate is in sight. A few final jumps down peaty steps.

At the road, I retrace my steps back to Brumston Bridge.

Sale Fell from the Ling Fell Corpse Road

52 Graystones, Broom Fell and Lord's Seat

Lord's Seat from Kelswick

Park / Start	Spout Force car park, Whinlatter Pass (NY 181 255)		
Map	OS Explorer OL4		
Exertion	•••		
Navigation	•••		
Terrain	•		
Distance	8 kilometres	Time	1 hour 10 minutes
Ascent	494 metres	On road	0 metres

A loop across rolling moors sweeping back through coniferous forests and needle-sprinkled trails

Three Wainwright's in the hour is the goal.

START There is space to park at the Forestry Commission's Spout Force car park close to Scawgill Bridge. I park at the entrance, metres away from the signpost to Spout Force (½ mile). I start my watch and head down to the ravine. ❶ Over the stile, down the steps and across the footbridge where I turn left beside Aiken Beck; I'm bracing myself for the climb. ❷ After 170 metres, I reach a gate and turn right to plant my feet on the scree still bleeding from the old quarry.

52 Graystones, Broom Fell and Lord's Seat

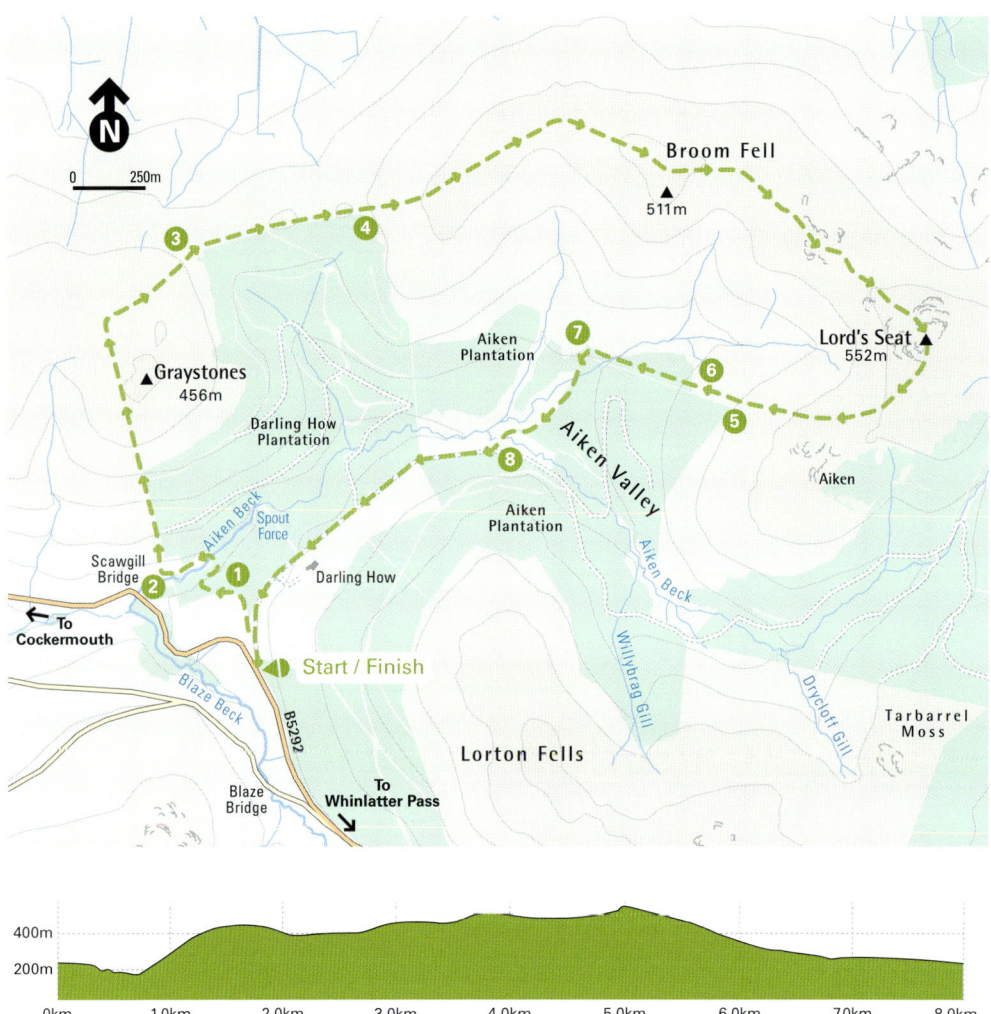

There can't be a more direct way to ascend a fell. Straight up the wall at the edge of the plantation, I keep to the left of the wall all the way to the top on a clear, well-used path. It is rocky at the start, with the residues of the stones that were apparently used to build the bridge over the beck, but these are the only rocks I will see on these grassy fells.

For 500 metres, I have my head down. With my quads pushing like clapped-out pistons, I rise 230 metres before the gradient finally eases. Now I can start running again, now I can lift my head and look around at the sun-warmed fells.

No one seems to be sure where the highest point of Graystones is. I plump for Wainwright's preference, a bump a few metres west of the wall marked with a small pile of stones. From here, the profiles of Skiddaw and Blencathra dominate the skyline to the west and the Grasmoor Massif stands prominent to the south. The most eye-catching view, though, is the broad sweep of the Scottish coast to the north, with the distinctive outline of Criffel beneath a cloudless sky.

I run east across the broken wall and take the obvious path north-east to the stile at the apex of the fence.

Graystones, Broom Fell and Lord's Seat

3 In the corner there is a strange enclosure that I climb in and out of before following the fence (and wall) east.

4 At the end of the plantation, I pass through the gate and follow a well-trodden path to the top of Broom Fell. A couple of steep slopes, just about runnable, with 500 metres of flattish moorland in the middle. A fell I love to run, unrestrained by scree or boulders.

On a clear day the imposing two metre column on the summit of Broom Fell can be seen a long way off. In the mist, I would keep to the clear path, just north of west, resisting any temptation to veer right down into the Aiken Valley.

Once beyond the column I cross the stile and continue on a well-defined path, first east then south-east. Down a grassy slope that becomes increasingly boggy as I reach the low point between the fells. From here, it is a runnable 80 metres of ascent to the top of Lord's Seat, where a rusty iron fence post marks the finish of the climb.

Fifty minutes to this point means that I will not achieve my target. I know that from here, the going will be swampy in parts and there is more than one beck to cross. I avoid the gravel trail south over the fence that leads down to Whinlatter Forest Visitor Centre. Instead, I take the grassy, westerly route that follows the wall for a while before dropping down towards the Aiken Plantation in the valley below. The path leads down to another fence, which I follow to a stile. **5** Ahead, across to another stile, the darkness of the forest awaits. **6** The path cuts through a dank fir-tree corridor following a bryophyte-swathed wall.

From here, bog and water dominate. I cross a beck and squelch west until I reach the wall I crossed on the top of Broom Fell. **7** Here the wall is broken. I turn left (south), climb clumsily over a couple of fallen trees, cross back over the beck and then wade through Aiken Beck before emerging onto a forest track. **8** Turning right I have an easy kilometre, mainly downhill running. On heavy legs I try to pick up the pace past Darling How, back to my car.

The direct route up Graystones, alongside the wall

The summit of Graystones, to the west of the wall

Broom Fell summit looking towards Lord's Seat

Fence posts on Lord's Seat summit

Over the stile to Aiken Plantation

52 Graystones, Broom Fell and Lord's Seat

Graystones from Whinlatter Pass

53 Whinlatter Top and Brown How

The Gruffalo, Whinlatter Forest Park

53 Whinlatter Top and Brown How

Park / Start	Visitor Centre, Whinlatter Forest Park, Honister Pass (NY 208 244)		
Map	OS Explorer OL4		
Exertion	•••		
Navigation	•••		
Terrain	•		
Distance	8.7 kilometres	Time	1 hour 12 minutes
Ascent	363 metres	On road	0 metres

Open fell and winding forest trails with an exhilarating descent

On windy wet days, I head for the shelter of the forest. This low-level fell barely pokes its head out above the trees but the views are spectacular and the woods atmospheric. In the winter beneath the firs, with snow on the ground, these wooded mountains exude a Scandinavian ambience.

Be wary of forests though, paths can change like Hogwarts' staircases and felled plantations change the aspect and play tricks with your memory.

START From behind the visitor centre, the walking trails start. The easiest way to navigate out of the forest is to follow the green trail for 560 metres. I go through a clearing with a viewpoint with some big benches and then follow the path up through a dense stand of spruce.

53 Whinlatter Top and Brown How

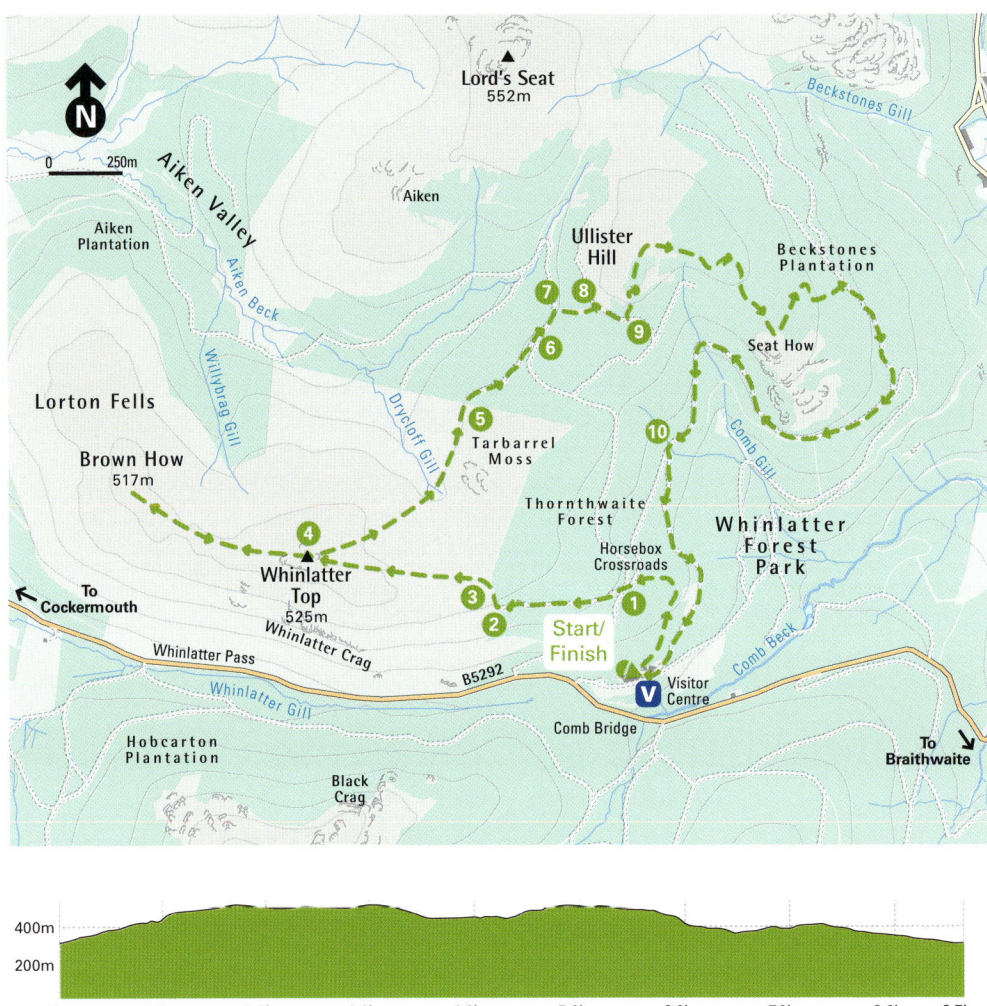

This brings me out at Horsebox Crossroads, a wide area where four forest tracks meet. ❶ I head directly across in a westerly direction, climbing on a broad track beneath the trees, which comes to an abrupt halt at a turning circle at the edge of the plantation. There is a gate in front of me giving access to the open fell. ❷ Immediately through the gate, I turn right and follow the fence up the rise. ❸ After 140 metres a path on my left leads west, away from the fence, and I head up the gentle slope through the flattened hibernating heather. I reach Whinlatter Top, the highest point of the fell, in 19 minutes and stop briefly to admire the panorama. From this minor summit, the views are surprisingly impressive. I am overlooked by the snow-topped peaks of Skiddaw, Clough Head and Great Dodd and, across from the forest I have just run through, a fair stretch of Derwentwater is visible in the valley below. Directly south, less than two kilometres away across Whinlatter Pass, Grisedale Pike and Hopegill Head, white and pristine, glare down at me.

I continue west towards Brown How, soon to pass over a broken wall before veering west-northwest across runnable terrain, traversing the occasional boggy moss. In Wainwright's day, the Ordnance Survey map

Whinlatter Top and Brown How

marked Brown How as the highest bump on the fell and this detour is an enjoyable 1.2 kilometre dogleg across soft grassy moorland.

I reach the wind shelter on Brown How in a few minutes, then retrace my steps to Whinlatter Top. A few metres east of the summit cairn the path divides. ❹ On my right is the path I came up from the forest; I take the left-hand branch which heads north-east in the direction of Lord's Seat. Down to a marshy hollow and the point where Drycloff Gill emerges, across saturated vibrant green sphagnum moss, then as the path rises up the drier bank, I contour around a grassy knoll on a clear path heading just east of north.

Ahead is the forest fence with a stile that takes me back into the subdued woodland. ❺ The minor path winds its way beneath the trees and 300 metres on from the stile I reach a wide forest road where I turn left. ❻

For a while, I have to pay more attention to my route. In 100 metres, when I see a clear track on my right, I turn to ascend through the trees. ❼ I climb towards Ullister Hill, the trail peters out into a path but in less than 200 metres, I once again reach a good forest track. ❽ This time I turn right and in another 100 metres, there is a path on my left leading up to the top of Ullister Hill and Seat How.

Navigation is easier from here. At the path junction there is wooden post, pointing downhill, marked 'Seat How Summit Trail'. I ignore this and instead I take a sharp left turn climbing into a wooded area along a well-maintained trail. ❾ This route skirts the top of Ullister Hill and within a kilometre reaches the rocky view point of Seat How. On a clear day, it is worth breaking your run here to survey the peaceful aspect of Derwentwater and its surrounding hills.

Back on the path, a twisting 500 metres descent brings me to another forest road where a right turn will take me back to the visitor centre. I make sure I keep right for the next 1.6 kilometres, ignoring any tracks or paths on my left. There are a couple of rises before a fast

The visitor centre, Whinlatter Forest Park

The gate to the open fell and Whinlatter Top

The path from Whinlatter Top to Brown How

Trail through the woods to Seat How

53 Whinlatter Top and Brown How

The view of Grisedale Pike from Whinlatter Top summit

decent begins around the hairpin at Comb Gill. Just beyond here, a wooden post points to a multitude of forest trails. ❿ I ignore the uphill track on my right; instead, I follow the arrow to the visitor centre.

I clatter downhill, past the finish line of the Whinlatter Forest parkrun, and within minutes, I reach the bike hire shop. I turn right at the barrier and soon I am back in front of the visitor centre.

Follow the arrow down to the visitor centre

Whiteside   54

Whiteside beneath the cloud, from Crummock Water

54 Whiteside

Park / Start	Parking area on the gated road between Hopebeck and High Swinside, Lorton (NY 168 241)
Map	OS Explorer OL4
Exertion	● ● ● ● ●
Navigation	● ●
Terrain	● ● ● ● ●
Distance	8.3 kilometres
Time	1 hour 22 minutes
Ascent	622 metres
On road	0 metres

A tough, rocky clamber with a grassy, heather-clad descent

Many circular fell runs can be completed in either direction. This one, however, is definitely one to run anticlockwise. Ascending the south-west spur over the summit of Whin Ben is definitely a better option than attempting to come down it.

START From the parking area, I climb the bank by the wall and cross Hope Beck at the ruined sheepfold. ❶ I now follow the path alongside the wall, south-west, contouring above the Vale of Lorton. Springs abound, flooding the start of this route but soon the path becomes a dry, undulating gambol all the way to Liza Beck.

I have no route choices, I merely follow the wall, I lose track of distance and time. Low Fell stretches out across the valley to my right, the knuckles of the Lorton Fells line up in front of me: Mellbreak, Hen Comb,

54 Whiteside

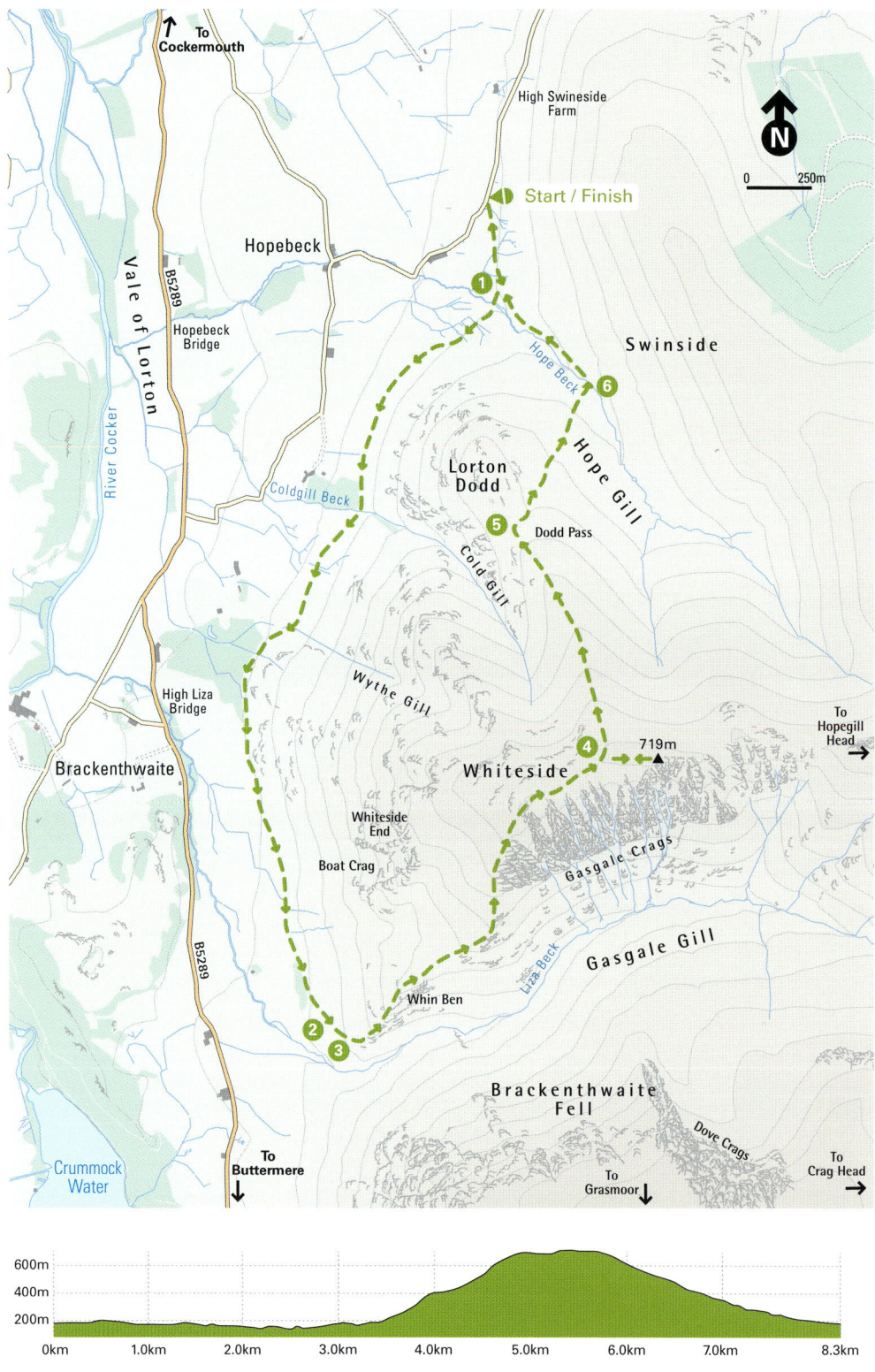

Whiteside

Gavel Fell, Blake Fell and Burnbank Fell. I am surrounded by the sound of bird song and, never far away, the burble of running water.

Almost four kilometres into my run I reach Liza Beck, at which point my relatively effortless canter is about to reach an abrupt conclusion. ❷ As soon as I see the footbridge over the beck, I begin to climb the path on my left that will take me up to Whiteside summit. ❸ After 200 metres the path divides, I know I have to keep ascending so I take the left-hand branch rather than the track up Gasgale Gill.

Steep through the heather, a smooth path to start with, becomes increasingly rocky, not hazardous, though, on the way up. Five hundred metres of distance travelled, 200 metres of ascent; the pace of a snail, but with the effort of a set of 400-metre intervals. I encounter a few scrambly sections, where I have to use my hands, and a rocky step just before the top of Whin Ben. This underscores the wisdom of tackling this loop in an anticlockwise direction.

Beyond here, the going gets less arduous, the gradient eases slightly and there are a few flatter sections. I can recover enough to glance at the valley below, glimpses of glass-flat Crummock Water attended by a restful Mellbreak. Then, suddenly, I reach the top of the ridge. On a clear rocky path, I reach the summit cairn at the western end of the ridge. I know I am not yet at the highest point, so I continue onwards on a track that becomes increasingly grassy, traversing the spine with Hopegill Head directly ahead.

I run past the path on my left where I will soon descend; from this point, I continue for 150 metres to the unassuming pinnacle. The Hopegill valley and the Solway plain look a long way down, Grasmoor and Crag Hill dominate from the south, Hopegill Head is now just a kilometre east along the arête. I am alone apart from a solitary buzzard that seems to be following me on my journey.

From the highest point, I turn to retrace my steps, 150 metres, and the path is obvious on my right, heading

The start of the Whiteside run, Lorton Dodd ahead

Whiteside, from the path below Whiteside End

Liza Beck and Gasgale Gill

The route up Whin Ben, Whiteside

Melbreak and Crummock Water from Whin Ben

Whiteside

The route down to Hope Beck from Lorton Dodd

down (northwards) towards Lorton Dodd. ❹ I begin to descend. The route is a steep but grassy and heathery slope, the kind I would have bounded down in my youth. ❺ A kilometre down to Dodd Pass, a distinct col filled with scree, where I turn right and continue my descent towards Hope Gill.

There are a number of paths traversing the fellside but I continue in a direct line running north-east towards Hope Beck resisting any temptation to climb. The slope begins to ease, the path becomes fainter but I head straight down to the beck and cross it at the point where the path down from Hopegill Head is at its closest. ❻

Rising up the bank, I turn left and follow the clear path back to the collapsed sheepfold where I first crossed Hope Beck over an hour ago. I now retrace my route, 400 metres to my right across boggy ground back to the parking area.

The col between Whiteside and Lorton Dodd

Barrow and Outerside   55

Barrow and Outerside from Latrigg

55 Barrow and Outerside

Park / Start	Braithwaite Village (NY 231 236)		
Map	OS Explorer OL4		
Exertion	●●●		
Navigation	●●		
Terrain	●		
Distance	7.3 kilometres	Time	1 hour 14 minutes
Ascent	599 metres	On road	400 metres

A grassy fairway to the brink of Force Crag and Coledale

Not surprisingly, Braithwaite Village, just a few minutes from Keswick and surrounded by a host of iconic Lakeland fells, is busy during peak holiday periods. In the summer, I arrive early in the morning or late in the afternoon to be sure of a place to park.

START I start my watch at the Royal Oak and run south along the Newlands Valley road. Once over the bridge above Coledale Beck it is just 100 metres to a driveway on the right, to Braithwaite Lodge Farm. ❶ This is the bridleway signposted to Newlands Valley.

Several slate signs at the farm make it clear that the path is to the right of the farmhouse through a metal field gate. I pass through the gate and cross the path to a wooden gate that leads onto the open fell. ❷

251

55 Barrow and Outerside

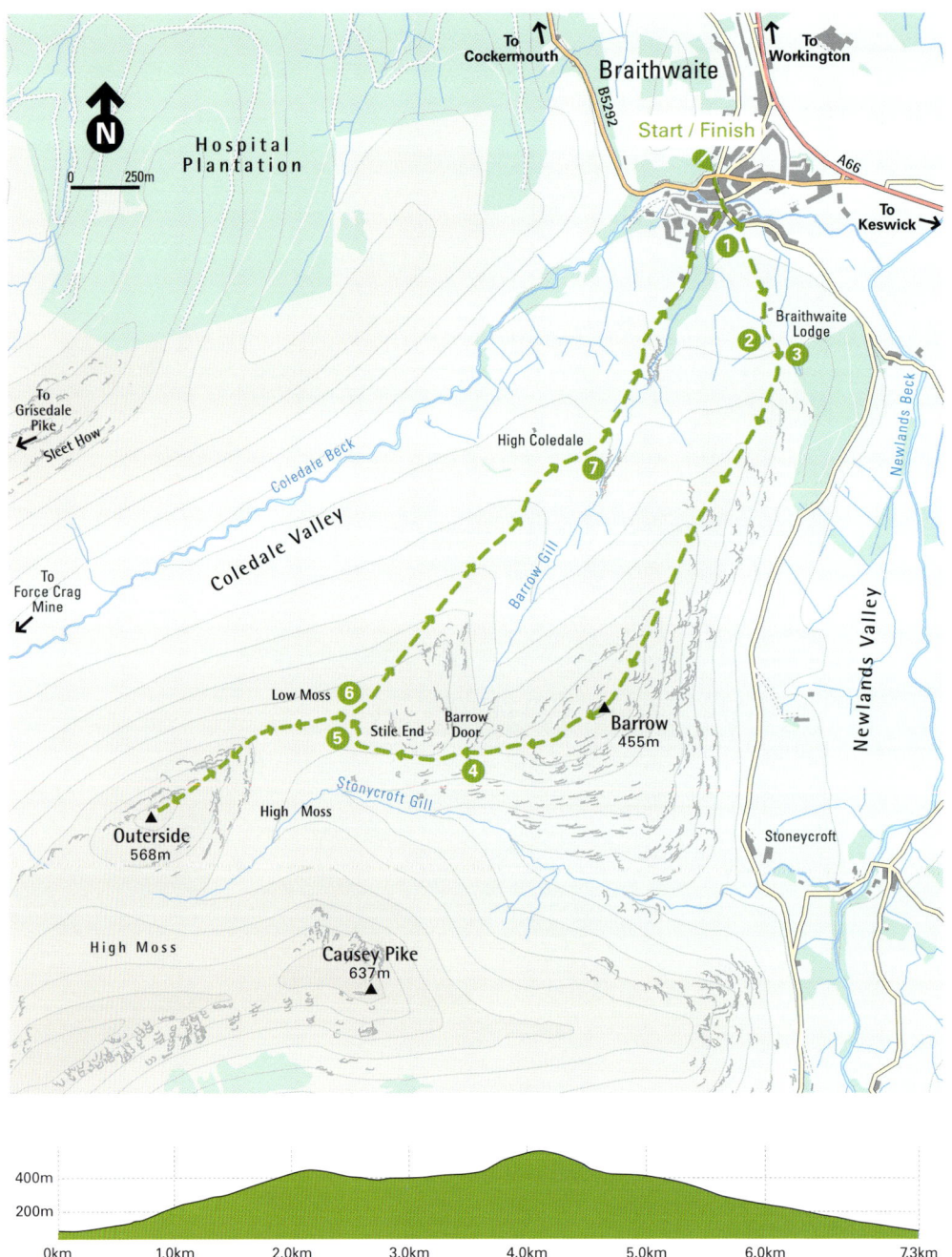

Immediately through the gate, there is a path on my right, which I ignore. The path I want is fifty metres further on, again on my right. ❸ A tiny three-way fingerpost points towards Barrow, on a clear green fairway up the fell through a border of brown bracken.

It is a broad, well-worn route formed by hordes of summer hikers, an easy slope to walk, but hard to keep going at a run. I gain 300 metres in 1.5 kilometres. It is unrelenting. My quads burn and my lungs work

Barrow and Outerside

flat out. The gradient doesn't ease until I reach the top. There is nothing to mark the highest point apart from a small heap of stones. Directly ahead, the distinctive outline of Causey Pike is revealed through shifting clouds. To my right, the cone of Outerside beckons. I catch glimpses of Derwentwater and Bassenthwaite Lake, but most of the surrounding tops are masked by clouds as grey as the lead that was once hewn from the local mines.

The bridge over Coledale Beck

I press on towards Barrow Door. A small dip and a large pile of stones, but this is not Barrow Door. Over the small hump then down to a junction of paths at a depression, this is Barrow Door. ❹ I take the path ahead, north-west, and climb up Stile End before dropping down to my left towards Low Moss. ❺ A bog with faint paths is not an easy place in the mist, but today Outerside stands out clearly to the south-west. This is an out-and-back spur, which somehow looks further away than it is. I should be back to the small tarn in the middle of this mire within 20 minutes.

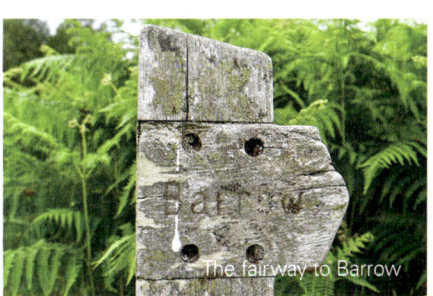
The fairway to Barrow

I wind my way through wintering heather on a path that is more of a fight in the summer months. It is a short sharp climb up to Outerside summit, sometimes tricky over wet slate slabs. My fell shoes fail miserably to grip. I push on to a pinnacle sandwiched between the twin pikes of Causey and Grisedale. Without real effort or power, I gain the height quickly. From Low Moss it takes me under 15 minutes to reach the top, where there is another nondescript pile of stones.

The higher Coledale fells limit my view, but the drop away west gives me a buzzard-eye view of the Coledale valley and Force Crag Mine. The treatment ponds lie like grey eyes on a scarred valley face. The rusting roofs of the abandoned processing plant tell of an industrial past within living memory. A time not too long ago when Braithwaite was home to miners, rather than a concentration of holiday lets and second homes.

Running up Barrow, Braithwaite in the background

I turn back the way I came as far as Low Moss. I aim to be back at the Royal Oak in 20 minutes. At first, I am

Looking down on Braithwaite from Stile End

55 Barrow and Outside

The route up Outerside from Stile End

circumspect down the green-grey slate. Then the marshy ground at Low Moss slows me down. Rather than heading back via Barrow Door, I pick up a path to my left just before the ascent of Stile End. ❻

I turn left and it is a clear path that at first contours around the fell. Once round the bend the route races north-east across the open moorland towards High Coledale. The grassy slope stretches out ahead. I bounce down soft peaty ground and the houses of Braithwaite are suddenly upon me. ❼ At High Coledale, I meet the path down from Barrow Door and follow the road down into the village.

Coledale Beck, the lane back to Braithwaite

Catbells Terrace

Cat Bells and the Terrace Path viewed from across Derwentwater

56 Catbells Terrace

Park / Start	Ullock Moss, Portinscale (NY 252 228)		
Map	OS Explorer OL4		
Exertion	● ●		
Navigation	●		
Terrain	● ●		
Distance	10.5 kilometres	Time	1 hour 8 minutes
Ascent	253 metres	On road	280 metres

An entry-level loop through woods and meadows with superb views of Derwentwater

There are some days when it's best to stay low. Sometimes the conditions dictate that even the least intimidating of fells can be hazardous or inhospitable, or both. This trail, by avoiding any summits and running north to south and back again, spares you from the brunt of the prevailing wind.

Tucked in a hollow surrounded by fells on three sides there is shelter from the foulest conditions, yet the views are still inspiring and the run is an off-road roller coaster with sufficient inclines to keep you warm on the coldest of days.

56 Catbells Terrace

Catbells Terrace

Today the 'feels like' temperature in the valleys is minus five and even on the lowest fells, this is down to minus thirteen with 50 kilometres per hour winds surging down from the Arctic. The Catbells Terrace route, returning by the shore of Derwentwater, is enticing.

START Close to the track down to Nichol End Marina, there is a signpost by the side of the road pointing up the hill, towards a small plantation called Fawe Park. This path is part of the Cumbria Way long distance footpath, although the signpost doesn't indicate this. The short, sharp ascent is a lung buster but it doesn't last long. Down the other side, I turn right and run past the entrance to Lingholm, the country house where Beatrix Potter spent her summer holidays. ❶ On my left, I reach the driveway to the house and to the right of this a sign directs me to the footpath to Cat Bells and round the lake.

The Alpaccas busy at Lingholm

Through the small gate, past the alpacas, I follow an enclosed path through the woods. Across a clearing, then more woods until I reach the road serving the Hawse End Outdoor Centre. ❷ The signpost across the road points towards Cat Bells and Newlands Valley. I cross the road and scramble up the bank, emerging after 200 metres at a cattle grid where I immediately turn left, ignoring the sign for Cat Bells summit.

A hundred metres up the slope I cross the road and head straight on up the broad path ahead. ❸ This is the Terrace Path to Grange (3 miles). As I climb, I can't help being affected by the view, one that has impressed poets and artists for centuries. The lake, fringed with crags and fragments of ancient woods, stretches down the valley towards the Jaws of Borrowdale. The mountains emerge, white capped and watchful: Skiddaw, Blencathra, High Seat, the Borrowdale Fells.

The Terrace Path beneath Cat Bells

Running freely on the smooth trail, back down to the road at the mudstone cliff, then up the other side keeping on the path until Manesty. I follow the signpost to Grange (1²⁄₃ mile), through the five-barred gate down

View across Derwentwater from the Terrace Path

56 Catbells Terrace

to the road, where I turn right (south). ④ After 300 metres, I reach a five-barred field gate on my left. ⑤ Here I pick up the Cumbria Way again, being directed to Lodore (1 mile) on a broad trail across wet pasture. Through a kissing gate, then another five barred gate. I bear right across the flood plain to reach a well-maintained path, grey and smooth, then over duckboards. ⑥ I turn left across land that becomes flooded in heavy rains.

The Cumbria Way across the duckboards

When I reach the lane, I turn right towards Brandelhow (¼ mile), through the gate to Abbots Bay, and try to pick up the pace down the slope. Another gate takes me past the teddy in the window at the Brandelhow Hut. There are a number of trails through Brandelhow Park and I choose the lakeshore path. ⑦ The flattest path with few undulations, just a few rocky outcrops and protruding tree roots to keep me on my toes.

The lake is deserted. Waves lap the shore. White horses skit across the surface, whipped up by the easterly wind. The wind blows without restraint through the leafless branches. Soft, dry ice-flakes begin to fall, gently stinging my face. I remain warm though, not wanting to stop to remove layers more suitable for exposed fells.

View from the Cumbria Way, Derwentwater east shore

I hug the water's edge until Hawse End where I keep to the main path, labelled as the Derwentwater Walk, rather than heading down to the jetty. ⑧ A gentle incline brings me up to the outdoor centre. Through the gate I turn right, and once beyond the entrance I retrace my steps back to Nichol End following the sign for Portinscale (1½ mile).

The Catbells Terrace run, overlooked by Cat Bells

57 Causey Pike and Scar Crags

Causey Pike across Derwentwater

Park / Start	Parking area at Uzzicar on the Newlands Pass Road (NY 232 217)		
Map	OS Explorer OL4		
Exertion	●●●●		
Navigation	●●		
Terrain	●●●●●		
Distance	8 kilometres	Time	1 hour 17 minutes
Ascent	606 metres	On road	0 metres

Over the snout of one of Lakelands most distinctive fells

Those visitors to the Lake District with only a vague knowledge of the locations and shapes of the fells will know the distinctive knobbly sculpturing of Causey Pike. Despite its rugged appearance and its dominant position above Keswick and Derwentwater, it is easily accessible to the average runner. The summit snout is a bit of a scramble, but this does not detract from the enjoyment of this loop.

START Directly across from the parking area, the old mine track starts. Rather than run on the road to Stonycroft Gill I take the track south a short distance. ❶ After 400 metres, a path off to the left eventually brings me back to the road and the bridge over the gill.

57 Causey Pike and Scar Crags

I cross to the south side of the bridge, and immediately on my right a short signpost points to a narrow path up the fell. ❷ This is the start of both of the main routes to the summit of Causey Pike. Today I am taking the direct route to Sleet Hause rather than tackling the steeper buttress of Rowling End.

❸ At the path branch, I take the right fork; a route that climbs more gradually with Stonycroft Gill and the mine track clearly in view on my right. It is still steep though, a steady 25 percent incline all the way to the summit.

In 25 minutes, I reach Sleet Hause, the col between Rowling End and the top of Causey Pike. ❹ The path is obvious. I turn right and continue to climb towards the rocky clenched fist. A short distance from the col I reach the base of the serrated, pink rocks that, close-up, suddenly look slightly daunting. It is a brief scramble though, and not hazardous. With plenty to hold on to, the rocks form rugged steps that are soon traversed. There is no single preferred route up through the slabs. I decide which way to go as the boulders present themselves.

Causey Pike and Scar Crags

Once on the cairnless top I can begin running again. People seem to spend a long time counting the knuckles, but I run down to the depression between the summit ridge and Scar Crags without noticing the bumps. On coral-coloured earth, I climb the few score metres to the cairn on the highest peak of Scar Crags. Directly ahead of me is Sail Pass and beyond it the grassy dome of Sail. From the pass, the path oscillating to Sail summit resembles a ribbon-like transverse wave. Within 400 metres from the top of Scar Crags, I reach the pass. ❺ Such a wide and worn path, the route is unmistakable. I turn sharp right and continue downhill. The descent is runnable. There is a section of stone pitching, but then the route is a rough, stony trail that swings to the right above the old cobalt mine. It's not technical though, there is nothing tricky, just a gentle slope and I have to focus on my feet. Time flies past.

I have Outerside on my left and ahead a mist-shrouded Barrow. A host of paths lead off to my left but I keep forging ahead. Soon I have Stonycroft Gill to my right, meandering towards the Newlands Valley. The clouds lift and Barrow is suddenly unveiled. It is a quintessential Lakeland circuit with a steep-sided valley, rocky mountain ridges, a twisting mountain stream and a mine track alluding to an industrial past.

Towards the end of track, the terrain becomes more even, with smooth, black rock spilling over the surface like ancient lava flows. ❻ I turn left beneath the eastern flank of Barrow and follow the mine track back to the parking area at Uzzicar.

The route up to Sleet Hause

Heading towards the distinctive first Knuckle of Causey Pike

On the summit of Scar Crags looking east

The path down to Uzzicar

57 Causey Pike and Scar Crags

Approaching Sail Pass and the path up to Sail

Maiden Moor and High Spy | 58

Maiden Moor and High Spy from across Derwentwater

58 Maiden Moor and High Spy

Park / Start	Chapel Bridge car park, Little Town, Newlands Valley (NY 231 193)
Map	OS Explorer OL4
Exertion	••••
Navigation	•
Terrain	•••
Distance	11 kilometres
Time	1 hour 31 minutes
Ascent	538 metres
On road	400 metres

**Floating above Newlands and Borrowdale,
an unmissable vantage point for Derwentwater**

I am deep in a valley traversed by Roman troops, settled by Vikings, mined by German migrants and heralded by Wordsworth for its peace and beauty. A valley lauded as one of the most picturesque in the Lakelands. I park near to Newlands Church, at Little Town, the stomping ground of Beatrix Potter's Mrs Tiggy-Winkle.

START North of the car park, a large sign informs me that if I want the public footpath to Dale Head it is up the road and I need to keep right. This is the way I am going.

❶ Two hundred metres up the hill towards the hamlet of Little Town I take a sharp right, clamber over a stile, and head up a grass bank to a footpath where I turn left. **❷** I pass a bench just before the houses and turn right to take a path that climbs first beside a fence, then a wall.

58 Maiden Moor and High Spy

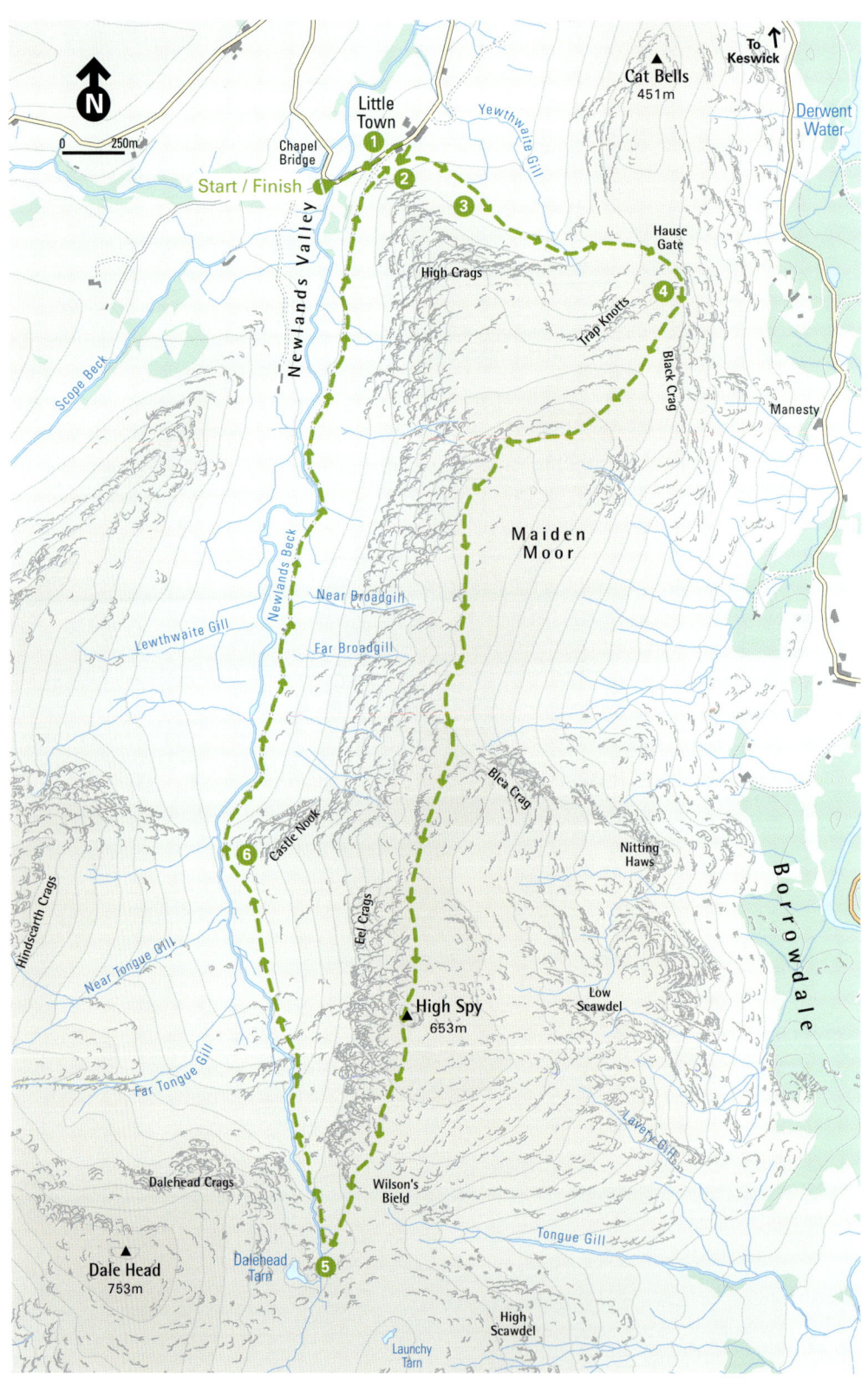

Maiden Moor and High Spy

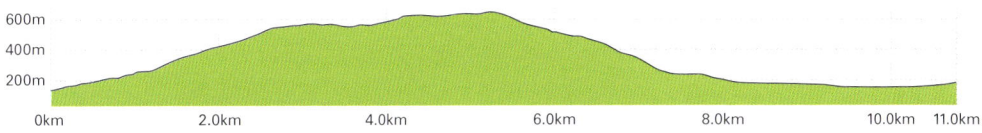

Soon the wall turns to the left and here, 860 metres into my run, the path divides. ❸ I take the right-hand branch up the fellside. This brings to an end my need to navigate on this run. The rest of the route is straightforward.

Past the broken rocks of the old quarry, over Yewthwaite Gill, I enter into bright, warm sunshine. It seems like no distance at all to Hause Gate, the col between Cat Bells and Maiden Moor. ❹ Justifiably, Cat Bells is a popular fell; walkers stream like ants over its summit in the summer to take in the view of Derwentwater. Maiden Moor, the next fell along the ridge, has equivalent views and a fraction of the traffic.

Yewthwaite Gill at Yewthwaite Comb on the path to Hause Gate

At Hause Gate, I turn right, head south and carry on climbing. Once I have reached the highest point on the moor I have half a kilometre of easy running until I start to climb once more, this time up High Spy. To my left the view is stunning. The late winter sky is a fierce blue, flecked with a few wispy clouds with a pinkish hue. The lake beneath is a sheet of blue steel, broken by reflections of Walla Crag and pastel pink clouds. High Spy rises before me in the shadow of Dale Head.

Rowan Tree at Hause Gate

My ascent begins again, a kilometre up the back of a giant, drab, grey lobster to the cairn on the highest point of the fell. Now begins a rocky kilometre of descent, and a 200 metre drop in elevation, down to Dalehead Tarn. ❺ Once at the col that houses the tarn, I turn right down the valley taking the path that follows the east bank of Newlands Beck.

Ascending Maiden Moor looking back to Hause Gate

I am now heading just west of north. I have to watch my footing as I scramble down the rocky route alongside the Newlands Beck canyon. Once past the waterfall the flatter valley bed is in sight. The path becomes more runnable and, before long, it joins a broad miners' track. ❻ I now have a good stretch, slightly downhill, following a route forged over hundreds of years of lead, copper,

The route from Maiden Moor to High Spy

Maiden Moor and High Spy

Cat Bells from Maiden Moor

silver and gold extraction. A glacial valley industrialised since the Elizabethan times, developed by German expertise – now remarkably tranquil, despite being just ten kilometres from the bustling town of Keswick. It's a straight run all the way back to Little Town following the meandering beck, sheltered by the slopes of Hindscarth and the crags beneath Maiden Moor. The pastures and the white farmhouses let me know I'm close to the end. A rise towards Little Town slows me down. I can see Chapel Bridge and I run past the car park before dropping down the slope to the road.

This is slightly longer than many of my other hour-plus fell runs, but the easy three kilometre finish compensates for this.

Looking down on Newlands Church

Knott Rigg and Ard Crags 59

Ard Crags swathed in heather

59 Knott Rigg and Ard Crags

Park / Start	Newlands Hause (NY 192 176)		
Map	OS Explorer OL4		
Exertion	●●		
Navigation	●●●		
Terrain	●		
Distance	7.4 kilometres	Time	1 hour 9 minutes
Ascent	432 metres	On road	0 metres

A ridge between two becks and a gently descending grassy trail, hugging a secluded valley

I am starting at an altitude of 333 metres and with the highest point of this loop being just 581 metres; this feels like cheating.

You can do this circuit in either direction, depending on your mood or the weather. A strong south-westerly would persuade me to run anticlockwise, which is the way I'm running today. The downsides to this are the uphill start, which begins straight from the car, and almost a kilometre of ascent at the end.

START The direct route up Knott Rigg is easy to locate, true north from the car park on the brow of the hause. While it is steep, there are much steeper fell ascents not too far away and at least this is on soft grass. Almost immediately, Keskadale Beck comes into view on my right meandering like a serpent along the valley

59 Knott Rigg and Ard Crags

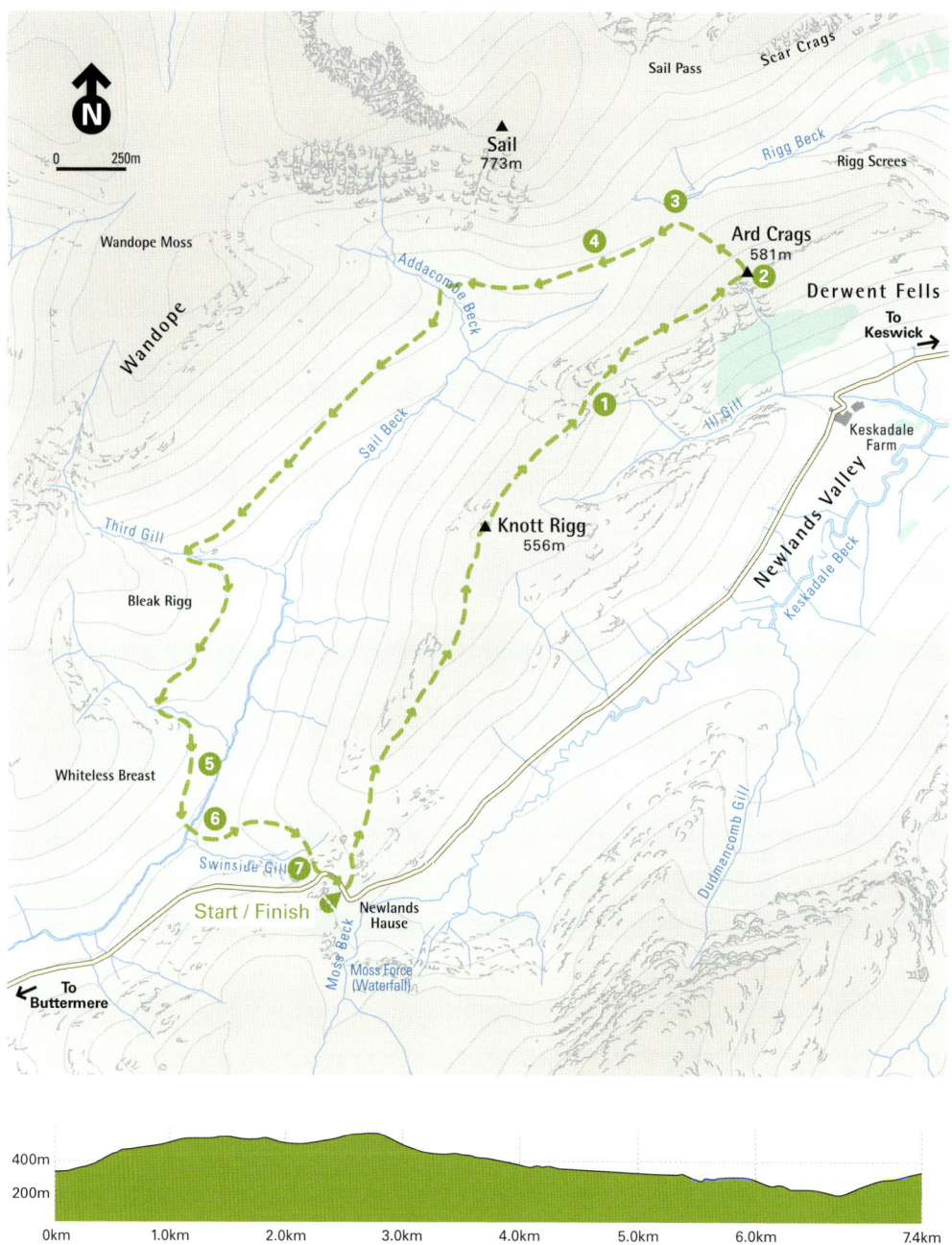

floor. Ahead are protuberances up the ridge, like the bumps of a rhino's back, which I will toil quietly over. After 500 metres, the slope eases and I'm soon on top of the ridge. The north-easterly wind is invigorating and somehow makes me feel more alive. For a while, I am completely alone beneath a cool, bright, spring sky. A dark shadow is cast over me; I glance skyward at a giant, solitary raven soaring low above my head. It follows me up to the summit, coming to rest like a sentinel on a small rocky outcrop. It waits, menacingly, for me to pass.

Knott Rigg and Ard Crags

Onwards to Ard Crags, down to the depression between the two summits on a soft ridge-path; glorious running terrain, rockless and undulating. ❶ From the hollow, the climb to the top of Ard Crags takes me little more than five minutes. ❷ I reach a small pile of stones marking the highest point and here I turn left to face north-northwest. Directly ahead is Sail summit and on my right-hand side I can see the col of Sail Pass. To the north-west, there is a path, not on the OS map, down the flank of the fell, a direct route to the head of Sail Beck.

The path is faint but easy to find and whilst it is steep, a 30 percent gradient, it is not hazardous. It is a grassy descent all the way down to a marshy basin. Within a couple of minutes, I'm at the watershed between the valley to the south-west holding Sail Beck and the valley to the north-east containing Rigg Beck. ❸

I contour along the fell on the other side and within 300 metres I reach a clear path where I turn left. ❹ I'm on the valley route linking Birkrigg in Newlands with Buttermere, running on a contour path heading south-west. Soon Sail Beck is beside me on my left. I am in a vale of tranquillity, hemmed in between the steep flanks of Sail and Ard Crags.

The path, too narrow for me to run on at a swift pace, sweeps serenely around the slopes of Wandope, Bleak Rigg and Whiteless Breast. I cut into, and cross, three gills – Addacombe, Third and one with no name – before looking out for Swinside Gill on the other side of the valley.

At the base of Swinside Gill is a ruined sheepfold, which marks the point where I will cross Sail Beck. Just before I am level with the sheepfold a path on my left, not on the map, leads down to the beck. ❺

❻ I ford the beck directly in front of the sheepfold, turn left then right, and head directly up the fell towards Newlands Hause. There is a faint path, again not on the map, heading east-northeast up the ridge that eventually meets the main route up to Knott Rigg – where I began this circuit just over an hour ago.

The route up Knott Rigg from Newlands Hause

Precarious cairn on Knott Rigg summit

The route up Ard Crags through the heather

Sail Beck heading west

59 Knott Rigg and Ard Crags

The Ard Crags ridge looking east

To my right I can see the road over Newlands Hause, it is within touching distance but the slope is steep and my progress has slowed. Three hundred metres on from the beck, still below the height of the hause, I reach a path on my left that climbs south-east round the head of Swinside Gill.

The climb to Newlands Hause from the Swinside Gill sheepfold

❼ Emerging onto the road, I am 130 metres shy of my start point. I turn left and struggle up the hill, round the bend to the parking area.

Rannerdale Knotts across Crummock Water

60 Rannerdale Knotts

Park	Road side, east of St James' Church, Buttermere (NY 174 169)		
Start	Opposite the Bridge Hotel, Buttermere (NY 174 169)		
Map	OS Explorer OL4		
Exertion	●●		
Navigation	●●		
Terrain	●		
Distance	8 kilometres	Time	1 hour 6 minutes
Ascent	457 metres	On road	300 metres

A rocky summit, a secret valley and a profusion of springtime bluebells

Great runs don't have to mean great heights. This is one of the smaller Wainwright fells but this route contains some of the most enjoyable fell running.

Straight up and down Rannerdale Knotts from Buttermere is little more than five kilometres, which makes a speedy training run if you don't have a lot of time. Today I am adding on a few more kilometres, with a tricky descent and a double climb.

There are numerous places to park in Buttermere village. I choose the off-road option at the start of Newlands Pass, just east of the St James' Church. It is a free spot and for this reason, it can get quite busy.

60 Rannerdale Knotts

🏃 **START** I begin my run opposite the Bridge Hotel. On the west side of the bridge there is a signposted path, which passes alongside Mill Beck through a cluster of trees. **❶** The path crosses the wall at a large contraption of wooden steps followed by a gate. Once over, I turn right onto a grassy path alongside the wall. Nine hundred metres from the start, just before the wall falls away to the beck, the path divides and I take the branch to the left. **❷** Going slightly up hill, I'm still running parallel to Newlands Pass on a narrow, runnable path, soft and dry, and not too steep.

❸ After another 600 metres, I take a sharp left. It is an obvious junction and, since it's opposite Swinside Gill and a ruined sheepfold on the other side of Mill Beck, it is easy to spot. I am now heading south-west, on another beautiful path for running – narrow and yielding with a steady incline.

In fact, the gradient is manageable all the way to the top. **❹** After a further 700 metres, I reach a busy path junction. To my right is Whiteless Edge. To my left is the direct route down to Buttermere, which I will be taking later. Ahead, on my right-hand side, is the path up from Squat Beck. This is where I will emerge on my return journey. Straight ahead, west-northwest up a grassy knoll, is my path to Rannerdale Knotts. A

Rannerdale Knotts 60

Running towards the summit of Rannerdale Knotts

ten percent incline of a cushiony, green carpet. Before long I can see Buttermere over my left shoulder and ahead Crummock Water comes into view, sliced in half by the peak of Rannerdale.

Grass gives way to a craggy summit. The path winds around rocky tufts. I'm looking at wispy clouds gathering over the lakes below. I have the flank of Mellbreak to my left and the slopes of Whiteless Pike to my right. There is deep silence, apart from a faint tumbling sound, which I can only assume is water cascading down Sourmilk Gill across the valley.

The highest point is a turret to the north of the ridge. ❺ From here, the path falls off to the west, steeply down an unrunnable section of rocks and steps. It's not long, though, before the gradient eases and I descend towards the road with Hause Point on my left.

When I reach the road, I head right (north) for 100 metres to the parking area south of Rannerdale Farm. ❻ Here, a fingerpost points north-east to Dale How and I take the path along the wall. Through the kissing gate into the National Trust's bluebell sanctuary, then

Through the gate by Mill Beck

Follow the path along Squat Beck

273

Rannerdale Knotts

The route alongside Squat Beck

out again, following the burbling Squat Beck on a good path to the right of the water. Further up the valley I cross the beck but continue to run alongside the water all the way up the blissful valley.

④ I reach the junction of paths at the head of the valley, the same intersection I crossed 40 minutes earlier on my way to the summit. This time I turn right, following a wide fairway of grass racing as fast as I can

Running down through the ferns, Buttermere in sight

downhill, straining my quads, as the slope steepens. There are numerous paths, a paradise for hill reps. From here any route down will get me to Buttermere. I hurtle on the broadest of paths towards a clump of boulders. ⑦ Beyond here, I reach the corner of Grassgarth Coppice from where I take the left-hand route. Down to a fence, a right-hand turn takes me back to the road and 300 metres left brings me back to the Bridge Hotel.

The Western Fells

The Western Fells is a diverse territory, chock-a-block with rugged peaks towards the east and outlined by softer, rounded, grassy hills towards its quiet western border. The runs described here take you over some of the most runnable and least visited fells in the entire Lakeland region, from the tops clustered around Loweswater to outposts of the flanks of Ennerdale.

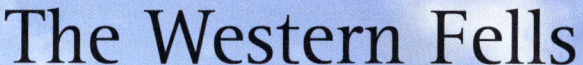

Cogra Moss (Murton Fell and Cogra Moss route)

The path to Fellbarrow from Mosser Road

61 Fellbarrow and Low Fell

Low Fell and Fellbarrow across Crummock Water from Rannerdale Knotts

Park / Start	Waterend, Loweswater (NY 118 224)		
Map	OS Explorer OL4		
Exertion	•••		
Navigation	•••		
Terrain	•		
Distance	8.4 kilometres	Time	1 hour 19 minutes
Ascent	516 metres	On road	0 metres

A roller-coaster canter over numerous tops beside the shore of Loweswater

Unusually for the Lake District, where hefted sheep are traditionally left to roam free, the fells in this triangle of moorland, wedged between the Vale of Lorton and Loweswater, are divided into compact parcels of grazing land. At least the lattice of fences makes navigation easier in the mist.

My parking spot is by the telephone box that now houses a defibrillator. **START** The lane opposite has signs for Miresyke and Askhill; this is the start of my run. At the entrance to Miresyke, the route divides and I take the right-hand branch, a bridleway, leading to the old Mosser Road. Through a couple of gates and a field full of fluffy Galloway calves, I soon reach the old road. ❶

61 Fellbarrow and Low Fell

Left along the lane, broken up and naturally greening, I am blown along by a strong wind. Immediately I know this is not a good thing. In a few minutes, on the tops, this wind will be in my face and significantly stronger. It is a kilometre from the bridleway to the turn-off for the fells. ❷ On my right there's a ruined sheepfold, a small clump of trees, a small brook – Mosser Beck – and a track leading from a metal gate that makes an acute angle to Mosser Road. Through the gate, I ford the beck and start to climb in an east-northeasterly direction up the gentle, grassy slopes of Fellbarrow.

On the map there are no paths shown, just a lot of fences. Ahead to my left I take the track through a patch of gorse bushes, which climbs up the side of Mosser Fell. The path becomes less distinct but is still visible. Then a fence appears on the horizon, from north to south, and I spot a heap of stones. This is where I head. It's a distinctive pile of stones arranged in a semi-circle, almost like a seat or a small shelter. Beyond this, almost touching the fence, I reach the trig point marking the summit of Fellbarrow.

Battered by the wind I don't dawdle. I turn right at the fence to face south and I am immediately confronted by a gale force blast. I follow the fence line south, with the peaks of Grasmoor and Whiteside draped

Fellbarrow and Low Fell

The route from Fellbarrow to Low Fell

beneath clouds on my left and the Solway Firth and the Scottish hills to my distant right. The barren Solway Plain skirts around these rolling fells; I am at the north-west reaches of the Cumbrian Mountains striding out over rounded, lower moorland.

There are paths on both sides of the fence, neither of which are on the map, and for now, I keep to the westerly side. Fences abound on these fell tops, unusually dividing this grazing land into well-defined enclosures. On these otherwise barren hills, this certainly helps with navigation.

This undulating moorland is splendid running country. Soft, peaty earth, easy on the joints with some fast descents. It is surprisingly tough, though, with numerous mini-summits – steep-sided cones – all the way to Darling Fell; over Smithy Fell, Sourfoot Fell and the double humps of Low Fell. Within the bogs between the tops, the views are limited to the pale greens and yellows, and the straws of the sedges and moorland grasses. I squidge through the sphagnum and turf mosses, following the zigzag line of the fence until I reach Sourfoot Fell. ❸ Left and down from here I pass through the gate below Watching Crag, joining the path up from Thackthwaite. ❹

Fellbarrow summit

I am pummelled by the wind on the top of the Low Fell ridge. Progress is difficult and it begins to rain. There is something strangely exhilarating about running across an open moorland fell, battling against a head-on wind that almost lifts me off my feet. I push into the incessant rain with a classic Lakeland view ahead: Mellbreak, Scoat Fell, Starling Dodd, Haycock. Three hundred metres below me, Crummock Water stretches

61 Fellbarrow and Low Fell

Low Fell summit looking towards Crummock Water

out to the south-west, drab beneath the thick clouds.
❺ From the cairn on the southernmost top of Low Fell, I head just west of north back to the fence and jog down the fence line to Crabtree Beck. **❻** Crossing the stepping stones at the beck, I make the 90-metre ascent to the cairn on the top of Darling Fell. **❼** The rains stops and the blackest of the clouds have moved west. Loweswater glimmers under a lightening sky. From the summit of Darling Fell, I follow a clear path that curves down the slope beneath Askill Knott. **❽** I cross the stile down to Mosser Road where a signpost points back towards Foulsyke (1¾ mile). After turning right, I have a 500 metre run to reach the top of the bridleway I ran up over an hour ago. From here, I turn left, through the field and down the track back to the road.

Mellbreak and Crummock Water from Low Fell

Darling Fell from Low Fell summit

Burnbank Fell and Blake Fell | 62

Carling Knott and Burnbank Fell across Loweswater

62 Burnbank Fell and Blake Fell

Park / Start	Fangs Brow, Loweswater (NY 109 228)		
Map	OS Explorer OL4		
Exertion	●●●		
Navigation	●●●		
Terrain	●		
Distance	8 kilometres	**Time**	1 hour 4 minutes
Ascent	439 metres	**On road**	0 metres

**On the north-western fringe of the Lakes,
quiet fells for contemplative running**

The north-western border of the Lake District arcs around the Loweswater Fells and these small grassy hills to the west of Loweswater provide ideal running terrain. Well-worn, rolling mounds of mudstone and siltstone undulate like a verdant rollercoaster. This run sweeps over the highest of the Loweswater Fells, up smooth slopes and down to green cols.

START From the parking spaces on the road to Lamplugh, south-west of Fangs Brow Farm, I pass through the gate and take the bridleway to the south-east, signposted to Loweswater (2 miles), a broad track reaching out across pastureland. Under high, slate-grey clouds, the path I will take up Burnbank is already visible.

62 Burnbank Fell and Blake Fell

I ignore the turn-off towards Loweswater through the gate on my left; instead I run onwards, beside the wall in the direction of High Nook. Through another gate, climbing steadily, running on the gravel and grass on a well-used path. ❶ At the next gate, the wall veers to the left and my route, a path up the shoulder of Burnbank, swings to the right.

Even though it's not on the map, it is a clear path, south then south-west, all the way to the summit. Steep to begin with, but the soft earth provides good grip and soon the gradient eases. Behind me,

Burnbank Fell and Blake Fell

The track to Burnbank Fell

Loweswater, a pool of quicksilver, mirrors the outline of the fells fringing its eastern shore. Ahead, I soon see the fence line that bisects the top of the Burnbank Fell from north to south.

The feeble-looking summit cairn lies just on the other side of the boundary line. ❷ I don't cross the fence. From the top, I turn left to follow the fence all the way to the top of my next goal – Blake Fell. I'm running with the fence on my right, down the dip into the spongy depression between the two tops. From here, it is a 120-metre climb, but not too steep and I'm able to run virtually all the way to the summit cairn.

Close to the top, I cross the fence at a place where it is obvious that many others before me have done the same thing. I stand at the top of a low-lying fell with views that stretch forever over the Irish Sea to the Isle of Man, and over the Solway Firth towards Criffel in the Scottish hills. Inland, a multitude of mountains fan outwards, from the Loweswater Fells in the foreground to Blencathra, Skiddaw and Helvellyn in a distant arc. On a misty day, returning the same way is a safe option. It is also a swift 3.6 kilometres downhill most of the way on firm grass. Today, however, I can clearly see the path north-east down to the fence and over Carling Knott; this is the way I will descend.

Following the path beside the wall towards High Nook

Blake Fell from Cogra Moss

Burnbank Fell and Blake Fell

Carling Knott – the descent to the wall

Down the hill, there is a hole in the fence, which I dip through. ❸ There is an incline to the top of Carling Knott but it is less than 50 metres of ascent. It is another runnable climb to a set of cairns. Beyond the summit, paths with great promise tend to deliver little, so I continue to head in a north-easterly direction. If I follow this course my actual route of descent doesn't really matter. I know that I will reach the wall by Holme Wood and from here I will turn left along the track.

The route I choose is steep but rockless, through heather and then bracken, and it brings me to the bridleway

Running on Blake Fell

by a gate. ❹ I have two kilometres of track running, cutting down to Holme Beck before an unexpected climb around the base of Burnbank Fell. A wooden ladder stile takes me back to where I began to climb up Burnbank 50 minutes earlier. ❶ From here, I retrace my steps along the track back to Fangs Brow.

Gavel Fell and Blake Fell

The path to Gavel Fell summit

63 Gavel Fell and Blake Fell

Park / Start	Maggie's Bridge car park, Loweswater (NY 134 210)		
Map	OS Explorer OL4		
Exertion	● ● ●		
Navigation	● ● ●		
Terrain	●		
Distance	9.2 kilometres	Time	1 hour 12 minutes
Ascent	531 metres	On road	0 metres

Off the beaten track, rolling, runnable fells with fast descents

Less inspiring fells for a walker can make superlative routes for a runner.
On the western margins of the Lakeland fells, there is a slight sense of forlornness. Within a few kilometres, the hills merge gently with the rolling pastures of the Cumbrian coastal plain, and the towns and villages on the coast of the grey Irish Sea have a story of their own.

START At the entrance to the car park is the gated access to High Nook Farm. South-west, through the gate, a sign points to a public bridleway to the farm (½ mile). I follow the track to the farmhouse and out through the gate at the end of the yard. The track veers left behind the farm and this brings me to a gate through the intake wall.

63 Gavel Fell and Blake Fell

Ahead is a part of the route where I have to be a little bit careful. ❶ Just fifty metres from the gate a grassy path leads off to the left; this is where I leave the track and head up the fell.

I rise quite steeply, but it isn't excessive. It is a clear route once I am on it, keeping to the left of Black Crag. I have to make sure I follow the path upwards here; if I go over the crest of the ridge, I'll descend to Whiteoak Beck.

Gavel Fell and Blake Fell

I climb through the heather, following the path with the small tarn, known unofficially as Highnook Tarn, to my right in the combe below. The gradient eases and soon I reach the first cairn, at a spot height of 488 metres on a nameless grassy knoll. ❷ The peace is sublime. There is no audible sound. No birds chirping, no insects whirring, no distant vehicle engines, no people. I look back at Loweswater, a picture of tranquillity with the gentle slopes of Low Fell and Darling Fell in the centre of the canvas.

If the cloud is down it might be easy to confuse this with the top of Gavel Fell, but Gavel Fell is 600 metres ahead and on the other side of a fence. I drop into a small, boggy hollow then continue to climb southwest reaching a fence junction. ❸ Over a stile, over a fence, a few metres to my left is the cairn, marking the top of Gavel Fell. I am struck by the proximity of the coast and the clarity of Snaefell on the Isle of Man.

The route to Gavel Fell

This is the kind of summit I can bound down. There is a path of sorts, but navigation is easy, I simply follow the fence, roughly north, down to Fothergill Head and another marshy depression. ❹ At the bottom of the dip, I cross a path heading to a stile over the fence on my right. This will be my route back to High Nook Farm once I have completed the dogleg to the top of Blake Fell and back.

I keep following the fence on my right and within 200 metres I reach a fence junction. In the corner, there is an unusual sandstone column, which used to form part of a strange hurdle contraption. Now I have to cock a leg over the fence and immediately climb the stile on my left to return to the path alongside the fence to Blake Fell summit. Another 600 metres, a runnable incline with the fence on my right all the way, brings me to the windshelter cairn.

High Nook Tarn and the route of descent from Gavel and Blake

The highest point of the Loweswater Fells provides a captivating set of views: Fleetwith Pike and a peek of Buttermere; Lank Rigg behind a fragment of Ennerdale Water; the panhandle water of Cogra Moss; Whiteside and Grassmoor, dusted with spring snow, slumbering by the bank of Crummock Water.

The run back down to Fothergill Head is the reason I make this detour. Almost a kilometre on yielding ground, a ten percent decline, no rocks, just soft grass if I fall. I can let myself go. Over the stile, over the fence, then down to the hollow.

The summit of Gavel Fell

63 Gavel Fell and Blake Fell

Running over Blake Fell and Gavel Fell

④ At Fothergill Head, I climb the stile, now on my left, to pick up the path that will take me down to Highnook Tarn. The path is a clear and easy running route; there is no real risk of descending into the ravine. I follow the bends all the way to the tarn; the path steepens, this slows me, but I can still canter freely down. In the valley I look out for a sheepfold on my left, this is where I cross Highnook Beck. ⑥ I keep the tarn to my right and follow the track to the intake wall at Highnook Farm. Through the gate, I now retrace my steps past the farm and back to Maggie's Bridge.

Hen Comb

Hen Comb from across Loweswater

64 Hen Comb

Park / Start	Loweswater, junction of road to Kirkstile Inn (NY 142 211)		
Map	OS Explorer OL4		
Exertion	● ● ●		
Navigation	● ● ●		
Terrain	●		
Distance	9.4 kilometres	Time	1 hour 18 minutes
Ascent	407 metres	On road	1.2 kilometres

A linear moorland ridge along Mosedale Beck, nestling in the shadow of Mellbreak

Along the road into Loweswater, not really a village or even a hamlet, just a church and a pub surrounded by isolated farmhouses. Mellbreak stares down domineeringly upon the scattered buildings; it is easy to miss Hen Comb.

START Past the church, left and then immediately right where one sign points towards Mosedale (1 mile) and a negative signpost points to *no through road*. I pass in front of the Kirkstile Inn and over Church Bridge. ❶

The road now heads to Kirkgate Farm and once through the farmyard the route becomes a rough lane of sharp stones up to a gate. ❷ Through the gate, I turn right following the wall with a thin plantation

64 Hen Comb

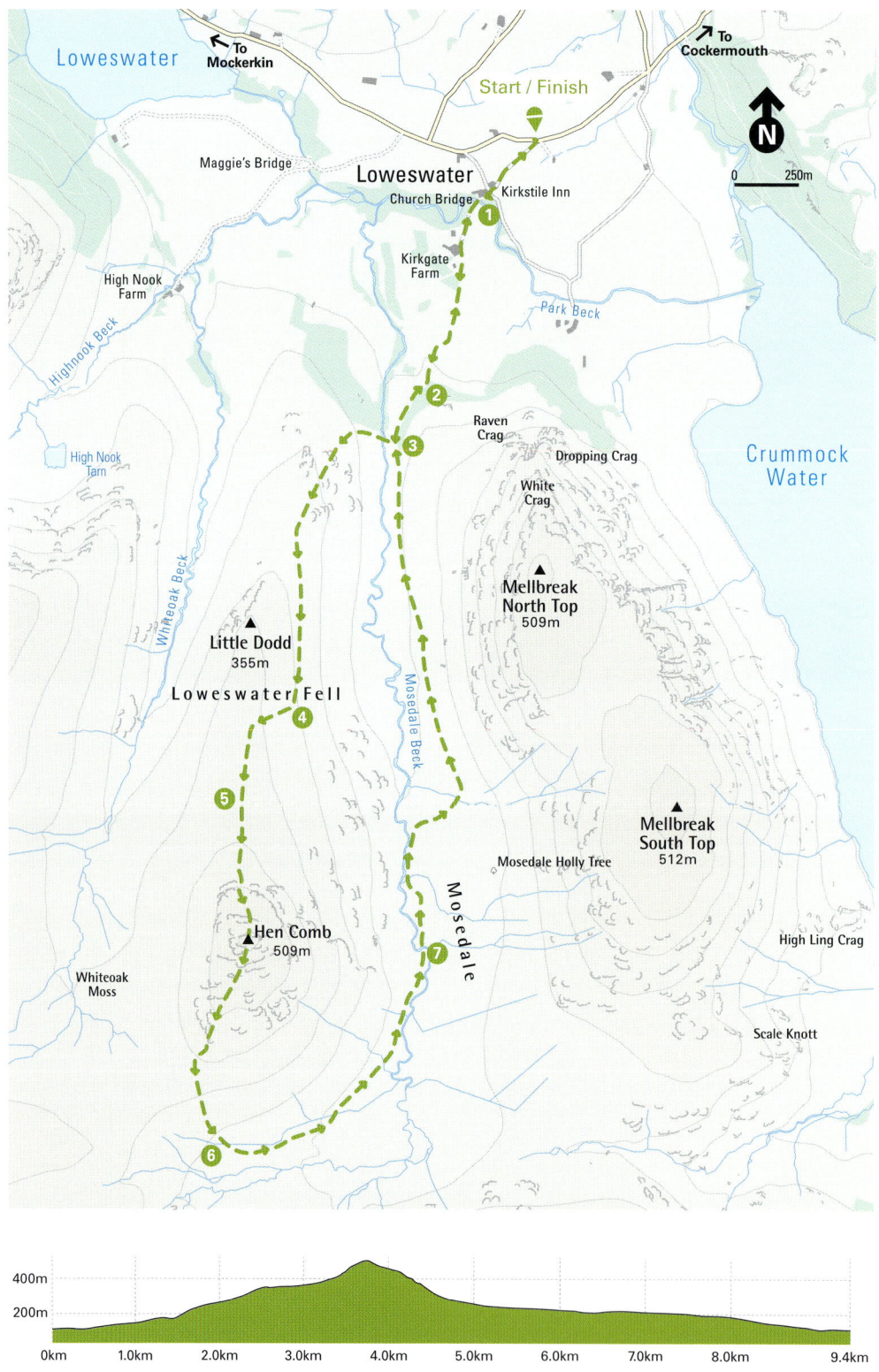

Hen Comb 64

Kirkstile Inn and St Bartholomew's Church

of conifers on my left. The wall turns right and so do I, through the gate down to Mosedale Beck. ❸
I wade through the beck at its shallowest point. Now the tricky part begins. My goal is to get onto the ridge leading over Little Dodd but the route is not obvious. I run up the bank keeping close to the wall for 270 metres. Here a path crosses through a gap in the wall and just beyond this, the wall sweeps away to my right. At this point, I bear left following a clear path south that climbs gradually up the fell. After a further 400 metres, I reach a stile where a fence meets a section of wall. ❹ Over the stile, I follow the path left, keeping my eye on the ridge up to Little Dodd, which I head for. Running in a southerly direction, I skirt around Little Dodd with Hen Comb looming ahead. Dry pasture has now given way to soggy moss, but at least the terrain has plateaued and running has become easier. I look around at Gavel Fell to my right and Mellbreak, still demanding attention on my left. Ahead stands Great Borne, a great dark wall hiding the water of Ennerdale. ❺ I step over a fence before commencing the final

Fording Mosedale Beck

The steep climb to Hen Comb summit

Hen Comb

Descent from Hen Comb to Mosedale Beck

climb. The last haul up to the summit gets surprisingly steep for such a low-level fell and I have to work hard up a 30 percent gradient. I pass the summit, an unobtrusive cairn, and follow the path south towards a marshy, boggy depression between Hen Comb and Great Borne. It is a clear footpath down a grassy bank towards Mosedale Beck, exercise for my quads as I brake to avoid hurtling too fast. The route veers right to pass alongside

Mosedale and the Holly Tree from Little Dodd

a fence, and a gate becomes visible at the bottom of the dip. The gate crosses the track of the bridleway I will follow. I pick up the path and head left (east) away from the gate. ❻

It is an indistinct path traversing an area consisting of a myriad of streams collecting in a poorly drained swamp. Very soon, the path divides and I need to take the left branch heading towards Crummock Water. I turn left into the Mosedale valley, knowing that the path will gradually become more distinct.

I negotiate the reeds, the pools and the mud and jump over puddles full of frogspawn, wondering whether the eggs will hatch before the puddles dry out. Mosedale Beck meanders alongside me. ❼ Over the metal bridge, I reach a drier place, an easier path on which to run. I have no choice of route; I keep running north towards Loweswater. The bridleway merges with the path from Mellbreak's southern ridge, the path harbouring the Mosedale Holly Tree, and I am now on a track proceeding gradually downhill. The river runs with me. This is a lonely valley, almost melancholic beneath the narrow confines of the flanks of Hen Comb and Mellbreak. I see the trees at the end of the track, the conifers by the ford.

At the gate, I follow the track back through the farm and the lane back to the road.

Murton Fell and Cogra Moss **65**

Late summer at Cogra Moss

65 Murton Fell and Cogra Moss

Park / Start	Felldyke car park, Lamplugh (NY 085 198)		
Map	OS Explorer OL4		
Exertion	•		
Navigation	• •		
Terrain	•		
Distance	8.2 kilometres	Time	1 hour
Ascent	282 metres	On road	0 metres

An entry-level circuit over fell, through dark woods, along fast forest tracks

Barely a kilometre from the Lake District's western boundary Murton Fell, not a Wainwright, provides a steep up and a steeper down on safe grassy paths leading to a sweeping forest trail above a secluded reservoir.

START At the back of the car park, a fingerpost points up a narrow path towards Cogra Moss (½ mile). At the top of the steps, I turn left onto the track and after 50 metres on my right there is another fingerpost pointing to Cogra Moss. ❶ To begin with there are a few turns to negotiate and a number of stiles to climb, but there are plenty of navigation aids to follow.

65 Murton Fell and Cogra Moss

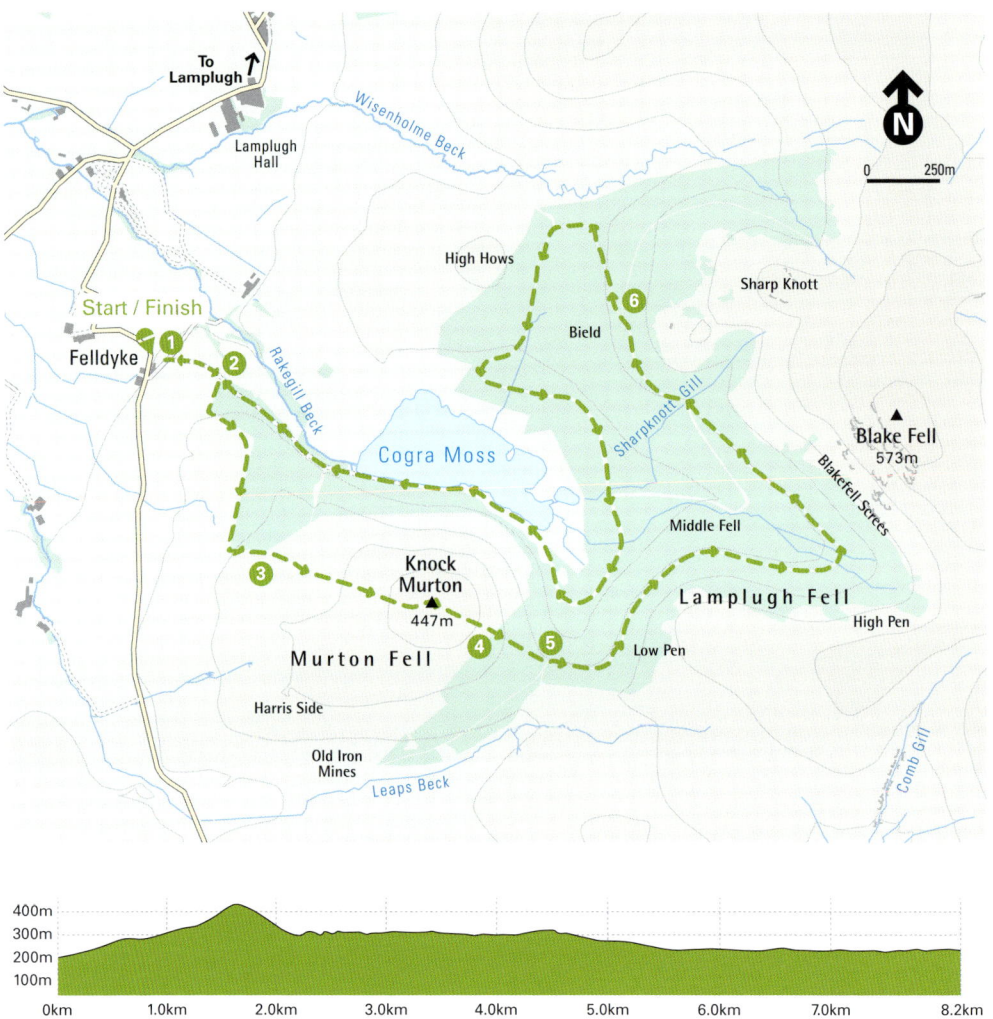

Through the wooden gate, I follow the route to the reservoir. Less than 200 metres up the track, just before a fenced plantation, I reach another gate, this time metal. ❷ At the gate, I cross the step stile on my right and run alongside the woodland fence. There is no real path but I know that the fence line will lead me to the route up the fell.

One hundred metres up the pasture a large tombstone-shaped slab at the corner of the fence marks another stile to cross, this time a couple of horizontal wooden bars. I turn left, then right, following the fence-line to a further timber-railed stile. I keep following the fence. I make one more ninety-degree turn (left) where, unexpectedly, two green MAFF waymakers attached to the corner post tell me I am in an environmentally sensitive area. Straight ahead is a rickety metal gate, which I have to climb to reach the open fell. ❸

Knock Murton lies ahead – Wainwright's forbidden peak. There is a faint path, which I follow, taking an east-southeast line up a steepening bilberry-draped slope. The path disappears, I continue to climb, and the summit is only a few hundred metres away. Just before the top of the dome, I join a clear path, the more southerly route up from Harris Side and the old iron mines.

Murton Fell and Cogra Moss 65

Descent off Knock Murton

A collection of stone constructions emerges. Firstly, an S-shaped shelter with a stone love seat, then three substantial cairns, the most easterly marking the highest point.

West and south, water dominates the view; the Irish Sea and the Solway Firth. East, the sweeping, unruffled crests of the Loweswater Fells. South, Starling Dodd and Great Bourne stand above the lower reaches of Ennerdale Water, less than three kilometres away across tight-walled fields.

This green mountain is quickly crossed. From the summit, there is a path ahead on my right, heading south of east towards the forest. I hurtle two hundred and forty metres down to the fence, braking under the strain of a thirty percent gradient. ❹ The path meets a stile, which I cross into the woods, and I continue to descend through a dark corridor of densely packed Sitka spruce.

Within minutes, I am out of the woods. Ahead of me, a broad, pink gravel forest track where I turn left. ❺ The track soon curves right, heading east, before sweeping

Following the fence towards the top of Murton Fell

Shelter on Murton Fell

Murton Fell and Cogra Moss

Late summer at Cogra Moss

north beneath Blakefell Screes. I will follow the track all the way down to Cogra Moss. On my left, flashing through windows in the conifers, is the green bell-shaped crown of Murton Fell, sitting above the still, silver-blue water. I keep left at the only path junction. ❻ The gravel turns grey. Slowly I descend towards the water's edge. The running is easy; the terrain changes from stone to grass to shale, I have no choice of route and it is a gentle descent.

Soon I am heading west along the edge of Cogra Moss. Buzzards soar above, wading anglers fish for trout, I run by the shore. Beyond the dam at Rakegill Beck, I have an 800-metre jog back to the wooden gate I passed through an hour earlier.

Cogra Moss from the forest trail

Mellbreak 66

Mellbreak from Kirkstile

66 Mellbreak

Park / Start	Parking area at junction of the B5289 and road to Kirkstile Inn, Loweswater (NY 142 211)		
Map	OS Explorer OL4		
Exertion	••••		
Navigation	••		
Terrain	•••••		
Distance	9.8 kilometres	Time	1 hour 28 minutes
Ascent	531 metres	On road	1.7 kilometres

Ascend an imperious mountain, gambol along a glorious lakeshore

From across Crummock Water, Mellbreak watches over me like an ancient brooding sphinx. A small mountain with a malevolent face and gentle haunches.

START The Kirkstile Inn is my starting point, along the road past the church, left, then directly right to pass in front of the pub. ❶ A fingerpost points to Mosedale (1 mile), over Church Bridge and along the lane to Kirkgate Farm. Through the farmyard, the route becomes a rough, stony track bordered by drystone walls, which I follow to a gate.

Through the gate, the track follows the wall to the right; I head straight on through the trees. ❷ The north-west face of Mellbreak is ahead of me, dark and ominous. If the Loweswater Fells are the digits of a hand, then Mellbreak is its knobbly thumb.

66 Mellbreak

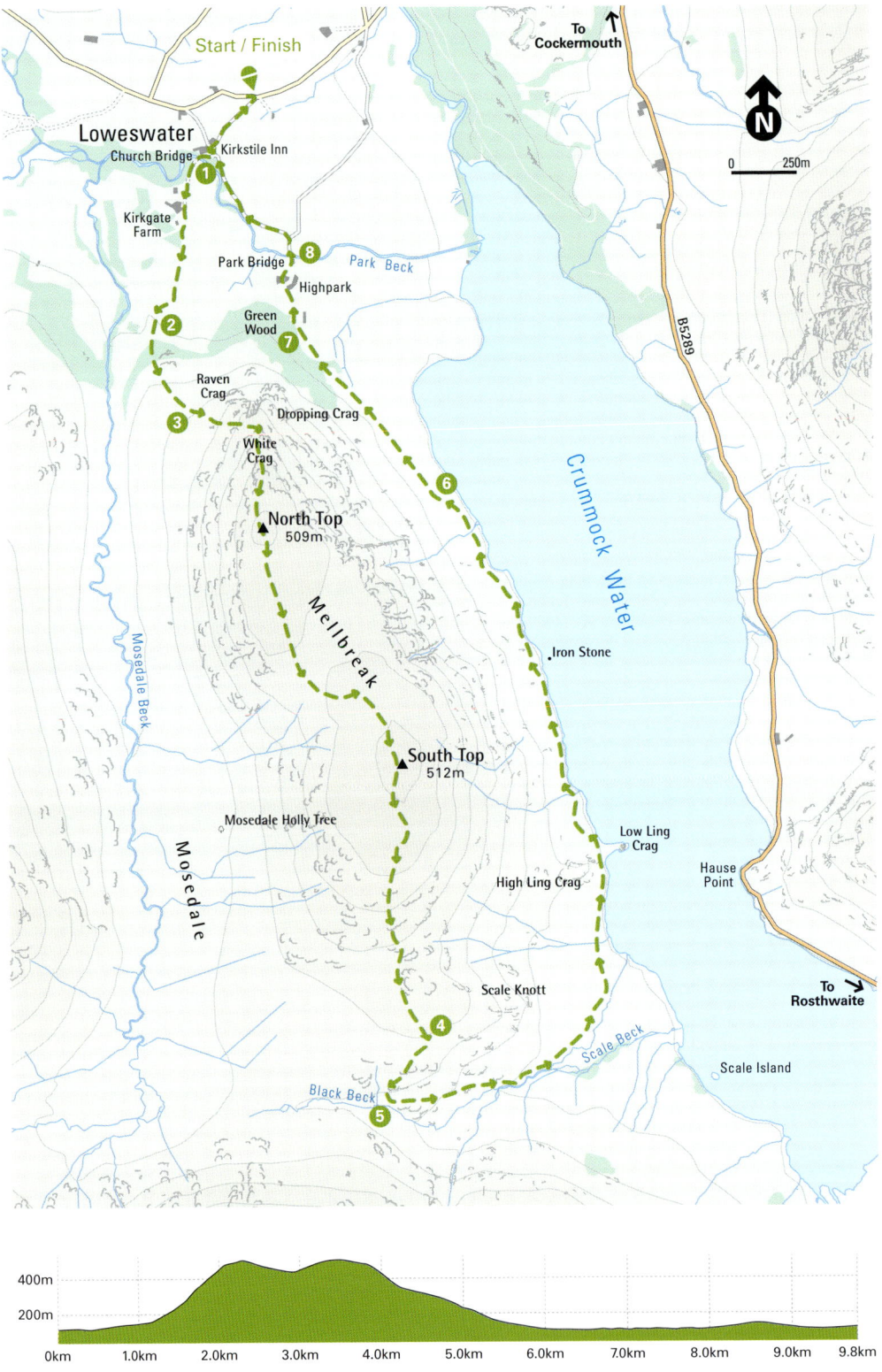

Mellbreak

Above the trees, I cross a track and continue on the path ahead, grassy to begin with but not for long. ❸ There is an obvious route up the spur and soon the gradient steepens. I have to ascend 330 metres in 900 metres distance travelled to reach the north top.

The scree begins and, of course, I am no longer running, in fact I am occasionally going backwards. I approach this section with a sense of amusement; it is a challenge to be appreciated. The scree provides more traction than the patches of bare earth I encounter, where I have to clutch onto clumps of heather to prevent me slipping down.

It is arduous but not hazardous and it doesn't last long. I enjoy the hard work and once I reach top I will be rewarded by stunning views and soft, grassy ground on which to run.

Around the rocky knolls, the path skirts close to the edge but the rock steps are solid and not too high. Another easier scree bleed takes me to another rocky outcrop; from here, the going gets easier. The north top is close.

I emerge out of the heather close to the first of two cairns and I can begin to run again, past the second cairn, heading south-southeast. The slightly higher south top is little more than a kilometre away, easy going across soft grass. Now, the sharp climb was worth the effort.

Five hundred metres down to the col between the twin peaks, 60 metres of descent and then a relatively easy 500-metre pull up the other side. Someone has placed a handful of stones on a slightly prominent flag-sized slab of bare rock; I assume this is the highest point.

I continue on the path, south, as it drops down steeply to the small depression before Scale Knott. Various paths meet here, but I head straight on the main path.

A swiftish descent over rockless terrain, so different from the north-western face, brings me to a fence with no stile. ❹ I cross and the path veers right down to Black Beck. ❺ Just above the beck, the route turns sharply left onto a bridleway to contour around the base of Scale Knott before dropping down to Crummock Water.

Kirkstile Inn with Mellbreak behind

The route to Mellbreak

Northwest face of Mellbreak from the Kirkstile Inn

Scale Beck, beneath Scale Knott

Mellbreak

Running past Low Ling Crag

I have an easy run north, along the water's edge for more than two kilometres. Beyond Low Ling Crag, quiet theatre unfolds. A single rowboat, a herd of fluffy calves, twin ducks in flight. ❻ I keep on the lakeside path to begin with and then, 800 metres beyond the solitary Iron Stone, I climb up to the higher path to my left, running north-west to the corner of a wall 400 metres ahead.

Iron Stone, Crummock Water

I run down through Green Wood, keeping above Highpark, until I reach the gate at the end. ❼ Through the gate, right, down the lane to the tarmac road where I turn left over Park Bridge. ❽ Another left turn at the road junction brings me within 500 metres of the Kirkstile Inn, from where I retrace my steps to my car.

Ennerdale Water from Crag Fell summit

67 Crag Fell and Grike

Park / Start	Roadside parking next to the Shepherds Arms Hotel, Ennerdale Bridge (NY 070 159)
Map	OS Explorer OL4
Exertion	•••
Navigation	••
Terrain	•
Distance	10.2 kilometres
Time	1 hour 13 minutes
Ascent	467 metres
On road	1.6 kilometres

Rising above the Cumbrian coastal plain, overlooking the waters of Ennerdale, soft grassy summits and forest trails

Ennerdale Water and its surrounding spruce forest evoke a wilderness on a grander scale, with undertones of Scandinavia or North America.

On this circuit, I have 1.6 kilometres of road running; by parking in Ennerdale Bridge, I can get most of this out of the way at the start. **START** From the Shepherds Arms I follow the road sign to Ennerdale Water (1½ miles). I run on the path by the roadside until I reach the junction, here I turn right following the sign to the lake.

67 Crag Fell and Grike

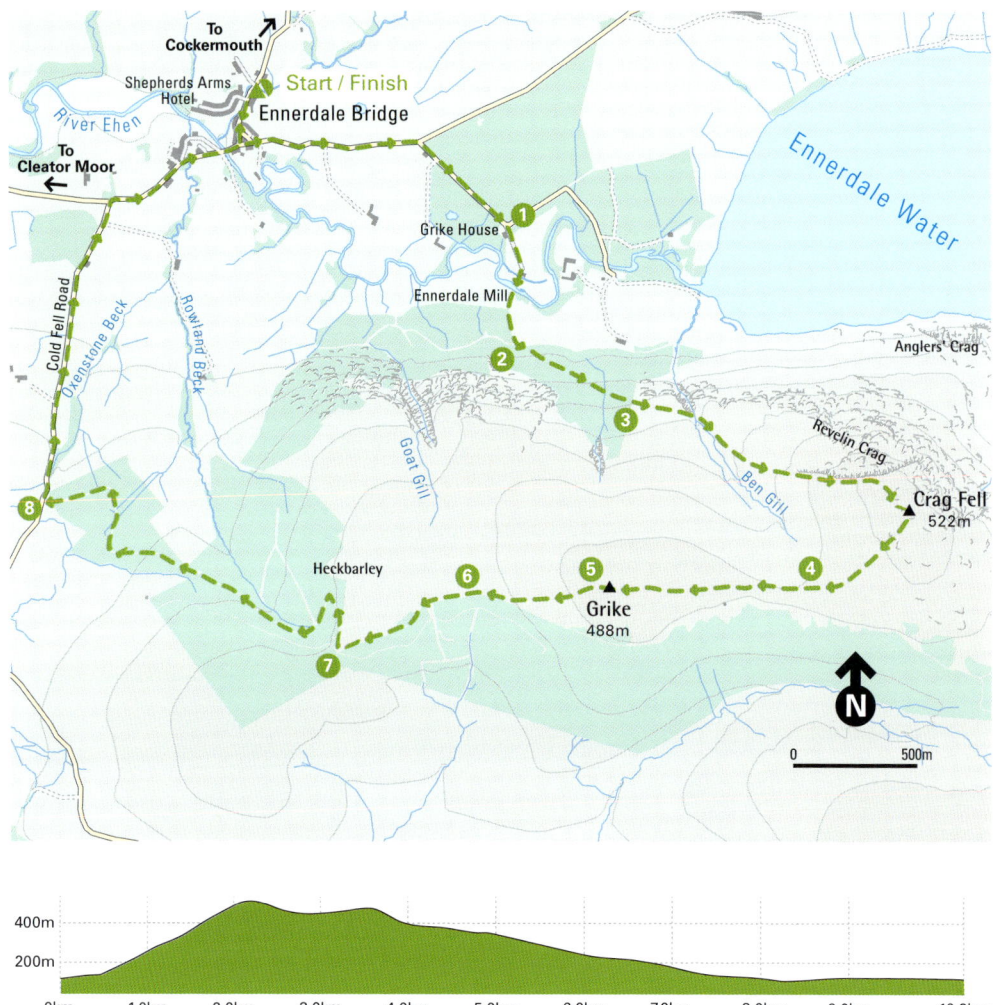

① Where the road turns sharply left, a fingerpost directs me straight on, past Grike House towards Ennerdale Mill (220 yards). Through the gate, I follow the track in front of the dilapidated old paper mill and wobble over a rickety bitumen-sprayed walkway to the footbridge. Once across the River Ehen, I turn left and immediately look for a path on my right climbing through the forest. ② The larch plantation has been felled and I have to scramble over branches and tree trunks to reach the trail.

Once on the path I follow a clear route rising gently towards Revelin Crag. The call of a solitary cuckoo reverberates across the empty water. From the naked fellside, views of Ennerdale Water, Great Bourne and Starling Dodd beyond have been revealed for the first time in decades.

Five hundred metres along a wasted forest trail, including 100 metres of ascent, leads me to a stile over a fence. ③ From here, I begin to climb more steeply on a grassy path heading towards Ben Gill and the higher ground above the rocky outcrop of Crag Fell's northern flank.

As I ascend, the western portion of Ennerdale Water disappears from view. Across Ben Gill, the path comes alongside a fence to my right; as the fence veers right, I follow the path straight on. I make surprisingly

Crag Fell and Grike

Running off Grike

good progress towards the top of the yielding turfy escarpment. Occasionally I catch glimpses of the top of Revelin Crag as it falls away sharply to my left. Soon the path turns its back on the scarp face and the large summit cairn on Crag Fell is suddenly revealed.

From the edge of the crag, my eyes are drawn towards the cone of Bowness Knott, tucked between Great Borne and the shoreline of an iron-grey lake. They are then pulled westwards, across the still water's surface, towards the head of the green valley and the towering heights of Starling Dodd, Red Pike and High Stile.

From the summit cairn, I turn away from the lake and take the path heading south-west towards Grike. A fast descent on bouncy grass towards a fence, 600 metres on from the summit. ❹ Today, high clouds mean that both the radio mast and Grike summit beyond are visible on the horizon. In misty conditions, I can use the fence on my left to navigate down to the boggy depression and up the other side.

I seem to reach the top of Grike, 1.4 kilometres from Crag Fell, in no time at all. An imposing wind shelter and two unnecessarily large cairns embellish the summit of the most westerly of the Wainwright fells.

Onwards I run towards the Irish Sea. ❺ Over a stile, just a 100 metres west of the summit, then 300 metres

The Shepherds Arms Hotel, Ennerdale Bridge

Summit cairn on Grike

67 Crag Fell and Grike

Descending west from Grike summit

across the pasture to another stile. ❻ I cross the fence onto the old mine road, turn right and follow the track through another denuded forest.

Following the fence on my right, I try to pick up the pace on the smooth surface. ❼ After 800 metres, I reach a junction, just beyond Red Moss, where various routes meet. Here the fence turns right; I follow the fence, ignoring the bridleway ahead, keeping on the main track as it swings back west through the re-planted forest.

An easy run, a gradual decline, almost two kilometres down to the Cold Fell road. ❽ I cross the road by the cattle grid and then turn right onto the public footpath signposted to Ennerdale Bridge (1¼ miles).

The path crosses the road before the junction and again at the junction. Here I turn right, following the path and then the road, over the River Ehen back to the centre of the village.

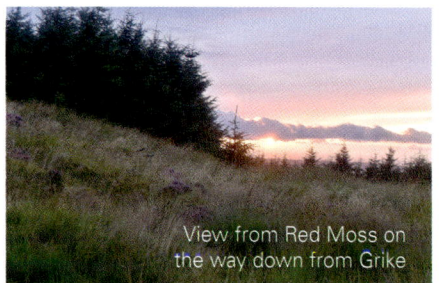
View from Red Moss on the way down from Grike

68 Hay Stacks

Hay Stacks from Buttermere

Park / Start	Gatesgarth Farm car park, Honister Pass (NY 194 149)
Map	OS Explorer OL4
Exertion	●●●●
Navigation	●●
Terrain	●●●●●
Distance	7.7 kilometres
Time	1 hour 27 minutes
Ascent	544 metres
On road	150 metres

A summit of variety, Wainwright's favourite, with picture-perfect panoramas

The Western Fells, rolling moorland in the far western hinterland, transform into crags of broken rock towards the central Lakeland region. A run over Hay Stacks is a run over stone steps and broken boulders. Apart from the central jaunt between the tarns, it is hard underfoot and you have to be prepared to use your hands on the way up. This is a slow run, a tough run, but one that strengthens the ankles and one that will fly by.

START Across the road from the car park a fingerpost at Gatesgarth Farm points to Scarth Gap (1½ miles), a mountain pass leading to Black Sail youth hostel in the Ennerdale valley. I pass through the farm

68 Hay Stacks

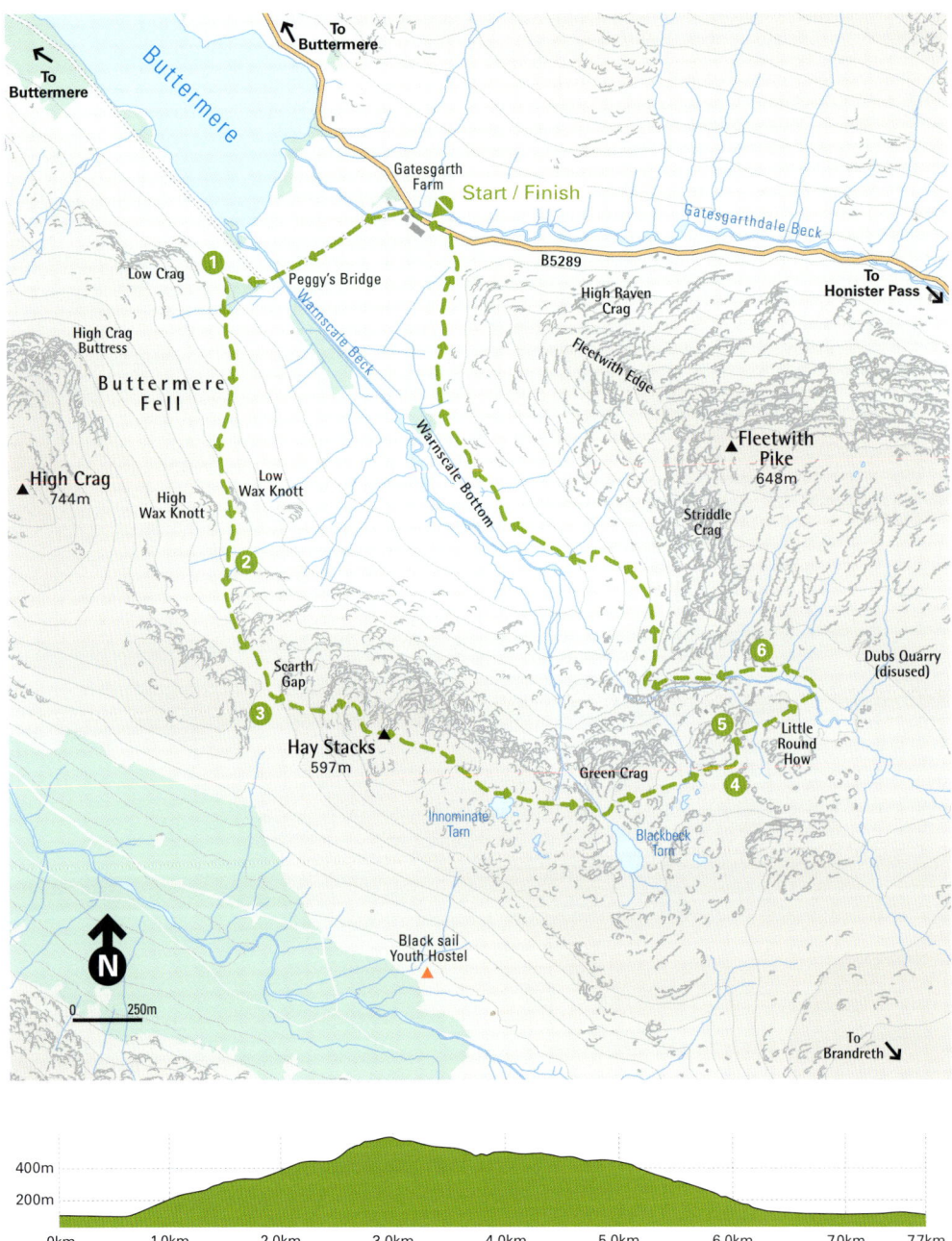

gates and run across the meadows at the head of Buttermere, crossing the leat-like stretch of Warnscale Beck at Peggy's Bridge. This is a useful 600 metre, flat warm-up before the climbing begins.

Beyond the bridge, the path turns right to Buttermere village or up and left towards the Scarth Gap pass.

❶ I follow the route to the pass and the hard work begins immediately. Apart from a brief respite at the top of the pass, I face a constant 20 percent gradient all the way to the summit. I struggle to achieve any gait resembling a run, even on the easier ground below Wax Knott.

Hay Stacks 68

Hay Stacks, scarred and rust-grey looms ahead. On my left, an indigo swathe of bluebells lights up Buttermere Fell. High above Warnscale Bottom hang the crags and quarries of Fleetwith Pike. ❷ At 1.8 kilometres, I cross a ruined wall and plough on up the steps towards the gap. ❸ A large cairn at the top of the pass marks the crossroads where I turn left up an obvious path. Stone steps soon give way to rough rock and the path is lost. I work my way up to the summit by selecting the easiest footholds. I don't feel exposed though; the ridge isn't narrow and there is plenty to grip onto in the rockier sections.

My climbing comes to an abrupt end as I emerge at the summit. I reach the second cairn with its protruding, rusting boundary post. This is the highest point. Despite its minor height, the views are stunning – intricate and varied – making the effort worthwhile. An amphitheatre of crowding fells – Great Gable, Green Gable, Robinson, Grasmoor, Whiteless Pike – look down on the tarns and tors of the summit platform.

I drop down to the south-east towards Innominate Tarn, choosing the softer boggier terrain wherever I can. I skirt the edge of the water imagining, like thousands before me, that I am kicking over Wainwright's ashes.

Running on an obvious path, I keep to the south of Green Crag. Within 400 metres east of Innominate Tarn, I reach the deep blue, tear-shaped Blackbeck Tarn, which reassures me that I am still on track. ❹ Five hundred metres from the tarn along the main path, still heading east, I arrive at a path on my right, which is the route from Brandreth.

I turn left and within 120 metres, at a large dome-shaped rock, I reach another path junction. ❺ Both routes lead to Warnscale Bottom, I head right choosing to take the less steep descent.

Around Little Round How, ahead is the abandoned Dubs Quarry with its ruined stone huts and heaps of 400 million year-old Westmorland Slate. The erstwhile home to scores of quarrymen living rough on the fellside

Passing through Gatesgarth Farm to the route up Hay Stacks

Looking up to Scarth Gap from Gatesgarth

Path up to Hay Stacks from Scarth Gap

The rocky route to Hay Stacks summit

Passing Innominate Tarn on the top of Hay Stacks

68 Hay Stacks

The route back along Warnscale Bottom

before a shortage of food forced a long march home to Keswick and beyond.

I cross Warnscale Beck, climb the path on my left and within 200 metres reach the miners' track that will take me back to Gatesgarth. ❻ Left again (west then north-west), down to the valley with the beck below me I run, slowly. A kilometre of steep decline, rocky and with loose stone, not dangerous but requiring me to concentrate on where I place my feet.

At last, I am nearing the flat valley floor. On my left, the violet haze of bluebells on the side of Buttermere Fell and ahead I meet a sweet fragrance drifting from a stand of flowering hawthorns. Now I have over a kilometre of running on a much smoother track contouring below Fleetwith Edge all the way to the road. At the road, I turn left back to the car park.

Warnscale Beck and the path back to Gatesgarth

Kinney How, Blakeley – the path into the forest

69 Lank Rigg and Whoap

Park / Start	Blakeley, the Cold Fell road (NY 066 130)		
Map	OS Explorer OL4		
Exertion	● ● ●		
Navigation	● ● ●		
Terrain	●		
Distance	9.1 kilometres	Time	1 hour 12 minutes
Ascent	477 metres	On road	0 metres

Gentle climbs over slouching grassy fells with expansive seaward views

Beware of the mist on these nondescript outlying fells. Rolling moorland bearing more resemblance to the North York Moors than to quintessential Lakeland mountains.

There is room to park on the grass verge on the west side of the Cold Fell road. The track on the bend on the east side is quite distinctive. 🏃 **START** Two old rusting iron gateposts mark the start – and finish; I find the remains of a wooden signpost strewn amongst yellowing tussocks.

I head north-northeast up Blakeley Raise. It is a clear day but out of habit I set a compass bearing (30 degrees) and it takes me a while to realise I need to stand away from the iron posts. There is a path, not on the map, which follows the short distance to the top of the fell at the apex of a forest fence ❶. For

69 Lank Rigg and Whoap

such a minor summit, there is an impressive pyramid cairn at the fence corner; the forest beyond is less impressive – a wasteland of timber debris.

From the cairn, I follow the fence to my right (north-east) along a faint path, again not on the map. When I reach Kinney How, where a metal gate leads into the ex-forest, the fence breaks right and heads down a gulley. A faint path climbs the grassy knoll south-east. I run parallel to the fence, which I lose sight of temporarily. ❷ I drop down to the unfortunately named Stinking Gill; pulling up the bank on the other side the path returns to the fence and I follow this south-east.

Seven hundred and fifty metres on from Stinking Gill I lose the security of the fence as it turns left keeping a high line. ❸ I maintain my course, heading east-southeast descending a steep mossy bank, fording the gill at Buck Hole then climbing up the sphagnum carpet on other side. My actual line is not vital; I know I will soon reach the grassy path leading up from the River Calder to the top of Whoap.

❹ I reach the path up from the Calder valley just 400 metres on from Buck Hole; this is an obvious route ascending Whoap's broad north-western flank. I turn left and follow the slope upwards; the gradient eases

Lank Rigg and Whoap

Heading up Blakeley Raise

towards the summit and my pace increases over soft, yellow-brown heath. I reach a large rock, described as a white stone, with a small cairn in attendance. The rock, more pink-grey with smudges of green lichen, lies just below Whoap's pudding-shaped summit.

At the boulder marking the highest point on the fell I take the path on my right (south-southwest). I canter down to the col between Whoap and Lank Rigg, noting the path off to the right down to the Whoap Beck valley, which will be my line of descent once I have completed the Lank Rigg dogleg. ❺ From the col, I have a half-kilometre climb to the Lank Rigg trig point. The small cairn next to the trig point bears a small white flag, probably marking the spot of Wainwright's treasure.

'White' stone on Whoap

My position on the western border of the Lakeland Fells is emphasised by the vast expanse of the Irish Sea from Morecambe Bay to the Solway Firth, with the mountains of the Isle of Man due west.

Back to the col the way I came, ❺ I turn left at the path junction down to Whoap Beck. The path is runnable, narrow and grassy with the occasional boggy section, heading due west. Directly ahead, in the window between Lowther Park and Flat Fell, the Isle of Man floats above the sea mist like a mystical Narnian kingdom.

Lank Rigg summit cairn

69 Lank Rigg and Whoap

The Whoap Beck valley back to Blakeley

❻ I keep Whoap Beck on my left and after fording Stinking Gill, again, the path leaves the valley, still heading west, up a surprisingly steep bank. I am careful not to follow the beck, now the River Calder, as it winds south-west beneath the flanks of Latter Barrow. I have Bomery Gill on my left as the track climbs back up to the two iron gateposts on the Cold Fell road.

Stinking Gill in the Whoap Beck valley

Middle Fell from Wastwater

70 Middle Fell and Seatallan

Park / Start	Off-road parking, Greendale, Wasdale (NY 144 055)		
Map	OS Explorer OL6		
Exertion	••••		
Navigation	••••		
Terrain	•		
Distance	7.2 kilometres	Time	1 hour 22 minutes
Ascent	726 metres	On road	0 metres

High above Wastwater, views of The Screes and a soft descent over moss and tussock

By the water's edge on a summer's day families play, cars line the roadside by the beach at Countess Beck Bridge, SUPs float on the crystal clear expanses of England's deepest lake and smoke from disposable barbeques fills the shimmering air. Less than a kilometre away, on a quiet country lane, I start my run through lush ferns, observed at close quarters by hefted Herdwicks.

START North of the road by the cottages the path cuts through the rumpled blanket of summer bracken. Middle Fell, rising to my right, is strewn with scree and boulders, but the path is well worn and largely smooth with a few sections of engineered steps.

70 Middle Fell and Seatallan

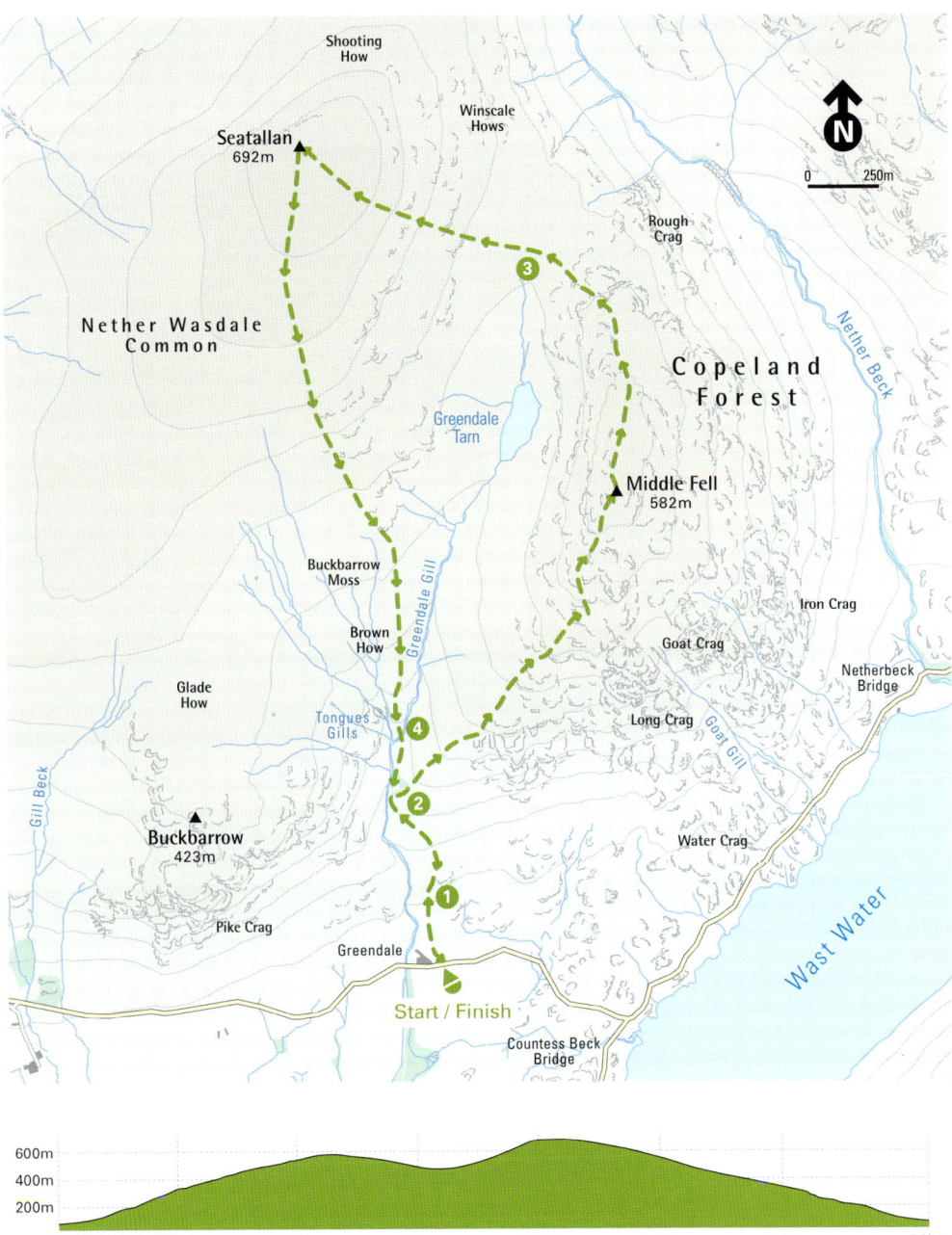

1 After 250 metres the path forks, I take the right-hand route away from Greendale Gill. **2** A little further on, after 650 metres, I reach another branch and again I head right to begin the steady climb to the summit.

The path is steep, for me not runnable, but not too precipitous. On my right Wastwater sparkles, a broken prism scattering the white light, and on the south-eastern shores the dark rubble of the Wastwater Screes, Britain's favourite view.

Middle Fell and Seatallan 70

The route up to Middle Fell from Greendale

On a constant gradient, easing slightly towards the top, I climb, parallel to the length of the lake heading into a lingering morning mist. I soon reach the summit cairn, Wastwater's western reaches shine but the tops of England's tallest mountains lurk behind dense white mist.

From the summit cairn, I continue on the path north across the short plateau. It is the height of summer but there is solitude here. The path drops down left towards the head of Greendale Tarn. ❸ Across the marsh, dry after weeks without rain, there are two paths visible beneath the swirling mist, one straight ahead, another to my right. I take the path ahead in an east-northeasterly direction, climbing steadily up the grassy mound that is Seatallan.

I leave the tear-shaped tarn behind. A lone runner and his dog lope across the col and disappear down the gill, the only person I see on this route. I ascend grassy steps worn into the earth, an uncomplicated route that brings me out directly at the triangulation pillar.

An obelisk-shaped trig column, a trivial cairn marking the fell's highest point and a large cairn (a massive pile of stones sculptured into a wind shelter) form a triumvirate of ornaments on an otherwise featureless moor. Grassy moors, often dull for walkers, are great for running.

View of Wastwater from route up to Middle Fell

Greendale Tarn

Middle Fell and Seatallan

The path to Seatallan summit

This morning the air is replete with moisture, further limiting the unspectacular panorama. Great End, Lingmell, Broad Crag, Scafell Pike, Scafell and Slight Side, normally dominating the western skyline, are obscured beneath a high shroud.

From the summit, I turn left. There is a faint path but, wary that the mist might descend, I set a bearing just east of south. My return to Greendale is all downhill on soft earth; to begin with, I bounce across cropped moorland before meeting tussocks of purple moor grass and soft rush. The path is intermittent across dry bogs of cotton grass and crunchy sphagnum, but I keep on my bearing, knowing that I will soon reach Greendale Gill. Buckbarrow, blocking my view of Wastwater, looms to my right, but I keep south, heading towards Tongues Gills. I pick up a clearer path that takes me down the

The path down from Greendale Tarn

gentle spur of Brown How and reach the ford, marked on the map, which takes me across Greendale Gill. ❹ The beck trickles across the stepping stones; in the winter, this is a surging torrent. I cross and turn right onto the main trail from Greendale to Greendale Tarn. Within 300 metres, I reach the point where I left the path to begin climbing Middle Fell. I retrace my steps through the dense bracken back towards the road, back towards the cottages.

Middle Fell and Seatallan 70

Through the bracken to Middle Fell

Nearly at the top of Hen Comb (Hen Comb route)

Appendices

Rating System Criteria

Exertion

This is a relative scale taking into account a combination of the elevation gain, the maximum gradients, the distance, the terrain and the time. For the time element, I have used the actual time it takes me to run these routes. Of course, the level of exertion ultimately depends on how much effort the runner puts in.

Exertion Level	Elevation gain (metres/km)	Maximum gradients (%)	Distance (kilometres)	Terrain Level (see below)	Time (minutes)
1	Less than 35	Less than 10%	8 or less	1	50-59
2	Less than 45	Less than 20%	9 or less	2	60-69
3	Less than 55	Less than 30%	10 or less	3	70-79
4	Less than 65	Less than 40%	11 or less	4	80-89
5	More than 65	More than 40%	More than 11	5	90+

Navigation

Level	Description
1	Clear waymarked paths and trails throughout. Obvious route choice. Compass not required.
2	Clear waymarked paths and trails most of the way. Few route choices. Compass not required (in good weather).
3	Some paths are not on OS maps but clear paths exist on the land. Clear aids to navigation, for example walls or fences and water features. The use of a compass may be needed to verify routes, especially when descending summits.
4	Much of the route is on open fell. Use of a compass may be needed to aid route finding. A compass will be relied upon in cloudy conditions.
5	Compass needed for navigation. No obvious paths.

Terrain

Level	Description
1	The route is all on rolling grassland moors and / or easy to run tracks and paths. Some roads.
2	Mostly rolling fells. Some stony ascents.
3	Some stony ground. Paths requiring caution in the wet.
4	Some rocky ground. Some rocky descents
5	Broken rock and rock steps. Hands needed on the way up or down.

Greenburn Bottom and Helm Crag from Steel Fell (Steel Fell route)

Appendices

Fell Races

The Fell Runners Association (FRA) is the place to go for all things related to fell racing (*fellrunner.org.uk*). The FRA classifies races as S (short), M (medium) or L (long). Since the majority of the routes described in this guide are ten kilometres or less, the FRA would place them in the short category. The FRA also categorises races as A, B or C depending on the height gained relative to the length of the race. It is possible to search for races by these categories and for your first race take a look at the AS, BS and CS races.

In addition, before entering a race, study the race details carefully and look for the following abbreviations:

- NS – navigational skills required
- ER – experience required
- PM – partially marked
- LK – local knowledge is desirable

Any race that does not require you to have navigation skills, experience or local knowledge will be your best option. The FRA emphasises that you are responsible for your own navigation and safety. Remember that visibility is likely to the biggest factor in getting round the course. If you are in the 'middle of the pack', you have the advantage of following others. However, do not assume that the person in front of you knows where they are going. For advice on fell races, including kit, rules and navigation see the FRA website. A list of some possible races within the Lake District, along with their classification and organizing group, is given below.

Arnison Crag Horseshoe (AS), Patterdale Dog Day, grid reference NY 391 161

Latterbarrow Loop (AS), Cumberland Fell Runners, grid reference NY 061 119

Loopy Latrigg (AS), Kong Adventure, grid reference NY 267 241

Rusland 5 (BS), Rusland Show, grid reference SD 331 891

Sale Fell Race (BS), Cumberland Fell Runners, grid reference NY 191 301

Shipman Knotts (AS), Helm Hill Runners, grid reference NY 461 041

SOB (Style End, Outerside, Barrow, (AS), Kong Adventure, grid reference NY 235 232

Steel Fell (AS), Borrowdale Fell Runners, grid reference NY 322 128

Wansfell Fell Race (AS), Ambleside AC, grid reference NY 337 044.

Eden Runners crossing Cow Bridge (Caudale Moor and Hartsop Dodd route)

Acknowledgements

Janet Quigley took many of the photographs for this book, checked many of the routes and gave up her time generously to proofread the text and offer suggestions. Ian Littlewood gave me valuable advice on equipment and techniques to help me elevate the quality of the photographs. I am indebted to the numerous runners, who kindly allowed me to photograph them as they ran the routes in this guide. I apologise to anyone who I have inadvertently missed from the following list: Abigail Jardine, Alex Myatt, Andrea Fell, Andrea Wightman, Andrew Walker, Andy Ridge, Angela Watson, Angus Wightman, Anna Larden, Arran Horne, Ben Grayson, Cal Pannone, Caryl Hartwright, Charlotte Tweddle, Chris Lockley, Dave Baglee, David Bowes, Debbie Walker, Dom Davis, Elaine Malyn, Emily Wightman, Emma Nielsen, Fiona McKean, Gina Mumford, Greg Simpson, Ian Robinson, Jack Eyre, James Jardine, Jamie Partridge, Janet Quigley, Jasmin Dobson, Jessica Critchlow, Jo Scott, John Stafford, Jonny Kent, Julie Gate, Katherine Neo, Katie Ainsworth, Katie Milburn, Kevin Whitemore, Kimberly Summers, Laura Benson, Lesley Allison, Malcolm Wood, Mark Osborne, Mark Pannone, Micah Wightman, Mike Allison, Mike Rosher, Natalie Myatt, Nick Irlam, Nigel Hierons, Paul Saagar, Peter House, Richard Down, Ross Bell, Sarah Wright, Scott Morley, Siobhan Jones, Sophie Wilson, Stephen Pearce, Stuart Lowthian, Teresa Douglas, Tim Slater, Trudie Newlove, Wade Tidbury, Wendy Johnson and Sam Braithwaite who nearly met me on Causey Pike. My special thanks goes to Caz Burns, Katie Milburn, Stuart Lowthian and Andrew Walker from Eden Runners for inviting me on club runs and enabling me to take photographs of club members on some of the stunning Lakeland Fells. Last, but not least, my gratitude goes out to Franco and his team at Pesda Press for guiding me through this project and turning my text and photos into an attractive and, hopefully, usable guide.

The Scar Crags ridge (Causey Pike and Scar Crags route)

Index

A
Abbots Bay 258
access 16
Aik Beck 73
Aiken Beck 241
Aiken Plantation 241
Aira Beck 31, 35, 36
Aira Force 30
Airy Crag 29, 30
Alcock Tarn 60, 63
Ambleside 99, 102, 145
Angle Tarn 89, 90
Angletarn Pikes 81, 87, 89
Applethwaite Common 104
Applethwaite Quarry 106
Ard Crags 267, 269
Armboth 129
Armboth Fell 129, 130, 131
Arnison Crag 47
Arthur's Chair 58
Arthur's Pike 73, 74
Artlecrag Pike 97
Askham 67, 70
Askham Fell 67
Askill Knott 280

B
backpacks (running) 13
Bannerdale Beck 82
Bannerdale Crags 209, 211
Barrow 251, 253
Barrow Door 253
Barton Fell 74
Baystones 99, 101
Beda Fell 79
Bedafell Knott 81
Beda Head 81
Bell Knott 51
Benn, The 123
Bessyboot 151, 153
Bewaldeth 195
Bield Crag 160
Binsey 193, 194, 195
Binsey Lodge 193
Birker Fell 187
Birk Fell 172
Birk Fell Hawse 173
Birkhouse Moor 41
Birkie Knott 77
Birks 46
Blackbeck Tarn 307
Black Crag 169
Black Fell 167, 169
Blackmoss Pot 153

Blake Fell 281, 283, 285, 287
Blakefell Screes 296
Blakeley Raise 309
Bleaberry Fell 117, 119
Blease Farm 224
Blease Fell 223
Blease Gill 221, 224
Blea Tarn 159, 162
Blencathra 221, 223
Blencathra Field Studies Centre 225, 228
Blindtarn Gill Falls 144
Blindtarn Moss 143
Boredale Hause 85, 90
Borrowdale 151, 155
Borrowdale Hotel 128
Bowscale 205, 208
Bowscale Fell 205, 207
Bowscale Tarn 205, 206
Braithwaite 251, 254
Braithwaite Lodge Farm 251
Brandelhow Park 258
Branstree 95, 96
Briar Rigg 229, 231
Broad Slack 164
Brock Crags 89
Brockle Beck 120
Brockstone 64
Broom Fell 239, 241
Brothers Water 49, 52, 91
Brotherswater Inn (Patterdale) 93
Brow Head Farm 146
Brown How (Lingmoor Fell) 161
Brown How (Seatallan) 316
Brown How (Whinlatter) 243, 245
Brumston Bridge 235, 237, 238
Brund Fell 125, 127
Brundholme 227, 228
Brundholme lead mine 225
Brundholme Wood 231
Buck Hole 310
Burnbank Fell 281, 283
Burthwaite Bridge 154
Buttermere 271, 274

C
Caiston Glen 51, 52
Caldbeck 197
Calebreck 197, 198
Captain Whelter Bog 97

Carling Knott 284
Carl Side 215
Carrock Beck 198
Carrock Fell 198
Castle Crag 122
Catbells Terrace 255
Cat Gill 115
Caudale Bridge 93
Caudale Moor 91, 93
Caudale Quarry 93
Causey Pike 259, 260
Chapel Bridge (Little Town) 263, 266
Chapel in the Hause 85
Chapel Wood 236
Christy Bridge 79
Clough Head 25, 26
Coast-to-Coast footpath 55
Cockpit stone circle 69, 73
Coffin Route (Rydal) 64
Cogra Moss 293, 296
Cold Fell road 304, 309, 312
Combe Gill 152
Common Fell 33, 35
compass 8
Corpse Road 98
Countryside Code 16
Cow Bridge (Patterdale) 49, 91, 94
Crabtree Beck 280
Crag Fell 301, 303
Crook Crag 185
Crummock Water 299
Cumbria Way 177, 201, 227, 229, 257, 258

D
Dale Head Farm 81
Dalehead Tarn 265
Dale How 273
Darling Fell 280
Darling How 241
Dead Pike 138
Demming Crag 181
Derwent Folds 228
Devoke Water 187, 189
Dockray 29, 32, 33, 36
Dock Tarn 135
Doctor Bridge 183, 186
Dodd Crag 237
Doddick Fell 223
Doddick Gill 222
Dodd Pass 250
Dodd Wood 213

Dodd Wood Sandbeds Gill trail 213
Dod Knott 179
dogs 16
Dowthwaitehead 35, 36
drink 13
Dry Cove Bottom 172
Dubs Quarry 307
Dunmail's crown 55

E
Easedale Beck 144
Elder Beck 73
emergencies 15
Ennerdale Bridge 301, 304
Ennerdale Mill 302
environment 16
equipment 10
equipment checklist 12
erosion 17
Eskdale 179
Eskin 237
Ewe Crag 147

F
Faeryland Tea Garden 141
Fairfield col 165
Fangs Brow 281, 284
Fat Man's Agony 161
Fawe Park 257
Fellbarrow 277, 278
Felldyke 293
Fell End Farm 195
fell races 320
Fell Runners Association (FRA) 10, 320
Fishercrag Plantation 132
Fisher Gill 129
Fix the Fells 17
food 13
footwear 11
Fothergill Head 287, 288
Foxbield Moss 185

G
Garburn Road 104, 106
Gate Gill 222
Gatescarth Pass 95
Gatesgarth Farm 305, 308
Gavel Fell 285, 287
Glenamara Park 46
Glencoyne Bay 37
Glencoyne Bridge 37
Glencoyne Wood 40

Index

Glenderamackin col 211
Glenderaterra Beck 227
Glenderaterra valley 225
Glen Mary Bridge 167, 170, 177
Glenridding 37
gloves 12
Goldrill Bridge 86
Gowbarrow Fell 29, 30
Gowbarrow Park 29
GPS 8
Grains Gill 158
Grange Fell 125
Grasmere 57, 141, 144
Graystones 239, 240
Great Carrs 163, 164, 165
Great Cockup 202
Great Rigg 58, 59
Greatrigg Man 59
Great Sca Fell 203
Great Wood 115
Green Crag 183, 185
Greendale 313, 316
Greendale Gill 314, 316
Greenhead Gill 57, 60
Green How 36
Greenside Mine Road 44
Green Wood 300
Grey Friar 163, 165
Grike 301, 303
Grike House 302
Grisdale Hause 55
Grisedale 46
Grisedale Beck 41
Grisedale Tarn 55

H

Hallin Fell 75
Hallinhag Wood 76
Hallsfell Top 223
Hardknott Pass 179, 181
Hare Shaw 84, 85
Harry Guards Wood 177
Harter Fell 179, 180
Hartsop 87, 94
Hartsop Dodd 91, 93, 94
Hartsop Hall 51, 52, 91
hats 12
Hause Gate 265
Hause Point 273
Hause Well 27
Haweswater 98
Hawse End Outdoor Centre 257, 258
Hayeswater 89
Hayeswater Gill 87
Hay Stacks 305

Hazel Bank Hotel 133
Hell Gill Pike 164
Helvellyn Range 26
Hen Comb 289, 292
Heron Pike (Glenridding) 38, 39
Heron Pike (Grasmere) 59
Heugh Scar 69
Heughscar Hill 69
High Coledale 254
High Hartsop Dodd 51
Highnook Beck 288
High Nook Farm 285
Highnook Tarn 287
High Pike (Caldbeck) 197, 199
High Rigg 109, 111
High Spy 263, 265
High Street 69, 74
High Tove 129, 131, 132
Hole-in-the-Wall 42
Hole Rake 173
Hollin Bank 170
Holme Fell 175, 176
Holme Wood 284
Hope Beck 247, 250
Hopegill Head 250
Horsebox Crossroads 244
Howe Grain 81
Howegrain Beck 82

I

Iron Gate 166
Iron Keld 169
Ivy Crag 176

J

Jobson Close 147
Jopplety How 127
Jubilee Bridge 179, 182

K

Kailpot Crag 76
Kelswick Farm 235, 237
Kepple Crag 185
Keswick 113, 229, 231
Ketley Gate 69
King's How 126, 127
Kinney How 310
Kirkgate Farm 289, 297
Kirkstile Inn 289, 297, 300
kit 10
Knight, The 85
Knock Murton 294
Knott Rigg 267
Knott, The 89
Knowe Crags 223

L

Lad Stones 173
Lang How 143
Langstrath Beck 153
Langstrath Country Inn 154
Lank Rigg 309, 311
Lanty's Tarn 44
Lanty Tarn 77
Latrigg 229, 230
Limefitt Park 104
Ling Fell 235, 237
Lingholm 257
Lingmoor Fell 159
Lingy End 134
litter 16
Little Carrs 164
Little Dodd 291
Little Hart Crag 51
Little Langdale 159
Little Round How 307
Little Sca Fell 203
Little Tongue bridleway 56
Little Town 263, 266
Liza Beck 249
Longlands 201
Longlands Beck 204
Longlands Fell 204
Longmire Road 104
Long Moss 126
Long Side 215
Longside Edge 213, 215
Lord's Seat 239, 241
Lorton Dodd 250
Loughrigg Fell 145
Loughrigg Tarn 147
Loughrigg Terrace 147
Low Arnside 169
Low Beckside Farm 219
Low Birker 183
Low Birker peat road 184
Low Birker Tarn 184
Loweswater 289, 292
Low Fell 277, 279, 280
Low Moss 253, 254
Low Oxen Fell 170
Lowthwaite Fell 204
Low Tilberthwaite 171, 172
Lucy's Wood 36
Lyulph's Tower 31

M

Maggie's Bridge 285, 288
Maiden Moor 263, 265
Manesty 257
maps 13
Mardale Head 95, 98
Martindale 75, 79, 81

Meal Fell 203
Mellbreak 297
microspikes 11
Middle Crag 131
Middle Fell 313, 315
Mill Beck 272
Mill Bridge 53, 56
Miller Bridge 145, 147
mindfulness 18
mitts 12
Moor Divock 68
Mosedale Beck (Loweswater) 291, 292
Mosedale Valley (River Caldew) 206
Mossdale Bay 40
Mosser Beck 278
Mosser Fell 278
Mosser Road 277
Mossmire Coppice 127
Mountain Road 168, 177
Mousthwaite Comb 218, 220
Mungrisdale 209, 212, 220
Murton Fell 293

N

Nab Crag 43
Nab Scar 61, 62
Nanny Lane 102
Nest Brow 117
Newlands Beck 265
Newlands Hause 267, 269, 270
Nick Head 39
north top (Mellbreak) 299

O

Old Coach Road 25, 27
Old Green Head Road 204
Old Saw Mill tearoom 213
Ordnance Survey 13
Outerside 251, 253
Oxen Fell High Cross 175, 177

P

Patterdale 41, 45, 83
Patterdale Hall 46
Peggy's Bridge 306
Pelter Bridge 61, 147
Penny Hill peat road 185
phones 13
Pictorial Guide to the Lakeland Fells 8
Pikeawassa 77
Place Fell 83, 85
Pooley Bridge 71
Pounder Sike 33

Index

R
races, fell 320
Rake Crags 140
Rakefoot Farm 116, 119
Rannerdale Knotts 271, 272
Raven Crag 121, 122
Red Screes 26
Rest Dodd 89
Revelin Crag 302
Riddings Beck 29
River Caldew 206
River Derwent 157
River Ehen 302
River Ellen 202
River Rothay 147
Robin Lane 102
Roehead 71, 74
Rooking 86
Rosthwaite 133, 136
Rosthwaite Fell 151, 153
Rough Crag 187
Roughten Gill 227
Round How 33
Royal Hotel (Dockray) 29, 33
Ruddy Gill 158
running shoes 11
running spikes 11
Rydal 61
Rydal Cave 147
Rydal Coffin Route 64
Rydal Mount 64

S
safety 14, 15
Sail Beck 269
Sail Pass 261
Sale Fell 235, 236
Sallows 103, 105, 106
Satura Crag 89
Scale Knott 299
Scales 217, 220
Scales Fell 222
Scaley Beck 222
Scandale Pass 52
Scar Crags 259, 261
Scawgill Bridge 239
Seatallan 313, 315
Seat How (Devoke Water) 190
Seat How (Whinlatter) 245
Seathwaite 155, 158
Seathwaite Fell 155
Seatoller 151, 154
Seat Sandal 55
Seldom Seen 38
Selside Pike 95, 97
Sheffield Pike 39
Shepherds Arms Hotel (Ennerdale Bridge) 301
Shivery Knott 131
Shivery Man 131
shoes 11
Shoulthwaite Gill 124
Side Gates 159
Side Pike 161
Silver How 141, 142
Sippling Crag 123
Skelghyll Wood 102
Skill Beck 213, 215
Sleet Hause 260
Smithy Fell 279
Sourfoot Fell 279
Sour Howes 103, 105
Souther Fell 217, 219
South Top (Mellbreak) 299
spikes 11
Spooney Green Lane 229, 231
Spout Force 239
Springs Farm 114, 116
Sprinkling Tarn 157, 158
Squat Beck 274
Steel Edge 85
Steel End 77, 137
Steel Fell 137
Steel Knotts 77
Stickle Brow 153
Stile End 253
Stinking Gill 310
St John's Church (St John's in the Vale) 109
St John's in the Vale 109
St Martin's Church (Martindale) 79
Stockley Bridge 157, 158
Stone Arthur 58, 59
Stonethwaite 134, 153
Stony Cove Pike 93
Stonycroft Gill 261
St Patrick's Church (Patterdale) 41, 45, 83
St Peter's Church (Martindale) 75
Strands Bridge 151
Swan Hotel, Grasmere 57
Swinburn's Park 30
Swinescar Pike 143
Swineside Knott 33, 35
Swinside Gill 269
Swirl How 163, 164, 165
Sykeside Farm 91

T
Tarn at Leaves 153
Tarn Crags 206
Tarn Hows 167, 175
Tarn Sike 206
Tarns, The 167
Taylorghyll Force 157
Terrace Path (Cat Bells) 257
Tewit Moss 190
Thirlmere Reservoir 129
Thirlmere Reservoir Dam 121
Three Shires Stone 163
Threlkeld 221, 223
Threlkeld Knotts 28
Threlkeld Quarry 28
Tilberthwaite Gill 172, 174
Tom Gill 167, 177
Tongue Gill 53, 55
Tongue, The 210
Torver Intake 168
Touchstone Sheepfold 174
trail shoes 11
Trough Head 47
Troutbeck 102, 103, 106
Troutbeck Institute 102
Troutdale Lodge 125

U
Uldale Fells 201
Ullister Hill 245
Ullock Moss 255
Ullock Pike 215
Ullswater Way 30, 37, 73, 74, 75, 83
Uskdale Gap 176
Uzzicar 259, 261

V
vests (running) 13

W
Wainwright, Alfred 8
Wainwrights (fells) 8
waist belts 13
Walla Crag 113, 115, 119
Wansfell Pike 99, 101
Wanthwaite 25, 27
Warnscale Beck 308
Watching Crag 279
Watendlath 135, 136
Watendlath Tarn 127, 133
Water Crag 188
Waterend 277
Watermillock Common 35
waterproofs 11
Wax Knott 306
weather 14
West Crag 194
West Fell 198
West Head Farm 137
Wetherlam 171, 173
Wetherlam Edge 173
Wet Side Edge 163
Whin Ben 249
Whinlatter Forest Park 243
Whinlatter Top 243, 244, 245
Whit Beck 227
White Horse Bent 212
White Moss Common 63
White Pike 189
White Raise Cairn 69
Whiteside 247, 249
White Stones 215
Whoap 309, 311
Whoap Beck 311
Willygrass Gill 134
Winder Plantation 70
Winter Crag 79
Woodend Height 189
Woodhall Park 200
Woolpack Inn (Eskdale) 183, 186
Wordsworth's Tarn 64
Wordsworth, William 30
Wrynose Bottom 166
Wrynose Pass 163, 166
Wythburn Dale 139
Wythburn Head Tarns 139
Wythop Beck 235
Wythop Church 236

Y
Yewdale Beck 171, 172
Yew Tree Farm 177
Yew Tree Tarn 170, 177
Yoadcastle 189

More running guides from Pesda Press

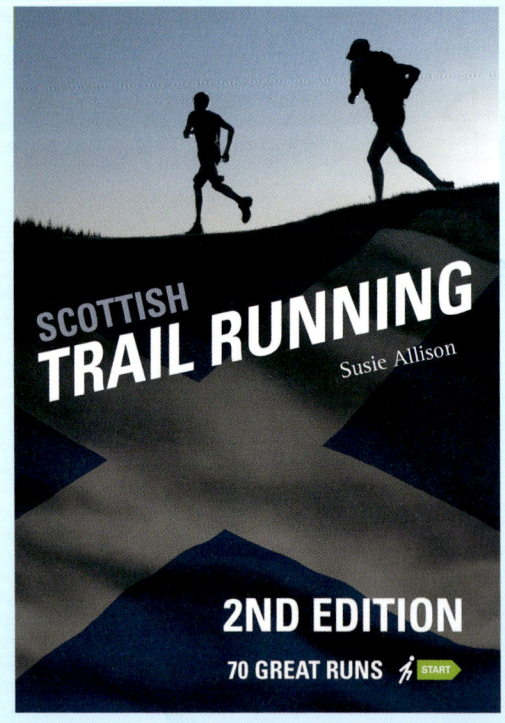

www.pesdapress.com